_M_

Memoirs of the Comtesse de Boigne

Adèle d'Osmond, Comtesse de Boigne

FROM A MINIATURE BY ISABEY

Memoirs
of the
Comtesse de Boigne

VOLUME I
1781–1815

EDITED AND WITH AN INTRODUCTION BY

Anka Muhlstein

AFTERWORD BY

Olivier Bernier

HELEN MARX BOOKS
NEW YORK

This edition of the *Memoirs of the Comtesse de Boigne*
is an abridgment of a three-volume version
originally edited by M. Charles Nicoullaud and
published in 1907 by William Heinemann, London.

LCCN 2002106465
ISBN 1-885586-63-9

Printed in Canada

CONTENTS

INTRODUCTION

Mme. de Boigne was born Adèle d'Osmond on February 10, 1781. Her father, scion of an old and illustrious family whose origins can be traced to the tenth century, was a brilliant young officer who, at the time of his marriage during the reign of Louis XVI, entered the diplomatic service. Her mother, Eléonore Dillon, was the daughter of Robert Dillon, a Catholic Irishman who had settled in France. Mme. d'Osmond was so beautiful and so charming and her manners were so impeccable that Madame Adélaïde, daughter of Louis XV, chose her as one of her ladiesinwaiting. This charge entailed living at Versailles. Contrary to custom, baby Adèle lived with her parents instead of being sent off to a wetnurse, and the pretty little girl became the pet of the court during the few happy years that remained before the end of the Ancien Régime. M. d'Osmond was about to be posted to St. Petersburg when the Revolution began. Feeling no responsibility towards the new government and discouraged by the ugly turn of events, he decided in 1790 to leave France with his family.

The Osmonds first took refuge in Italy, then settled in England, where they lived the difficult life of *émigrés*. The relative lack of social amusements available to the young couple had the happy consequence of giving M. d'Osmond the leisure to take a very close interest in his daughter's education. As a result, she was certainly better read and more serious than would have been the case had she spent her adolescence at court. Her father was remarkably intelligent and well educated, and he had a reasonable outlook on the world around him. M. d'Osmond was that rare political bird in times of turmoil: a true moderate. It was no easy task to remain so in exile, where ambitions and judgements are not weighed down by reality. Mme. de Boigne probably learned first from her father to observe and judge her friends, her acquaintances, and her natural milieu with a cold and amused eye.

With time, the financial situation of the family worsened. So at seventeen, Mademoiselle d'Osmond decided, quite on her own, to marry and to marry for money. It seemed the only way to help her impoverished parents, even if it had to be at the cost of ruining her prospects of personal happiness. Having first openly declared that she had no affection for him, and most probably never would have, she married General de Boigne, very rich but thirty years older than she, on the condition that he would support her parents. The General agreed and proposed in writing very generous terms, probably hoping that the sweet young thing would in the end prove to be an agreeable companion and would assure him of a peaceful, happy, and elegant home. It was not to be. Mme. de Boigne did not disclose the details of her unhappy marriage, nor did M. de Boigne. They separated several times. Much to Mme. de Boigne's dismay, her married life became the stuff of gossip until she and her husband finally came to an agreement on how they would live. They moved back to France in 1804 during Napoleon's reign: Adèle stayed in Paris while M. de Boigne spent most of his time in Chambéry in Savoy. Ultimately, he remained there. From then on, relations between husband and wife became both cordial and distant. M. and Mme. d'Osmond also left England and shared a house in Paris with their daughter. Adèle claimed her heart was broken, but she made the best of the situation and, as we shall see, a very discreet and durable affair came to make her solitude much lighter.

Mme. de Boigne was careful not to provoke Napoleon. Contrary to her friend Mme. de Staël, she never advertised her political views, and when asked to attend a court function, she accepted without further ado. Her rare and short exchanges with the Emperor were always marked by extreme politeness. Like many women, she was not insensitive to the charm and energy he exuded.

In 1814, the Bourbons returned to power. M. d'Osmond resumed his political career and was given the post of Ambassador, first in Turin, and then in London. His daughter followed him and, as her mother was often sick, played the role of junior Ambassadress. This position enabled her to meet everybody of importance in Europe, and to observe from a privileged point of view the various European upheavals of the time. After her father's retirement, she established herself in Paris. An invitation to her salon became one of the most sought-after favors in high society.

She started to jot down her memories of Louis XVI's court in 1835, convinced by a friend that all these fascinating details would soon be forgotten, and kept going. Eight years later, she had a book on her hands, and with the true coquetry of an aristocrat, she declared that she never kept notes, consulted any documents, and never reread her manuscript or corrected it. She said: "I do not know how to write and I am not going to learn the trade at my age." One thinks of Saint-Simon declaring proudly that he was not "un sujet académique."

The *Memoirs of Mme. de Boigne* extend from the 1780s to the 1830s and thus cover fifty years of one of the most troubled periods of French history, marked by three revolutions and the succession of six different political regimes. Loyalty was tested, and so was political instinct. Duty to one's country could mean switching allegiance from the King to the Republic or the Emperor, or vice-versa. Personal interests, moral convictions, and patriotic obligations clashed. It was an era during which neither virtues nor vices could be masked. Character was everything. One had to show one's hand when called. It was a memorialist's heaven, and memoirs of the time abound. Mme. de Boigne's recollections stand out for many reasons.

As a private person, without any political role, she did not have to justify her conduct. She had no axe to grind, nothing to prove. Her memoirs do not retrace her career—she had none. She just wrote down what she saw and she saw quite a lot—not always from the same point of view. For instance, she stayed twice in England, first as a vulnerable *émigré* and, fifteen years later, as the daughter of the French Ambassador. In France, during the reign of Napoleon, she lived a quiet, secluded life, in complete contrast with her very public existence after the Restoration, hence her entrenched sense of relativity. Interested in everything and surprised by nothing, she was extremely well informed and remained as such all her life, with her information not limited to one milieu. Her father was a Royalist; her husband, born in Savoy and thus a subject of the King of Sardinia, was a self-made man who had earned a fortune in India and had many connections in the business world. She refused to let politics dictate her affections and had close friends in Napoleon's administration. Above all, her thirty-year love affair with the Chancelier Pasquier, an unusually intelligent politician who served in turn Napoleon, the restored Bourbons, and Louis-Philippe, gave her an incomparable inside view of the political world. Finally, she had lived long enough in England to observe France with an outsider's eye, taking nothing for granted.

All these advantages might have produced little had Mme. de Boigne not been such a startling bundle of contradictions. Having ancestors who had fought in the Crusades and raised in the intimacy of the royal family, she remained all her life conscious of her exalted origins, but abandoned early on the conservative views of her environment, understanding better than most of her friends and relations that times had changed. She admired England but hated its customs. She loved French society but detested its political stagnation; a staunch Royalist, she respected Napoleon and was appalled by the stupid rigidity of the two last Bourbon kings. Most important for a memorialist, she was both chatty and immensely serious, never petty but always sharp.

Mme. de Boigne had no children and left what she called "une causerie de vieille femme, un ravaudage de salon qui arrivera à mes héritiers comme un vieux fauteuil de plus"* to her grand-nephew. He did

---

* "Tales of an old woman, a bit of tapestry that shall be bequeathed to my heirs as if it were one more armchair."

not know what to do with it but showed it to a friend, Charles Nicol-laud, who was interested in history. Nicollaud published a slightly condensed version after the death of the d'Osmond nephew in 1907. A more complete edition appeared in 1921. The most careful reader of Mme. de Boigne's *Memoirs* was Marcel Proust, who wrote an article about them as soon as they were first published. He relished the description of a society in flux; he adored the gossip, he admired the incisive portraits, and, above all, he was fascinated by the author. He proved his admiration by giving one of his characters, Mme. de Ville-parisis, many of her traits. The old, rich, impertinent, and slightly déclassé marquise, who loves to tell stories about her father, writes her memoirs, claims with the arrogance of an old aristocrat to have no social prejudices, and lives a quiet conjugal life with her old lover, the diplomat M. de Norpois, often seems the spitting image of Adèle de Boigne. To be remembered thus by the greatest writer of the twentieth century is an amazing but fitting homage to an amateur of genius.

Anka Muhlstein

DICTIONARY OF CHARACTERS

Adélaïde, Madame, daughter of Louis XV, 1732–1800. Of Louis XV's seven daughters, only the eldest, Elisabeth, married. Adélaïde and her sisters lived at Versailles and Bellevue, a château built for Mme. de Pompadour. At the onset of the Revolution, the two surviving Princesses, Adélaïde and Victoire, fled to Italy.

Adélaïde, Princesse d'Orléans, Mademoiselle, Madame, sister of Louis-Philippe, 1777–1847. She emigrated to England in 1792, and was not welcome in the circle of *émigrés* as her father, Philippe-Egalité, had voted for the execution of Louis XVI. She lived with her brother, Louis-Philippe, after he returned from his voyage to the United States in 1800, and always remained very close to him.

Alexander I, Emperor of Russia, son of Paul I and grandson of Catherine II, 1777–1825. Educated by a French tutor, he instigated a series of liberal reforms at the beginning of his reign in 1801, but by its end had become a reactionary. His alliance with Napoleon did not last long (1807–1812). In 1812, Napoleon invaded Russia and entered Moscow on September 14. The next day a huge fire destroyed the capital and Napoleon had to order the retreat of his troops. In 1815, Alexander and his allies triumphed over the French in the Battle of Waterloo.

Angoulême, Louis de Bourbon, Duc d', Monsieur le Dauphin, son of Charles X, 1775–1844. He emigrated to England where he married his first cousin, Marie-Thérèse, the daughter of Louis XVI, and joined Wellington's army to fight against Napoleon. He renounced his rights to the throne after the Revolution of 1830 in favour of his nephew, the ten-year-old Comte de Chambord.

Angoulême, Marie-Thérèse de Bourbon, Madame Royale, Duchesse d', Madame la Dauphine, daughter of Louis XVI, 1778–1851. She was imprisoned with her parents and her brother in 1792 and liberated in 1795 in exchange for French prisoners held in Austria. The Orphan of the Temple, as she came to be known, was then conducted to London where she married her cousin. Quite unpopular in all circles of society, despite her tragic past, she did not help the Bourbon cause during the Restoration.

Arago, François, 1786–1853. Celebrated astronomer and secretary of the Bureau of Longitudes. At the age of twenty-three, he was a member of the Academy of Sciences, taught at the Polytechnic School. In 1830, he was elected deputy and appointed director of the Observatory.

Artois, Comte d'. See Charles X.

Beauharnais, Hortense de, Queen of Holland, Duchesse de Saint-Leu, 1783–1837. Daughter of Joséphine, stepdaughter of Napoleon, she was married to Louis Bonaparte, King of Holland. Their son became Napoleon III.

Bernadotte, Jean-Baptiste, King of Sweden under the name of Charles XIV, 1764–1844. After a quick and glorious military career in Napoleon's army, he became Ambassador to Vienna and Minister of War. He backed Sweden against Napoleon in 1808. The grateful Swedes proceeded to elect him Prince Royal, and King Charles XIII adopted him. He became King in 1818, thus founding the dynasty that still reigns today.

Berry, Charles-Ferdinand, Duc de, son of Charles X, 1778–1820. Second son of the Comte d'Artois, future Charles X. Married Marie-Caroline de Bourbon-Sicile. He held extreme conservative views and was assassinated by Louvel in 1820. His posthumous son, the Duc de Bordeaux, was born seven months later.

Berry, Marie-Caroline de Bourbon-Sicile, Duchesse de, 1798–1870. Daughter of the King of Naples, she married the Duc de Berry and gave him two children, la petite Mademoiselle and the "miraculous" Duc de Bordeaux, the posthumous son. She followed Charles X into exile into Prague but soon made her way back to France and tried to inspire a Royalist insurrection. She failed miserably and ended in prison, where it was discovered that she was pregnant. She had to confess her secret marriage to an Italian count and was sent back to Palermo, humiliated, dishonoured, and deprived of the custody of her children.

Bertrand, Henri, General, Comte, 1773–1844. He remained faithful to Napoleon and followed him first to Elba, then to Saint Helena, where he returned in 1844 to bring back the Emperor's ashes. He is buried next to him in the Invalides in Paris. Bertrand married Fanny Dillon, a cousin of both Empress Joséphine and Mme. de Boigne.

Blacas, Pierre, Duc de, 1771–1839. This Ultra-Royalist politician was counsellor to Louis XVIII from the beginning of the Revolution. He was named Minister of the Royal Household in 1814. Always faithful to the Bourbons, he followed the royal family into exile in 1830.

Boigne, Benoît Leborgne, General, Comte de, 1751–1830. He was born in Chambéry, then a possession of the King of Sardinia, where his father was a furrier. He first entered an Irish regiment serving in France, then, finding that promotion was slow, switched to a Greek regiment in the service of Catherine of Russia. Having reached the rank of Major, he resigned and went to India, where he offered his expertise to several Hindu Princes. A Maharajah, Sindiah, accepted his services, and Leborgne, who had not yet changed his name to de Boigne, organised the Prince's army on European principles, won great victories over the neighbouring rulers, was appointed General of all the infantry and Governor of the conquered provinces, and was thus entitled to a share of the tribute—the origin of his enormous fortune. Sindiah died in 1794. Two years later, the General arrived in London, where he married Mlle. d'Osmond in 1798. The King of Sardinia made him a count, and Louis XVIII, a Knight of Saint Louis. The General became an important benefactor of his native town.

Borghese, Camillo, Prince, 1775–1832. Married Pauline Bonaparte, the beautiful sister of Napoleon, in 1803, and was Governor of the Piedmont from 1807 to 1814.

Bourbon, House of. From 1572 the Bourbon Princes were at different times Kings of Navarre, France, Spain, Naples, and Sicily. The senior line in France ran directly from Henri IV to Charles X. The names and titles of the different Princes are sometimes confusing because they change during their lifetimes. At the beginning of Mme. de Boigne's *Memoirs,* the King is Louis XVI. The Dauphin is his eldest son. His daughter is Madame Royale (a younger daughter would have been simply Madame). The King's immediate brother is always called Monsieur, the term preceding his actual title, which in this case is Comte de Provence. His youngest brother is the Comte d'Artois. Louis XVI is executed in 1793, and the Dauphin, though imprisoned, is King Louis XVII, at least for the Royalists. He dies in 1795 and his uncle, the Comte de Provence, becomes King in exile under the name of Louis XVIII. His brother, the Comte d'Artois, is then called Monsieur. Louis XVIII has no children and Monsieur, Comte d'Artois, has two sons. The eldest, the Duc d'Angoulême, is married to his cousin, Madame Royale, who is then known as Madame, Duchesse d'Angoulême. The second son is the Duc de Berry. When Louis XVIII dies, his brother becomes King Charles X. The Duc d'Angoulême, as eldest son of the reigning king, is then given the title of Dauphin and his wife that of Dauphine.

Calonne, Charles-Alexandre de, 1734–1802. He replaced Necker in 1783 and tried in vain to reform the financial administration of the kingdom. He was forced to resign in 1787 and fled France during the Revolution.

Cambacérès, Jean-Jacques, Duc de Parme, 1753–1824. A lawyer and a judge, he embraced the Revolution and worked on the new Civil Code. He was named Second Consul at Bonaparte's suggestion and during the Empire worked on the reform of the administration and the elaboration of the Imperial Civil Code. He rallied to the Bourbons in 1814 but abandoned their cause during the Hundred Days.

Carignan-Savoie. See Charles-Albert.

Caroline of Brunswick, 1768–1821. She married the Prince of Wales in 1795. The wedding night was an irreparable disaster and soon after the birth of their daughter, Charlotte, the Prince refused to have anything to do with his wife and did not allow her near her child. She travelled extensively in Europe and remained popular in England, where she was perceived as a victim. On her husband's accession as George IV, she returned to claim her rights as Queen but he initiated a bill to dissolve the marriage and refused her admittance to Westminster Abbey for the Coronation. She died shortly thereafter.

Castlereagh, Henry Robert Stewart, Viscount, 1769–1822. His role at the Foreign Office was crucial in consolidating the alliance against Napoleon in 1812. He committed suicide in 1822.

Caulaincourt, Armand, General, Marquis de, Duc de Vicence, 1772–1827. Though born to an aristocratic family, he adopted the new ideals and served in the Revolutionary Army. Napoleon noticed him and sent him as his Ambassador to Russia in 1801, then took him as his aide-de-camp. He returned to Russia from 1807 to 1811, where he gained the Tsar's respect. He traveled in Napoleon's carriage when the Emperor raced back from Moscow in 1811 and left an extraordinary account of their week-long conversation.

Cayla, Zoé Talon, Madame du, 1784–1850. She was the daughter of a secret agent of Louis XVIII before the Restoration. Admitted to court, she became the favourite of the old King, who left her a vast fortune.

Charles X, Comte d'Artois, Monsieur, 1757–1836. As a young man, the Comte d'Artois was a frivolous, fun-loving, unpopular Prince. The early stirrings of the Revolution scared him and he was the first to flee France on July 17, 1789. During exile, he became quite religious and more and more conservative. On his return, he became the head of the Ultra-Royalist party. He succeeded his brother Louis XVIII in 1824. His reactionary politics caused the 1830 Revolution. Once more, he fled his country and this time took refuge in Prague. He accepted the nomination of his cousin, Louis-Philippe d'Orléans, as the Lieutenant-General of the kingdom and as regent, while abdicating in favor of his grandson, the Comte de Chambord. His fall marked the end of the Bourbon reign in France.

Charles-Albert de Carignan-Savoie, King of Sardinia, 1798–1849. He was recognised by the Congress of Vienna as heir to the throne of Sardinia in the absence of male successors in the senior branch. He became King in 1831. His son, Victor-Emmanuel, would be the first King of Italy.

Chateaubriand, François-René, Vicomte de, 1768–1848. One of the most important figures in French literature, he would probably have preferred a great political career. He spent the first years of the Revolution in America, where he traveled extensively, and emigrated to England upon his return to Europe in 1793. Though he admired Napoleon and lived in France during his reign, he remained faithful to the Royalist cause. He was Ambassador to London and Foreign Minister from 1822 to 1824, and retired from politics during Louis-Philippe's reign. He married when quite young a friend of his sister's, Mademoiselle de Lavigne. She was loyal and intelligent, but they had nothing in common; she claimed she had never read a page written by her famous husband.

Clary, Désirée, Maréchale Bernadotte, Queen of Sweden, 1770–1860. The daughter of a rich merchant of Marseilles, she caught Bonaparte's eye on his way to Egypt, but he was already married to Joséphine. His brother Joseph was still single. He fell in love with her sister, Julie, and married her. When Désirée met Bernadotte, one of Bonaparte's officers, he proposed immediately and she accepted because he always stood his ground in front of Napoleon. She became Queen of Sweden in 1818 but hated her new country and succumbed to a mad passion for the Duc de Richelieu. After his death, she left France and rejoined her husband in Stockholm.

Condé, House of. A junior branch of the House of Bourbon. Louis I, first Prince of Condé, was the brother of Antoine de Bourbon, King of Navarre and father of Henri IV. The Condés were thus the first Princes of the blood. The junior branch of the Condé family took the name of Conti. Louis de Bourbon, eighth Prince of Condé, emigrated upon the fall of the Bastille in 1789 and set about raising the *émigré* "armée de Condé." He went to England in 1801 and returned to Paris in 1814. His son, the Duc de Bourbon, did not choose to assume the Condé title on the death of his father. His grandson was the Duc d'Enghien.

Constant, Benjamin, 1767–1830. A novelist and political writer, he was the epitome of the cosmopolitan European of the time. In 1794, he chose the side of the new regime under the influence of Mme. de Staël.

Cuvier, George, 1769–1832. A zoologist of genius, his work is at the origin of modern biology.

Damas, Baron, Duc de, 1758–1829. Followed Louis XVIII to Belgium during the Hundred Days. He was then nominated First Gentleman of the King's Household. Both his brother and his son also loyally served the Bourbon Princes.

Decazes, Elie, Duc de, 1780–1860. Decazes started his political career at the side of Louis Bonaparte, King of Holland. He switched allegiances in 1814 and was nominated Minister of the Police by Louis XVIII. The King took an immense liking to Decazes, who represented the moderate wing of the Royalist party, and entrusted the government to him. The Ultra-Royalists, led by Monsieur, detested him and forced his resignation after the murder of the Duc de Berry. In 1830, he went over to the side of Louis-Philippe.

Dillon, Edouard, Comte, uncle of Mme. de Boigne, 1751–1839. Fought in the War of Independence and went into exile to serve with the *émigré* army. Returned to France in 1814 and became Ambassador to Dresden and Florence and First Chamberlain of Charles X.

Elchingen, Duc d'. See Ney.

Elisée, Père, Marie, Vincent Talochon, 1753–1817. An excellent surgeon, Talochon, who was known as Père Elisée, emigrated to England. He cured Louis XVIII of an illness that had resisted all sorts of treatment and received a snuff-box filled with gold as a token of his gratitude. During the Restoration, he resided at the Tuileries and was one of the most influential men in the royal entourage.

Enghien, Louis de Bourbon, Duc d', 1772–1804. The last descendant of the Condé branch settled in Baden during the Empire. Napoleon, who suspected him of organising a plot, ordered him seized at Ettenheim. A military court hastily condemned the Prince. He was shot the next day. This execution roused the utmost indignation in France and throughout Europe.

First Consul. See Napoleon.

Fouché, Joseph, Duc d'Otrante, 1759–1820. One of the most amazing careers of the period. In 1789, Fouché, a teacher in a religious school, embraced the revolutionary cause and became one of the most efficient organisers of the Terror. He shifted in 1794 and contributed to the fall of Robespierre. His political skills and his incomparable network of spies led to the post of Minister of Police under Napoleon. Astoundingly, for the same reasons, he maintained his position during the Restoration.

Genlis, Félicité de Saint-Aubin, Comtesse de, 1746–1830. This interesting woman was given the responsibility of raising the children of the

Duc d'Orléans, including the future King Louis-Philippe. She was inspired by Rousseau's theories, and the enthusiasm of her charges for her was quite remarkable. Mme. de Gontaut said that she had seen them kiss the ground upon which she had walked. After the execution of her husband in 1793, she finally emigrated to England but returned to France during the Empire. Napoleon named her inspector of all the grade schools of the country.

Girardin, Emile, 1806–1881. He was the founder of the first moderately priced newspaper. He was extremely well-informed, and his salon was always full of people of different opinions. He was married to Delphine Gay, a writer and a poet.

Gontaut, Marie, Duchesse de, 1772–1857. She shared the responsibility for the education of the children of the Duc d'Orléans before the Revolution and became attached to the Duchesse de Berry in 1816. In 1819, she was named to the much-desired post of governess to her children.

Guizot, François, 1787–1874. A Protestant who opposed Napoleon and supported the Restoration and the July Monarchy. The Ultras hated his moderate policies, and he soon resigned from his ministerial post and resumed his academic career as a historian. He returned to politics under Louis-Philippe.

Jordan, Camille, 1771–1821. A constitutional Royalist, he emigrated to Switzerland in 1793. He returned to France in 1815 and was then elected to Parliament.

Joséphine Tascher de La Pagerie, Empress of the French, 1763–1814. She was first married to Alexandre de Beauharnais, who was executed during the Revolution. She met Napoleon Bonaparte in 1795. He fell violently in love with her, married her in March 1796, and was always kind and generous to her children, Eugène and Hortense. Unfortunately, she was unable to give him a child and he divorced her in 1809. She retired to Malmaison and stayed on very good terms with him.

Krüdener, Mme. von, 1764–1824. After the death of her husband, she became a disciple of Swedenborg, the Swedish founder of a mystical sect. For some years, she had a great influence on Tsar Alexander I.

La Fayette, Marie, Joseph, Marquis de, 1757–1834. The hero of the American War of Independence served in the French revolutionary army until August 1792. He was taken prisoner by the Austrians who surrendered him, as an American citizen, to the United States consul in Hamburg in 1797. He returned to political life under the Bourbons but his Liberal views put an end to his career. In 1830, he publicly espoused the Orléanist cause in a theatrical apparition on the balcony of the Hôtel de Ville. He died, disappointed by the new regime, four years later.

La Tour Du Pin, Henriette, née Dillon, Marquise de, 1770–1853. She left a very interesting account of her life as an exile in America during the Revolution, returning to France during the Empire. Her life ended sadly in Italy after she and her husband plotted against Louis-Philippe.

La Valette, Antoine, Comte de, 1769–1830. Aide-de-camp to Napoleon and Postmaster-General, he joined the Royalists in 1814 but wavered during the Hundred Days. He was condemned to death upon the return of the Bourbons but saved by the devoted intercession of his wife and friends.

Louis XVI, 1754–1793. He became King at twenty years of age. Immature and irresolute, he was torn between the influence of the court faction and the reform-minded Ministers. When the Revolution broke out in 1789, he was unable to respond to the challenge of the Liberal and democratic forces. After his failed attempt to escape the country on June 20, 1791, and his arrest in Varennes, he never regained any semblance of authority. Moreover, he was suspected of secret dealings with foreigners. In August 1792, he was imprisoned in the Temple with his wife and children, brought to trial for treason, and executed on January 21, 1793.

Louis XVIII, Comte de Provence, Monsieur, 1755–1824. He fled France at the time of Varennes but took a different route from his brother Louis XVI and managed to reach Brussels and Coblentz, where he put himself at the head of the *émigrés* and took the title of King after the death of his nephew on June 8, 1795. He settled in England in 1807, and returned to Paris on May 3, 1814, after issuing the declaration of Saint-Ouen, in which he promised to grant the nation a constitution. He did so by signing a Constitutional Charter. He had to flee once more during the Hundred Days and reentered his realm on July 8, 1815. By then he was sixty, suffered from gout and obesity, and though his personal policy tended towards prudence and common sense—except in questions of etiquette—he found it more and more difficult to oppose the ultra-reactionary bent of his brother and heir Charles X, his nephews, and their wives.

Louis-Philippe, Duc de Chartres, Duc d'Orléans, King of the French, 1773–1850. At the beginning of the upheaval, following his father's example, he joined the Jacobin club and fought in the revolutionary army. Later, Louis-Philippe deserted, although his father had changed his name to Philippe-Egalité and voted for the execution of Louis XVI. He did not choose, however, to fight on the side of the enemies of France, but settled in Switzerland and earned his living as a teacher of mathematics. After his father's execution, he sailed to America and lived in Philadelphia. He returned to Europe in 1800, made peace with his Bourbon cousins, married a distant cousin, Marie-Amélie of Naples, and stayed in England until the Restoration. During the reign of Charles X, Louis-Philippe became the center of the Liberal opposition. The July Revolution of 1830 gave him his opportunity. On August 9, 1830, he was proclaimed by the provisional Government "King of the French by the grace of God and the will of the people." He was to reign for eighteen years. A great revolutionary movement swept through Europe in 1848, and Louis-Philippe's growing conservatism and authoritarian attitude united many divergent interests against him. Faced with a revolution, he abdicated and escaped to England, where Queen Victoria placed the estate of Claremont at his disposal.

Madame. *See* Angoulême, Marie-Thérèse.

Marchand, Comte, General, 1765–1851. He commanded the department of Isère for Louis XVIII. Accused of surrendering Grenoble to Napoleon during the Hundred Days, he was tried and acquitted in 1816. He was appointed Peer of France during the July Monarchy.

Marie-Amélie, Princesse de Bourbon-Sicile, Duchesse d'Orléans, Queen of the French, 1782–1866. The daughter of Ferdinand IV, the King of Naples, and Marie-Caroline, elder sister of Marie-Antoinette, she married Louis-Philippe, with whom she had a very bourgeois and happy union. Their five sons, contrary to the royal tradition, were educated in public schools.

Marie-Antoinette, Archduchess of Austria, Queen of France, 1755–1793. The pretty, young, frivolous Queen was unpopular from the start. She was childless for eight years and took too energetic a part in the pleasures of the court. She changed when she became a mother, but it was too late to save her reputation. When the Revolution began, she was perceived as a reactionary influence on the King, and she did imprudently participate in secret intrigues. She was imprisoned with her family in August 1792, placed in solitary confinement in a tiny cell of the Conciergerie for the last three months of her life, and was guillotined in October 1793. She died with the utmost dignity and courage.

Marmont, Auguste Viesse de, Maréchal, Duc de Raguse, 1774–1852. Attached to Bonaparte since 1793, Marmont had a brilliant career in the *Grande Armée.* In 1814, he negotiated the surrender of Paris to the Tsar and withdrew his troops to Normandy without waiting for Napoleon's order. This action was considered treason by the Bonapartists. He then served the Bourbons and commanded the Royalist troops in 1830. His life ended in exile.

Martignac, Jean-Baptiste, Comte de, 1778–1832. His government lasted from 1828 to 1829 and marked the last effort of Charles X to work with the Parliament. He was replaced by the reactionary Polignac, whose politics led to the Revolution of 1830.

Metternich, Clemens, Count, then Prince, 1773–1859. Austrian statesman who stood as a resolute champion of conservative principles. He was Ambassador to Paris in 1806–1807. His triumph was the agreements reached at the Congress of Vienna, which reorganised Europe after Napoleon's defeat. As Foreign Minister and Chancellor, he remained in power until 1848, when he resigned as a result of the insurrectionary movements in Austria and in Italy.

Montmorency, Mathieu, Duc de, 1767–1826. He started out life as a Liberal, fought in the War of Independence, and adopted the first revolutionary reforms enthusiastically. He prudently emigrated in 1793 but came back under the Empire. During the Restoration, he turned into a rabid Ultra-Royalist.

Mortier, Edouard, Adolphe, Duc de Trévise, 1768–1835. A brave and talented young officer of the revolutionary army, he served Napoleon with distinction. He went over to the side of Louis XVIII, but refused to be a member of the court-martial that tried Marshal Ney. He was named Ambassador to Russia under Louis-Philippe and Minister of War.

Murat, Joachim, Marshal, then King of Naples, 1767–1815. The son of an innkeeper, Murat became Bonaparte's aide-de-camp in 1796 and participated in all the campaigns. His courage and his luck were legendary. In 1800, he married Caroline, Napoleon's sister, and became King of Naples in 1808. Though he intrigued against Napoleon in

1814, he lost his kingdom to the Bourbons after the Congress of Vienna. During the Hundred Days, he encouraged an Italian nationalistic movement, but he was caught in Calabria and shot.

Napoleon, 1769–1821. Born at Ajaccio in Corsica, he attended military school in France. He participated in the revolutionary campaigns. Seizing his opportunity during the troubled times of the Directory, he organised the coup of 18 Brumaire and set up a new Government, the Consulate. From then on, he was the master of France. He was First Consul from 1799 to 1804, Emperor of the French from 1804 to 1814, then, after he escaped from Elba, Emperor during the Hundred Days in 1815. Defeated at Waterloo, he was exiled to Saint Helena.

Necker, Jacques, 1732–1804. This Swiss financier established himself in Paris as a banker in 1763. Talented and unusually honest, he was called to the Government in 1776. He tried vainly to reform the system. The King demanded his resignation on July 11, 1789. His departure was an important element in the upheaval which ended three days later by the fall of the Bastille. His daughter was Mme. de Staël.

Ney, Michel, Maréchal, Duc d'Elchingen, Prince de la Moskova, 1769–1815. As "the bravest of the brave," he was an immense asset to Napoleon and participated in all his campaigns. In 1814, he was in favour of the Emperor's abdication, then switched to the side of the Bourbons. He was ordered to stop Napoleon's march on his return from Elba but instead joined him. Ney fought bravely at Waterloo and tried to hide after the defeat. But he was caught, accused of treason, and shot.

Orléans, Duc d'. See Louis-Philippe.

Orléans, House of. The title of Duc d'Orléans was traditionally given to the King's closest brother. The heir to the duchy was the Duc de Chartres. The house that survived as a major branch of the House of Bourbon issued from Philippe, the only brother of Louis XIV. His heir was regent from 1715 to 1723, during the childhood of Louis XV. King Louis-Philippe was his great-grandson. The pretender to the throne of France is a direct descendant.

Osmond, Rainulphe, Marquis d', 1788–1862. Adèle de Boigne's little brother, whom she always called "darling boy," was a charming, light-headed young man. He married an extremely rich girl, Aimée Destil-lières, who refused some of the greatest French aristocrats for him. His grandson inherited Mme. de Boigne's manuscript.

Osmond, René-Eustache, Marquis d', 1751–1838. Entered the diplo-matic career in 1787 and emigrated first to Italy, then to England during the Revolution. A very intelligent, moderate man, he did not participate in the excesses of the emigration. Though he returned to France during the Napoleonic regime, he refused to serve the Em-peror. Louis XVIII rewarded him by posting him first to Turin, then to London. He was extremely close to his daughter. His marriage with the daughter of Robert Dillon, a Catholic Irishman who had set-tled with his wife and their thirteen children in Bordeaux, was a love match. Needless to say, she was extremely beautiful and also quite penniless.

Otrante. See Fouché.

Oudinot, Nicolas, Duc de Reggio, 1767–1847. Had a brilliant career in the army, though Napoleon once said "it was impossible to have less brains than Oudinot." He welcomed the Bourbons in 1814 and be-came Governor of the Invalides in 1842.

Pasquier, Etienne-Denis, Baron, Duc, 1767–1862. A descendant of the great Renaissance humanist, Estienne Pasquier, he followed his fa-ther's example and became a counsellor in the Paris Parliament. During the Terror, his father was guillotined, and he was arrested. He re-sumed his career in 1795 and served the Empire, the Restoration, and the July Monarchy. Immensely respected, he was named Chancellor of France when this office was revived in May 1837. He may have been se-cretly married to Mme. de Boigne.

Philippe-Egalité, Louis-Philippe, Duc d'Orléans, 1747–1793. He was very hostile to Marie-Antoinette and rarely came to Versailles, either staying in the Palais Royal—he built the shops in the arcades to increase his income—or living abroad. Extremely popular, he was elected deputy of Paris to the assembly. He voted for the death sentence of Louis XVI but was arrested and executed one month after Marie-Antoinette.

Pichegru, Charles, General, 1761–1804. Fought the War of Independence and participated brilliantly in the revolutionary campaigns. During the Directory, his politics changed. He supported the right-wing opposition and made his way to England, where he became a Royalist agent. Sent secretly to France in 1804 to join Georges Cadoudal in a plot against Napoleon, he was arrested in Paris and found strangled in his cell.

Polastron, Louise, Comtesse de, 1764–1804. Sister-in-law of the Duchesse de Polignac, Marie-Antoinette's favourite, and aunt of Jules de Polignac, she had a long affair with the Comte d'Artois and was instrumental in bringing him back to the Church.

Polignac, Jules, Comte, Prince de, 1780–1847. This faithful companion of the Comte d'Artois was opposed to any concession to Liberal opinion. With little brains and no political acumen, he had a disastrous influence once Charles X gave him the highest government posts. He was judged after the Revolution of 1830, condemned to perpetual confinement and loss of civil rights, and locked up in the fortress of Ham until the amnesty of 1836.

Pozzo Di Borgo, Charles-André, Comte, Duc, 1764–1842. He was born in Corsica three years before Napoleon. Unlike the Bonaparte family, Pozzo was in favor of Corsica's independence and therefore refused to serve Napoleon. He entered the service of the Tsar, who sent him to Paris as his Ambassador during the Restoration. He was transferred to London in 1834.

Raguse. *See* Marmont.

Récamier, Jeanne, Mme. de, 1777–1849. One of the most enchanting women of her times, she was married at fifteen to the rich banker Jacques Récamier. From the early days of the Consulate until the end of the July Monarchy, her salon attracted fashionable, literary, and political society. She had many admirers but no lovers. Chateaubriand was a constant visitor and became the centre of her salon, where he read extracts from his works.

Regent, Prince of Wales, 1762–1830. Eldest son of George III, he became Regent during his father's illness and reigned as George IV from 1820 to 1830. He was married to Caroline of Brunswick (*see* Caroline), though his attachment to Mrs. Fitzherbert (see p. 9, Volume One) had been blessed by the Church.

Richelieu, Armand Emmanuel du Plessis, Duc de, 1766–1822. He joined the Russian army during the Revolution and was greatly appreciated by Tsar Alexander I. In 1803, he was appointed Governor of Odessa and, two years later, Governor General of the whole Odessa region. During his remarkable tenure, he established schools, reformed finances, and encouraged agriculture and exports. He returned to Paris in 1814, and was President of the Council twice. A moderate man, in constant opposition to the extreme Royalists, he resigned in 1821. His last years were clouded by the unwanted attentions of the Queen of Sweden, who pursued him wherever he went.

Sabran, Elzéar de, 1774–1842. A charming, witty poet with surprisingly strong conservative political views.

Salvandy, Achille, Comte de, 1795–1856. One of Napoleon's youngest officers, he energetically opposed the allied occupation of France in 1816. He became Minister of Education during the July Monarchy and founded the French School of Archeology in Athens.

Schlegel, August-Wilhelm von, 1767–1845. The great German proponent of Romanticism. His literary criticism and university lectures were crucial to the development of the movement.

Sièyes, Emmanuel, Abbé, 1748–1836. One of the chief theorists of the Revolution and an architect of the coup that replaced the Directory with the Consulate and marked the start of Napoleon Bonaparte's political career. He played an important, though discreet, role in political life until 1815. He spent the Restoration years in exile in Brussels and returned to Paris after 1830.

Staël-Holstein, Germaine Necker, Baronne de, 1766–1817. A brilliant woman of letters who wrote novels, plays, and political essays and was the main theorist of Romanticism. She was the daughter of Necker and married the Swedish Ambassador to Paris, whose diplomatic status allowed her to stay in France during the Revolution. Her salon flourished at the end of the Terror. She was too much of an aggressive female intellectual not to irritate Napoleon, who banished her from Paris. She spent the seven years of her exile either in Coppet in Switzerland or travelling extensively in Russia, Germany, Italy, and England. She returned to Paris in 1814.

Sweden, Queen of. See Clary, Désirée.

Talleyrand, Charles-Maurice de Talleyrand-Périgord, Prince and Duc de Bénévent, 1754–1838. A statesman and diplomat notable for his capacity for political survival. He held high office during the French Revolution—prudently spending the two years of the Terror in the United States—under Napoleon, during the Restoration, and under Louis-Philippe.

Talma, François-Joseph, 1763–1826. The most famous actor of the period. He imposed a more natural diction and a search for historical truth in both attitude and costume, and Napoleon regarded him highly.

Trevise. See Mortier.

Victor Emmanuel I, King of Sardinia from 1802 to 1821, 1759–1824. His possessions in Piedmont had been annexed by France during the Empire and returned to him in 1814. His reactionary politics provoked insurrections, and he was forced to abdicate in favor of his brother Charles Félix in 1821.

Villèle, Jean-Baptiste, 1773–1854. A naval officer whose Ultra-Royalist political career took off in 1815. He was named President of the Council during the last years of Louis XVIII's reign. He retired in Toulouse after the Revolution of 1830.

Wales, Prince of. See Regent.

Wellington, Arthur Wellesley, Duke of, 1769–1852. Born in Dublin, educated at Eton and at a military academy in France, he was the principal architect of Great Britain's victory over Napoleon.

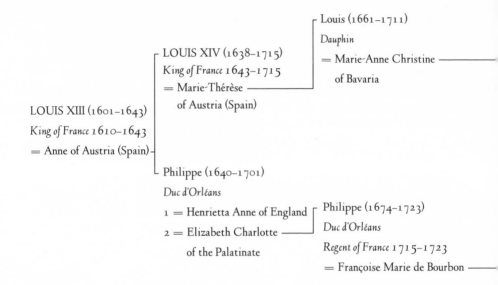

LOUIS XIII (1601–1643)
King of France 1610–1643
= Anne of Austria (Spain)

LOUIS XIV (1638–1715)
King of France 1643–1715
= Marie-Thérèse —————
of Austria (Spain)

Louis (1661–1711)
Dauphin
= Marie-Anne Christine —————
of Bavaria

Philippe (1640–1701)
Duc d'Orléans
1 = Henrietta Anne of England
2 = Elizabeth Charlotte —————
of the Palatinate

Philippe (1674–1723)
Duc d'Orléans
Regent of France 1715–1723
= Françoise Marie de Bourbon —————

Bourbon Family Tree,
with the House of Orléans to 1830

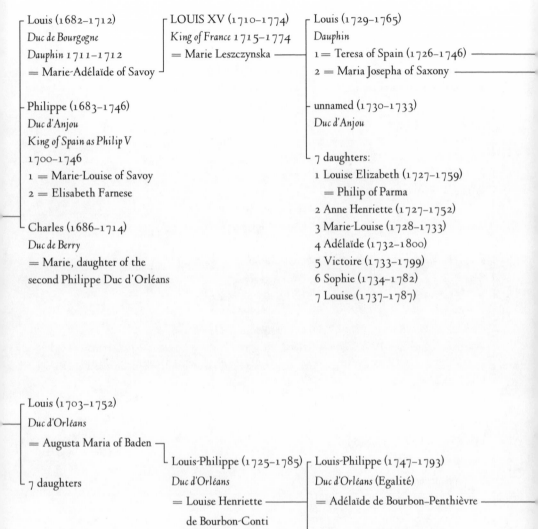

Louis (1682–1712)
Duc de Bourgogne
Dauphin 1711–1712
= Marie-Adélaïde of Savoy

Philippe (1683–1746)
Duc d'Anjou
King of Spain as Philip V
1700–1746
1 = Marie-Louise of Savoy
2 = Elisabeth Farnese

Charles (1686–1714)
Duc de Berry
= Marie, daughter of the
second Philippe Duc d'Orléans

LOUIS XV (1710–1774)
King of France 1715–1774
= Marie Leszczynska ———

Louis (1729–1765)
Dauphin
1 = Teresa of Spain (1726–1746) ————
2 = Maria Josepha of Saxony ————

unnamed (1730–1733)
Duc d'Anjou

7 daughters:
1 Louise Elizabeth (1727–1759)
  = Philip of Parma
2 Anne Henriette (1727–1752)
3 Marie-Louise (1728–1733)
4 Adélaïde (1732–1800)
5 Victoire (1733–1799)
6 Sophie (1734–1782)
7 Louise (1737–1787)

Louis (1703–1752)
Duc d'Orléans
= Augusta Maria of Baden

7 daughters

Louis-Philippe (1725–1785)
Duc d'Orléans
= Louise Henriette ———
  de Bourbon-Conti

Louis-Philippe (1747–1793)
Duc d'Orléans (Egalité)
= Adélaïde de Bourbon-Penthièvre ———

Louise (1750–1822)
= Louis Henri Joseph
  de Bourbon-Condé

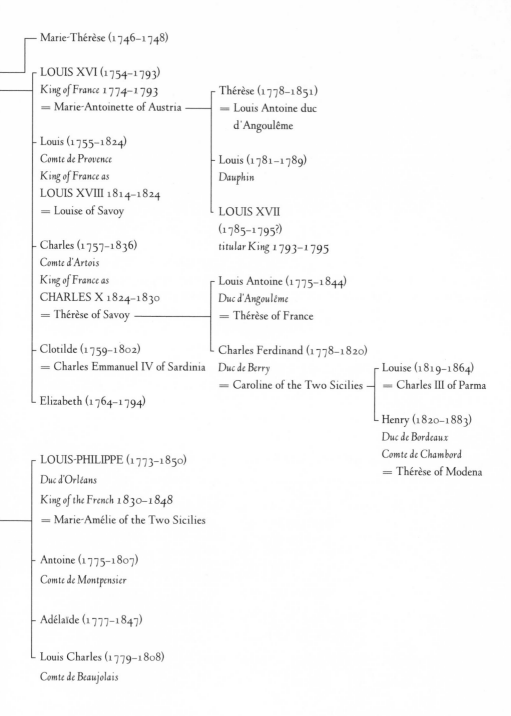

Marie-Thérèse (1746–1748)

LOUIS XVI (1754–1793)
King of France 1774–1793
= Marie-Antoinette of Austria ——

Louis (1755–1824)
Comte de Provence
King of France as
LOUIS XVIII 1814–1824
= Louise of Savoy

Charles (1757–1836)
Comte d'Artois
King of France as
CHARLES X 1824–1830
= Thérèse of Savoy ———

Clotilde (1759–1802)
= Charles Emmanuel IV of Sardinia

Elizabeth (1764–1794)

Thérèse (1778–1851)
= Louis Antoine duc
 d'Angoulême

Louis (1781–1789)
Dauphin

LOUIS XVII
(1785–1795?)
titular King 1793–1795

Louis Antoine (1775–1844)
Duc d'Angoulême
= Thérèse of France

Charles Ferdinand (1778–1820)
Duc de Berry
= Caroline of the Two Sicilies

Louise (1819–1864)
= Charles III of Parma

Henry (1820–1883)
Duc de Bordeaux
Comte de Chambord
= Thérèse of Modena

LOUIS-PHILIPPE (1773–1850)
Duc d'Orléans
King of the French 1830–1848
= Marie-Amélie of the Two Sicilies

Antoine (1775–1807)
Comte de Montpensier

Adélaïde (1777–1847)

Louis Charles (1779–1808)
Comte de Beaujolais

CHRONOLOGY

Events in the life of Mme. de Boigne are in italic.

February 21, 1781   *Birth of Adèle d'Osmond*

May 1783   End of the War of Independence

May 1789   The Estates General assemble in Versailles

July 14, 1789   Fall of the Bastille

October 6, 1789   The royal family is forced by the mob to leave Versailles

February 1791   *Adèle and her mother follow the King's aunts to Italy*

October 1791   Constitutional regime is installed in France

June 1791   Louis XVI tries to flee but is caught at Varennes

April 1792   France declares war on Austria

August 10, 1792   Louis XVI is deposed and imprisoned with his family

September 2, 1792   The First French Republic is proclaimed and the Terror begins

September 20, 1792   French victory at Valmy

December 1792   Trial of Louis XVI

Chronology

January 21, 1793	Execution of Louis XVI
February 1793	Extension of the war: Great Britain, Russia, and Spain constitute a coalition with Austria against France
September 1793	The regime of Terror intensifies
October 16, 1793	Marie-Antoinette is executed
February 1794	*The d'Osmonds leave Italy to settle in England*
July 27, 1794	The Terror ends with the execution of Robespierre
June 11, 1798	*Marriage of Adèle d'Osmond and General de Boigne*
November 9, 1799	Napoleon Bonaparte seizes power (18 Brumaire)
May 18, 1804	Napoleon is proclaimed Emperor of the French
September 1804	*Mme. de Boigne returns to France*
January 1811	George III is declared insane. His son becomes Prince Regent
January 1812	*General and Mme. de Boigne separate*
April 4, 1814	Napoleon I abdicates and is exiled in Elba
June 4, 1814	Louis XVIII enters Paris. Beginning of the Restoration
September 1814	*Mme. de Boigne and her parents settle in Turin during her father's ambassadorship*
March 20 to June 22, 1815	The Hundred Days
August 1815	*Mme. de Boigne returns to Paris*
January 1816 to 1819	*Mme. de Boigne follows her father, who is named Ambassador to Great Britain*
January 1820	The Prince Regent becomes George IV

Chronology

February 1, 1820	Assassination of the Duc de Berry
May 5, 1821	Death of Napoleon
September 16, 1824	Death of Louis XVIII. His brother, Charles X, becomes king
June 21, 1830	*Death of General de Boigne*
June 26, 1830	William IV succeeds his brother, George IV
July 26, 1830	A series of reactionary ordinances provoke an uprising
July 27, 28, 29, 1830	A three-day revolution puts an end to the Bourbon regime
August 9, 1830	Louis-Philippe is crowned King of the French
April 1835	*Mme. de Boigne starts writing her memoirs*
November 6, 1836	Death of Charles X
June 20, 1837	Victoria becomes Queen of England
February 1848	Louis-Philippe is dethroned and takes refuge in England
July 4, 1848	Death of Chateaubriand
December 1, 1848	Louis-Napoleon is elected President of the Republic
December 2, 1852	The Second Empire is proclaimed. Louis-Napoleon takes the title of Napoleon III
August 26, 1850	Death of Louis-Philippe
May 10, 1866	*Death of Mme. de Boigne*

Memoirs of the Comtesse de Boigne

CHAPTER ONE

Versailles

1781–1791

My childhood ~ A dog and a doll ~ Opening of the Estates

General ~ Versailles invaded ~ Journey to England ~

Mrs. Fitzherbert ~ The buckles of the Prince of Wales ~

My father's position in 1790 ~ His crossing to Corsica

~ Last meeting with the Queen ~

Departure from France and arrival in Turin

I was brought up literally upon the knees of the royal family. King Louis XVI* and Queen Marie-Antoinette* especially overwhelmed me with kindness. It was a time when children were put out to nurse, then weaned and sent to a convent, or dressed up like little ladies and gentlemen, and appeared only to be wearied and made peevish and ill-tempered; in my cambric frock, a profusion of fair hair framing a pretty little face, I was extremely striking. My father had taken pains to develop my intelligence, and I was honestly regarded as a little prodigy. I had learnt to read with such facility that at the age of three I could read and repeat the tragedies of Racine for my own pleasure, and, it is said, for the pleasure of others.

My father[1] often took me to the theatrical performances at Versailles. After the first piece I was taken away, that I might be sent to bed, and I remember that the King sometimes called me into his box and made me tell him the story of the play that I had just seen. I generally added my reflections on it, which were usually highly appreciated. On one occasion, in the middle of my literary observation, I told

---

* Names that appear in the *Dictionary of Characters* (see p. xv) are asterisked at their first appearance.
1. See Osmond, René-Eustache, in the *Dictionary of Characters*.

him that I very much wanted to ask him a favour, and encouraged by his kindness, I admitted my desire for two of the smallest glass drops from the chandeliers, to use as earrings, as my ears were to be bored the next day.

My parents had eventually come to spend the whole summer at Bellevue,[2] and my room was on the ground floor, looking into the courtyard. Madame Adélaïde* took long walks every day to supervise her workmen. She used to call me as she passed; my hat was put on, I climbed out of the window, and went off with her without any nurse. She was generally followed by a number of servants, and a little carriage drawn by one led horse, which she never entered, but which I often occupied. I preferred, however, to run by her side and to carry on what I called a conversation. My rival and friend was a large white spaniel, a very intelligent dog, who shared these walks. If the road happened to be very muddy, he was put into a large white linen bag and carried by two of the servants on duty. I was extremely proud of being able to pick my steps without getting muddy as he did.

When we came back to the château, I fought with Vizir for his red velvet cushion, which he abandoned more readily than he did the cakes which were broken up for us on the floor. The good Princess would often go down on all fours and join in our romps, to restore peace or to obtain the prize of the race. I can still see her tall, thin figure, her tucked violet dress (which was the uniform at Bellevue), her butterfly hat, and two large teeth, which were the only ones she had. She had been very pretty, but at this time was extremely ugly, and so I thought her.

Madame Adélaïde had made for me, at great expense, a magnificent doll, with a complete wardrobe, basket, and jewels, including a watch by Lépine, the King's watchmaker, which I still possess, and a

2. Bellevue had been built by Louis XV for Mme. de Pompadour in 1748. When she died, the King gave it to his daughters. At the end of Louis XVI's reign, only two of the Princesses, Adélaïde and Victoire, occupied it. Mme. de Boigne's mother, Mme. d'Osmond, who was lady-in-waiting for Madame Adélaïde, stayed there with her family for part of the year. The château was badly damaged during the Revolution.

duchesse bed, in which I slept at the age of seven, so that the size of the doll can be imagined. The presentation of this doll was a festival for the royal family. The family went to dine at Bellevue and sent for me when they rose from the table. The folding doors were opened, and the doll arrived, dragged forward upon her bed and escorted by all her property. The King held me by the hand.

"Who is that for, Adèle?"

"I believe it is for me, Sir."

Everybody began to play with my new property. They wished to put me in the bed instead of the doll, and the Queen and her sister-in-law, Madame Elisabeth, on their knees, on either side of the bed, amused themselves in making it, with much delight at their cleverness in turning the mattresses. The poor Princesses alas did not think that a very few years later, they would be reduced to making their own bed. How extravagant such a prophecy would then have seemed!

I was no less a favourite with the younger generation. The Dauphin[3] who died at Meudon was very fond of me, and was continually asking that I might play with him, while the Duc de Berry got himself into disgrace because he would not dance with anyone but myself at a ball.

The misfortunes of the Revolution ended my successes at court. Events had become too serious, and the affectations of a child no longer had interest; the year 1789 had begun.

My father was well aware of the gravity of the situation. The opening of the Estates General was a solemnity conducted with magnificence, which attracted strangers from all parts of Europe to Versailles. My mother, in full court dress, told my father that she was about to start. As she did not see him, she went into his room and found him in his dressing-gown.

"Do be quick, we shall be late."

"No, I am not going. I cannot go and see that unhappy man abdicate."

3. The eldest son of Louis XVI and Marie-Antoinette, who was born in 1781 and died in 1789.

It must not be concluded from this that my father was opposed to concessions. On the contrary, he was persuaded that the spirit of the time urgently demanded concessions, but he wished them to be made from a definite plan—to be large and generous, and not exaggerated. It was with mortal fear that he saw the opening of the Estates General, for, knowing the vagueness of individual wishes, he was aware that no one had settled any point at which concession or demand should cease.

My parents lived in town as the apartments in the château were in-convenient for people definitely established at Versailles. On October 6, 1789, I do not know who came to warn my father, while he was at table, of the rumours, only too well founded, which were beginning to go about. He went off immediately to the château; my mother was to meet him there at the time when the Princesses began their card game. But shortly after his departure, the streets of Versailles filled up with a flood of horrible-looking people, uttering wild cries, while gunshots could be heard in the distance. Such part of their language as could be heard was even more frightful than their appearance. Communica-tions with the château were cut off. When night came, my mother took up her position in a darkened room and attempted, with her face against the closed shutters, to discover the nature of events from what she could hear and see. I was on her knee, and eventually went to sleep. They put me on a sofa to avoid waking me, and she decided to go and reconnoitre for herself, taking with her a *valet de chambre*. She went to several gates of the château without being able to get in, till at last she found on sentry duty a member of the National Guard who recognised her, and said, "You had better go home, Marquise; you must not be seen in the street. I cannot let you in, my orders are too strict; and it would be no use if I did, for you would be stopped at every door. You have nothing to fear for your friends, but there will not be a Life Guardsman left tomorrow morning."

This was said at nine o'clock in the evening, before the massacre had begun, and the words were those of a reasonable and moderate man, as can be seen from their purport; yet he was privy to this horrible secret, and was by no means revolted by it, to such an extent had everybody's head been turned.

My mother did not recognise the man at the time, but afterwards learnt that he was a hosier. She went home again, frightened, as may be imagined, but less despondent than when she started, for the street rumours declared that every throat in the château had been slit.

At midnight my father arrived. I was aroused by the tumult and by the joy of seeing him, but it was not for long. He came to say good-bye to us and to get some money. He ordered his horses to be saddled and led to the neighbouring town of Saint-Cyr by a circuitous route. His brother, the Abbé d'Osmond, who accompanied him, was to go with the horses and wait for him there. These gentlemen proceeded to change their court dresses for travelling suits. My father loaded his pistols. Meanwhile my mother was sewing all the money that she could find in the house into two belts, which she made them put on. These proceedings occupied half an hour, and then they started. I wished to embrace my father, but my mother pulled me away, with a roughness to which I was not accustomed, and which surprised me.

The door closed, and I then saw her fall on her knees in an outburst of grief which absorbed my complete attention, and I understood that she had wished to spare my father the unnecessary pain of seeing our sufferings. This practical lesson made a great impression upon me, and thenceforward I never gave way to any demonstrations which might increase the grief or the anxiety of others.

I have heard my father relate that when he had reached the meeting-place, the terrace of the orange garden, he walked about alone for a long time; a man then arrived, wrapped in a cloak. At first they kept aloof, but then they recognised one another: it was the Comte de Saint-Priest, a Minister at that time and a man of sense and courage. They continued their walk for a long time, but no one came, and the hour grew late. Uneasy and astonished, they did not know what to think of this delay in the King's proposed departure, as it was arranged that he should go to Rambouillet that same night. They did not dare to appear in the royal apartments in their travelling dress; not only would this have been contrary to etiquette, but it would have been a revelation of the plan.

M. de Saint-Priest, who had rooms in the château, decided to go and change his clothes, and made an appointment with my father in a distant spot. My father waited a long time, and at length the Comte appeared. "My dear d'Osmond, go home and reassure your wife; the King is not going to start." And shaking his hand, "My friend, M. Necker* has won the day, and the King and the monarchy are alike ruined."

The King's departure for Rambouillet had been decided, but the orders for the carriages had been given with the full formalities usually in force. The rumour had thus been amplified. The grooms had hesitated to harness the horses, the coachmen to drive them. The populace had gathered before the stables and refused to let the carriages out. M. Necker, informed of these facts, had gone to discuss them with the King, who was persuaded to stay rather by these obstacles than by the Minister's arguments. Though he was accustomed to ride twenty leagues while hunting, to go to Rambouillet on a troop horse would have seemed to him an inconceivable solution. There, as later at Varennes,[4] the chance of safety had been destroyed by those habits of formality which had become second nature to the French royal family. My father was obliged to go home to change his clothes, and as he did not return to the château that night, he escaped the spectacle of the horrors which were there perpetrated.

As soon as the King's consent to his removal to Paris had opened the château doors, my mother went to her Princess. She found the two sisters, the Princesses Adélaïde and Victoire, in their room on the ground floor, with all the shutters closed and one single candle

4. On June 20, 1791, Louis XVI, Marie-Antoinette, and their children attempted to escape. They were recognised in the small town of Varennes and brought back to Paris as virtual prisoners. The King was then compelled to accept the Constitution. Meanwhile, his two brothers, the Comte de Provence and the Comte d'Artois, had taken refuge in Coblentz in Germany.

lighted. After their first words she asked them why they were making so sad a day still gloomier. "My dear, it is in order that they may not aim at us, as they did this morning," replied Madame Adélaïde, with extreme calm and gentleness. In fact, the mob had fired into their windows in the morning, and not a single pane of glass remained unbroken.

My mother stayed with them until the moment of their departure. She wished to accompany them, but the Princesses obstinately declined, and accepted this mark of devotion only from their ladies of honour, the Duchesse de Narbonne and Mme. de Chastellux. They followed the sad procession which carried off the King as far as Sèvres;[5] from there they took the road to Bellevue, where my parents went to join them the next day.

However, the uproar did not subside. The excitement at Versailles was intense, and terrible threats were uttered against my mother. It was said that Madame Adélaïde had full power over the King, while she in turn was under my mother's influence, who was thus at the head of the aristocrats. This feeling became so violent that at the end of three days the danger was obvious, and we started for England.

My recollections of the journey are but scant. I can only remember the impression which the sight of the sea made upon me. Child that I was, I conceived a devotion for the sea which has never faded. Its grey and green tints always held a charm for me which Mediterranean blue has never been able to efface.

We disembarked at Brighton. By chance my mother met there Mrs. Fitzherbert, who was walking on the jetty. Some years before she had come to Paris to avoid the attentions of the Prince of Wales.* My mother, who was her cousin, had seen a great deal of her. Since that time the blessing of a Catholic priest had sanctified, though not legalised, her relations with the Prince; she lived with him in an intimacy which gave the appearance and the form of ordinary married life. They inhabited together a little house at Brighton like ordinary citizens. My

5. After the invasion of Versailles by the mob on October 6, 1789, the King, the Queen, and their children were forced to return to Paris, where they settled in the Tuileries.

parents were received with much effusion, and were induced to spend several days there.

I remember that I was taken one morning to Mrs. Fitzherbert, and that she showed us the Prince's dressing room, where there was a large table entirely covered with shoe buckles. I expressed my astonishment at the sight, and Mrs. Fitzherbert, with a laugh, opened a large cupboard, which was also full; there were enough buckles for every day of the year. It was a fashion of the times, and the Prince of Wales was the most fashionable of men. This collection of shoe buckles struck my childish imagination, and for a long time I only thought of the Prince of Wales as owner of these buckles.

My parents were made much of in England. French visitors were rare at that time. My mother was a pretty and fashionable woman, and her family overwhelmed her with kindness. Life there was very magnificent as far as I can remember, but I was too accustomed to magnificence to be greatly impressed. On several occasions I saw the three youngest English Princesses. They were much older than I, and I did not like them. The Princess Amelia called me a little thing, which shocked me greatly. I spoke English very well, but did not then understand that this was a term of affection.

In the month of January 1790, my father returned to France, and three months later we joined him there. I have forgotten to say that he had left the army in 1788 to take up a diplomatic career. Formerly he had been colonel of the infantry regiment of Barrois, in a garrison in Corsica. He went there every year.

One of these journeys gave rise to an episode which was of little importance at the time, but afterwards acquired interest. He was at Toulon, staying with M. Malouet, the naval commissary and a friend of his, waiting for a change of wind to permit his embarcation, when he was informed that a Corsican gentleman desired to see him. The gentleman was shown in, and after the preliminary courtesies, explained that he wished to return as quickly as possible to Ajaccio, and, the only felucca in the harbour being chartered by my father, he begged him to allow the captain to accept him as a passenger.

"That is impossible, Sir, as I have chartered the felucca, but I shall be very happy to take you on board as my guest."

"But, Marquis, I am not alone; I have my son with me and my cook, whom I am taking home."

"Well, Sir, there will be room enough for all of you."

The Corsican thanked my father profusely, and came to see him frequently for several days, at the end of which the wind changed and they embarked. At dinner, to which my father invited the passengers, he requested an officer, M. de Belloc, to call the Corsican's son, who was wearing the uniform of the military school and reading at the end of the boat. The young man refused. M. de Belloc came back irritated, and said to my father, "I should like to throw the unsociable little fellow into the sea. He has an unpleasant face. Will you grant me permission, Colonel?"

"No," said my father, laughing; "and I am not of your opinion. His face shows character, and I am sure that he will be heard of some day."

The unsociable fellow was the future Emperor Napoleon.* Belloc has related this scene to me at least ten times, adding with a sigh, "Ah, if the Colonel had only allowed me to throw him into the sea, he would not be turning the world upside down today."

The day after the arrival at Ajaccio, M. Buonaparte, the father, accompanied with his family, called upon my father to express his thanks. My father called upon Mme. Buonaparte. She lived at Ajaccio in one of the best little houses in the town, on the door of which was written out in snail shells, *Vive Marbeuf*. M. de Marbeuf had been the patron of the Buonaparte family, and history records that Mme. Buonaparte had been very grateful for his services. At the time of my father's visit she was still a very beautiful woman; he found her in the kitchen, without her stockings, in a cotton skirt, making sweets. Notwithstanding her beauty, the task seemed appropriate.

After he was ordered to undertake a commission with respect to the Dutch refugees in 1788, my father was appointed Minister at The Hague, which position he held at the time of our stay in England. A quarrel between the Prince of Orange and the French Ambassador had decided the court of Versailles to send only a Minister to Holland. The Republic, however, wished to have an Ambassador. This quarrel prevented my father from taking up his post. He waited with great patience, as he hoped thus to secure the rank of Ambassador, which he would not have been able to do forthwith under ordinary conditions.

The town of Versailles had begun to realise the loss that was caused by the absence of the court. Excitement had subsided, and the sad days of October were regretted. Upon my mother's return, she was most kindly received by the very persons who had inveighed most strongly against her at the time of her departure; however, we did not stay long. We began by going to Bellevue for the summer, and we spent the next winter in rooms in the Pavillon de Marsan in the Tuileries.

I can recall in full detail a scene that happened during that summer. It was many months since I had seen the Queen. She came to Bellevue under the escort of the National Guard, a uniform that I had been taught to detest. The Queen was even then, I think, practically a prisoner, for the escort never left her. At any rate, whenever she sent for me I found her on the terrace surrounded by National Guards. My little heart was affected by this sight, and I began to sob. The Queen knelt down, put her face against mine, and hid both our faces beneath my long fair hair, begging me to hide my tears. I felt that hers were falling. I can still hear her words, "Hush, hush, Adèle!" She remained for a long time in this position.

All the spectators were affected, but only the carelessness of childhood could have shown emotion at a moment when there was danger in every action. I do not know if any report was made of this scene, but the Queen did not return to Bellevue, and that was the last time I saw her, except from a distance, during my stay at the Tuileries. The impressions of that moment, which I still preserve, are very distinct. I could describe her dress. She was in a white *pierrot de linon* with a lilac-coloured pattern, a full fichu, and a large straw hat, the broad ribbons of which were tied in a large knot at the point where the fichu crossed.

Poor Princess, poor woman, poor mother! Terrible was the fate reserved for her! She thought herself very unhappy at the time, but it was only the beginning of her troubles. Her son, the second Dauphin,[6] had accompanied her to Bellevue, and used to play in the sand with my brother. The National Guards joined in these games, and the two children were too young to object to their company. I would not have approached for all the kingdoms of the world. I stayed near the Queen, who held my hand. I have since been told that she thought herself obliged to explain to her attendants that the first Dauphin was very fond of me, that she had not seen me since his death, and that this was the reason of our mutual affection.

Far from subsiding, the Revolution became more and more formidable. The King, who was proposing to leave France, wished to remove his aunts. They applied to the National Assembly, and obtained permission to go to Rome. Before their departure they remained at Bellevue.

My father had been appointed Minister at Saint Petersburg, to replace M. de Ségur in 1790. The Minister's public report explained that this choice had been made because the Empress Catherine would not consent to receive a "patriot" envoy. This circumstance was eventually to make my father's position extremely dangerous. He had, however, no idea of resigning, but wished his wife and his children to leave France. It was arranged that as soon as the Princesses should have crossed the frontier, my mother was to follow them.

Our journey passed off without incident, and we rejoined the Princesses at Turin. My mother then spent several months in Rome, in keen anxiety owing to the dangers to which my father was exposed. Her health, which was becoming more alarming, eventually decided my father to tear himself from the Tuileries, where he did not wish to stay, and whence he could not easily depart. We were reunited in the spring of 1792, some months after the flight to Varennes.

6. He was to die imprisoned at the Temple in 1795.

In his last interview with the King, the monarch had awarded him a pension of twelve thousand francs from his private purse. "I am not very rich," he said, "but on the other hand, you are not grasping. We shall perhaps meet again at a time when I can make better use of your zeal, and reward it more worthily."

CHAPTER TWO

Emigration

1792–1804

I shall say but little of our stay in Italy. My recollections of it are too vague; I merely remember hearing stories of the quarrels in the little court of the Princesses, which even then seemed to me extremely ridiculous.

I often saw Mme. Vigée Lebrun, the portraitist, or rather her daughter, who was one of my playmates. Mme. Lebrun was an excellent person, still pretty, somewhat tactless at times, of remarkable talent and abounding in all those little affectations which she could claim the right to practice as an artist and a pretty woman. If the term *petite maîtresse* enjoyed a better reputation, it might well apply to her.

Towards the outset of 1792, Sir John Legard arrived at Rome with his wife, who had been a Miss Aston and was a first cousin of my mother. This family relationship led to great intimacy. The money which my parents had brought from France was running low, and only one quarter of the pension granted by the King had been paid. Sir John asked my parents to accompany him to Naples and then to return with him to his Yorkshire estate, where he offered them the most friendly and generous hospitality. My parents agreed to spend some time with him at Naples, but would not further pledge themselves, and Sir John did not insist.

At Naples we stayed ten months. My mother was very kindly

received by Queen Marie-Caroline, the eldest sister of Marie-Antoinette, who enjoyed her society and made her give a full account of the French court and of the beginning of the Revolution in which she was interested as both Queen and as sister. I was introduced to the Princesses, her daughters, and there began my connection, if I may use the term, with Princess Amelia, afterwards Queen Marie-Amélie* of France.

The time for leaving Naples approached. Sir John Legard again invited my parents to accompany him to England. It was easier to communicate from that country with Santo Domingo from which some help was expected. My father had stored all his ambassadorial furniture in Holland, and some use of this might be made. Finally, and as a last resource, Sir John Legard, with all possible tact, placed his house at our disposal. During the six months we had spent at Naples, he had overwhelmed my parents with marks of friendship. If we stayed in Italy, we should become dependent on the Princesses, who were beginning to find their circumstances straitened, while those about them would not welcome a new family to their circle.

These reflections induced my parents to accept the pressing offer of Sir John, after securing the consent of Madame Adélaïde. She agreed to their departure, adding that if they were unable to live in England, she was ready to share her last piece of bread with them. The Queen of Naples attempted to keep my mother there; she even offered her a small salary, but the family resources then held out some hope. The Queen, moreover, was reputed to be capricious, and Lady Hamilton was coming into favour. This Lady Hamilton became so notorious that I think a few words should be devoted to her.

Mr. Greville happened to enter his kitchen one day, and saw a young girl by the fireside with one foot bare, as she was mending the stocking of black wool which had covered it. Her angelic beauty attracted his notice, and he discovered that she was a sister of his groom. He found no difficulty in bringing her upstairs and installing her in his drawing-room. The young man lived with her for some time, and had her taught to read and write. When his affairs became completely upset, he found himself obliged to leave London very suddenly. At that moment his uncle, Sir William Hamilton, the English Minister at Naples, happened to be at home on leave. His nephew informed him that his chief vexation was the necessity of abandoning a beautiful young girl who was in his house, and who was likely to be turned into the street. Sir William promised to look into the matter.

As a matter of fact, he went to look for her at the moment when the bailiffs were turning her out of Mr. Greville's house, and soon he fell desperately in love with her. He took her with him to Italy. What their connection was I cannot say, but at the end of some years he married her. Previously he had treated her with that paternal affection which was natural to his age and allowed him to introduce her to Italian society, which is less strict than ours upon these matters.

The girl, who was as beautiful as an angel, though she had never been able to learn to read or write with any fluency, had great artistic talent. She turned to full account the advantages offered by her stay in Italy and by the taste of Sir William Hamilton. She became a good musician, and developed a unique talent which may seem foolish in description, but which enchanted all spectators and drove artists to despair. I refer to what were known as the attitudes of Lady Hamilton.

In conformity with her husband's taste, she was generally dressed in a white tunic, with a belt round her waist, her hair down her back or turned up by a comb, but dressed in no special way. When she consented to give a performance, she would provide herself with two or three cashmere shawls, an urn, a scent-box, a lyre, and a tambourine. With these few accessories and her classical costume, she took up her position in the middle of a room. She threw a shawl over her head which reached the ground and covered her entirely, and thus hidden, draped herself with the other shawls. Then she suddenly raised the covering, either throwing it off entirely or half-raising it, making it form part of the drapery of the model which she represented. But she always appeared as a statue of most admirable design.

I have heard artists say that if a perfect reproduction had been possible, art would have found nothing to change in her. She often varied her attitude and her expression from grave to gay, from trivial to severe before dropping the shawl which concluded that part of the performance.

I have sometimes acted with her as a subordinate figure to form a group. She used to place me in the proper position, and arrange my draperies before raising the shawl, which served as a curtain enveloping us both. My fair hair contrasted with her magnificent black hair, to which many of her effects were due.

Apart from this artistic instinct, Lady Hamilton was entirely vulgar and common. When she exchanged her classical tunic for ordinary dress she lost all distinction. Her conversation showed no interest and little intelligence. Yet she must have had some power of intrigue to reinforce her incomparable beauty, for she completely dominated anyone whom she wished to govern. There was first her old husband, whom she overwhelmed with ridicule; then the Queen of Naples, whom she plundered and disgraced; and finally Lord Nelson, who tarnished his glory under the influence of this woman at a time when she had become prodigiously fat and had lost her beauty.

In spite of all that she had extracted from the Queen of Naples and from Sir William Hamilton, she died at length in distress and poverty, as well as in disgrace. Upon the whole, she was a bad woman, and had a low mind within a magnificent form.

My father's resources were not entirely exhausted, and it had been decided that we should travel with Sir John Legard, dividing the expenses; from that moment the latter proceeded to rack his brains upon every occasion to reduce expenses to their lowest point. Hence the idea of buying mules, obstinate and hateful animals, which were a constant source of trouble, while the journey was rendered unbearable and sometimes dangerous by constant cheese-paring.

For instance, Sir John would not have the carriages mounted upon runners, or engage guides and local horses for the passage over the Saint-Gothard, in which we were nearly lost. Mounted on a little Neapolitan mule, which had never been ridden, and had never seen the snow, I crossed the mountain led by my father, who plunged into the snow up to his knees at every step through a dreadful storm. I remember that my tears froze on my face. I said nothing, lest I should increase the anxiety which I saw depicted on my father's face.

"Hold your bridle, child."

"I cannot hold it any longer, papa."

In fact, my skin gloves had been wet and then frozen, and had frozen my fingers, which had to be rubbed with snow. My father wrapped them up in a man's coat which he had, and we continued our route. When we reached the hospice, the weather had cleared up a little. Our luggage had been sent on and was at Urseren, so that we could not change our drenched clothes. My father found Sir John at the door talking with a monk, who was urging him to stay.

"What is your opinion, Marquis?"

"Well," said my father, "as the wine is drawn, we shall have to drink it."

"Certainly, gentlemen," replied the candid monk. "There are two bottles on the table right now, and we have a lot more if that is not enough."

This reply made me laugh and distracted my attention from my sufferings. In early youth there is a certain elasticity which cheerfulness can always restore. Notwithstanding the two bottles, we continued our journey. The storm did not extend to this side of the mountain. My father talked to me, and explained the reason for the avalanches which we saw falling, and the descent seemed to me as pleasant as the ascent had been painful. From there, we went down the Rhine by boat and reached Rotterdam. My father went to The Hague to fetch the boxes which had been stored there. We took ship, reached Harwich, and started directly for Yorkshire, where we lived with Sir John for two years, from 1794 to 1796.

My mother, who was threatened by a weakness of the chest, was obliged to go to London for a consultation, and in consequence it was thought advisable to remain within reach of the doctors. Her family subscribed to meet the expense. Lady Harcourt, her friend, and Lady

Clifford, her cousin, undertook this business. The Queen of Naples, with whom she had continued a correspondence, insisted that she should be close to medical advice and sent her three hundred louis, telling her that every year the Ambassador from Naples would hand her that same amount. Her relatives got together five hundred pounds with which it was possible to vegetate in London. My father then returned to Yorkshire to fetch my brother* and myself, who had remained there awaiting his decision.

As I shall constantly appear upon the scenes which I have to relate, I must devote a few words to my position. My education had been more thorough and serious than most young girls of my age had received, my taste was more developed, and I had a wide knowledge of the literature of three languages, which I spoke with equal facility. At the same time my ignorance of what is known as the world was profound, and in it I felt myself extremely ill at ease.

Though I was not beautiful, I had an attractive face. My eyes were small, but very dark and bright, and contrasted with a complexion remarkable even in England. My lips were red, my teeth excellent, while I had a great mass of fair hair. My neck, shoulders, and figure were correct, and my foot small; but these compensations did not reassure my anxiety for the redness of my arms and for hands which never recovered from their freezing during the passage of the Saint-Gothard, and caused me mortal embarrassment.

I do not know when I discovered that I was pretty, but it was not until some time after my arrival in London, and was then only a vague opinion. The exclamations of the lower classes in the street were the first announcement of the fact.

"You are too pretty to be kept waiting," a carter said to me, pulling up his horses.

"You will never be like that pretty lady, if you go on crying," said an apple-woman to her little daughter.

"God bless your pretty face, it's a sight for sore eyes," said a porter as he passed me, et cetera.

In any case, it is precisely true that these compliments, like all others, never struck my attention except (I cannot say if all women feel as I did) that I only noticed them when they stopped. The first compliments to vanish are those of the passers-by, then those heard as one crosses an ante-chamber, then those uttered in public places. As for drawing-room compliments, however inconsiderable one's elegance, one can live long enough on one's reputation.

To return to my youth, I was so excessively shy that I blushed whenever anyone spoke to me or looked at me. This failing is not always regarded with due sympathy. It was a real suffering in my case, and reached such a pitch that I was often choked by tears aroused by nothing but an excessive embarrassment which was quite unjustifiable.

Such being my character, I readily resigned myself to remain by my mother's bedside, for she had eventually become almost a complete invalid. I rarely went out for a walk, and was then always accompanied by my father. My amusements were to play chess with an old doctor, or to listen to the conversation of men who came to see my father.

M. de Calonne* was one of these; he conceived an affection for our household, and eventually spent his whole time there. I listened eagerly to his stories, which were as interesting as they were gracefully told, until I perceived that the same transaction was related by him in a wholly different manner upon different occasions, and soon discovered that he rarely told the truth. With the intolerance of early youth, I forthwith conceived a deep contempt for him, and hardly deigned to listen to him.

No one could have been more affectionate or better company, more frivolous or a greater liar. His talent and capacity were infinite, and were only equalled by his mistakes and the foolishness of his actions. Whenever it was possible to go astray, he would listen neither to remonstrances nor advice but would rush onwards, head first. However, as soon as his errors had been committed, even before he experienced the disagreeable consequences he foresaw the results, accused and condemned himself, and abandoned the line of conduct he had chosen with a readiness only comparable to his previous obstinacy.

I never entered the society of the *émigrés*, but I saw something of it, and gathered recollections which are difficult to coordinate by reason of their contradictory nature: actions highly praiseworthy and even moving could be related of persons whose carelessness, foolishness, and villainy were revolting.

Women of the highest rank worked for ten hours a day to get bread for their children; in the evening they dressed in their best, met together, sang, danced, and enjoyed themselves for half the night. This was the fair side of the picture; the unfortunate side was the fact that they slandered one another, told falsehoods about their work, and complained if one was more successful in her business than another, in the style of ordinary work-women. This mixture of ancient society claims and new-born petty malignities was distressing.

I have seen the Duchesse de Fitz-James, who lived in a house on the outskirts of London and preserved her ancient state, invite all her acquaintances to dinner. It was understood that each guest should put three shillings under a cup upon the mantelpiece as he left the table. Not only were the shillings counted when the company had gone, but if among the guests any one was thought to be in easy circumstances, he was considered mean if he did not put down half a guinea instead of three shillings, and the Duchesse pronounced her opinion on the matter with considerable acerbity. Nonetheless, a kind of luxury reigned in these houses.

I have seen Mme. de Léon and the whole of this society make up very expensive parties, to which they went in full dress on the top of an omnibus, to the great scandal of the English middle classes, who would not have ridden in that position. These ladies were constant visitors to the pit of the opera, which was chiefly occupied by women of bad repute, among whom they were not greatly conspicuous by their behaviour.

There were a large number of dual establishments which had never enjoyed the blessing of the Church. Reduced means and the necessity of joining incomes in order to live were the motives in some cases and the pretext in others. Moreover, everything was pardoned, provided that the offender held the "right" political views. Society was wholly tolerant upon every point but this. These are cases which I have seen, but they are not representative of the main body of the *émigrés*. These, as a whole, led irreproachable lives; such, indeed, their lives must have been, for it was their prolonged stay in England that originally changed English opinion in favour of the French nationality. As for political opinions, they were everywhere as irrational as possible, and those of the *émigrés* who led the most austere lives were the most ridiculous in this respect. Anyone who hired rooms for more than a month was regarded with disapprobation; it was better to take them only by the week, for at any moment the tenants might be recalled to France by the counterrevolution.

My father had taken our little house in Brompton on a lease of three years, and this act would have injured his reputation, if he had had anything to lose. But his disapproval of the army of emigration, and in particular his well-known attachment to King Louis XVI and the Queen, and his fidelity to their memory, were crimes which the *émigrés* could no more pardon than the sagacity with which he judged their immediate extravagances.

M. de Frotté, the General's brother, came to London. His mission was to warn the Comte d'Artois* that the Vendée[1] was lost unless some Prince appeared there. It was admitted that the presence of the Comte d'Artois was necessary for success. The difficulties of the journey then came forward, and these he surmounted. The question then arose as to how many *valets de chambre*, how many cooks, physicians, et cetera, the Comte should have (there was no question of almoners at that time).[2] All was discussed and agreement was secured. The Comte d'Artois took no great part in the discussion, and seemed ready to start.

1. The Wars of the Vendée is the name given to the insurrectionary counterrevolutions that took place in the west of France, the most important of which happened between 1793 and 1796. The introduction of military laws in 1793 calling to arms three hundred thousand men and the anti-Catholic policy of the Revolutionary government brought about a violent reaction of the peasants of the region, who gave full support to their priests and their nobility. The fighting was incredibly violent on both sides and ended in 1796 after a campaign of scorched earth led by the Republican Generals. Smaller Royalist uprisings subsequently occurred. The last one took place in 1832 when the Duchesse de Berry raised the Vendée for the Bourbon cause against Louis-Philippe.
2. Mme. de Boigne alludes ironically to the fact that before the Comte d'Artois turned ardently Catholic, as we shall see later, he had no use for priests or almoners.

M. de Frotté said in conclusion, "I may inform my brother, then, that my lord will be upon the coast at such and such a date?"

"Excuse me," said the Baron de Roll, with his German accent. "Excuse me. I am captain of the bodyguard of the Comte d'Artois, and am consequently responsible to the King for his safety. Can M. de Frotté assure us that the Comte will run no risk?"

"I tell you that a hundred thousand of us would die before a hair should fall from his head, and I can say no more."

"I appeal to you, gentlemen, is that a sufficient security on which to stake the Comte's safety? Can I consent?" the Baron replied. All answered in the negative, asserting that it was impossible. The Comte d'Artois dismissed the meeting, wishing M. de Frotté a good journey, and regretting the necessity of renouncing an enterprise which he would himself recognise to be impracticable.

M. de Frotté, who was stupefied for the moment, banged the table with his fist, and cried with an oath that they did not deserve that so many brave men should risk their lives for them. It was directly after this scene that he arrived at our house, and he was still so excited that he could not keep silence. He related these details with a burning eloquence of anger and indignation which impressed me greatly, and which I have never forgotten.

We must not be too hard upon the Princes. Consider what influence power and success can exercise upon men. A Minister in power for a few months, a pretty woman, a great artist, a fashionable man, are they not under the yoke of flattery, and do they not honestly think themselves extraordinary beings? If a few moments of flattery can produce this result this rapidly, can we be astonished that Princes, impressed from their cradles with the idea of their privileged importance, should be guilty of those aberrations which proceed from the foolish fact that they think themselves beings apart, whose intercourse is an essential necessity for mankind? I am persuaded that the Comte d'Artois represented to M. de Frotté in all honesty the impossibility of risking his safety, and that these arguments appeared to him final and definite.

When we tell princes that we are but too pleased to die in their service, it is to us but a form of words, as the formula which concludes a letter. But if they take the expression literally and believe that it is a happiness, are they entirely to blame? The fault is much rather attributable to their environment at all times and under every system.

I do not propose to relate the romance of my life: every individual has his own romance, which may be made interesting by truthfulness and talent, but talent I have none. I shall only say as much of myself as is necessary to explain in what way I became a spectator of the scenes I shall attempt to describe, and how I reached that point. For that reason I shall have to give some details concerning my marriage.

My mother's health caused less uneasiness, and she attempted to find some distraction for me. In London she had met Sappio, formerly music master to the Queen of France. He had called to see her, had made me sing to him, and showed much enthusiasm at my powers, which he cultivated with the more zeal, as he thus increased his reputation. His wife, a very pleasant little person, was a good musician. Our voices blended so admirably that when we sang together in thirds, the windows and glasses vibrated. The only other instance of this fact I have known is the case of Mmes. Sontag and Malibran. Its rarity made this power a valuable acquisition, especially to artists. Sappio often brought musical friends to see my mother. They grew into the habit of coming by preference on Sunday morning, on which day a kind of impromptu concert was eventually held by artists and amateurs. Listeners increased in number, the thing became fashionable, and at the end of some weeks my mother had infinite trouble to drive away the crowd.

A certain Mr. Johnson, whom we saw sometimes, asked leave to bring a friend, a General de Boigne,* who had just returned from India. He knew very few people as yet, and wished to make some good acquaintances. He came and went without attracting particular attention from us.

Several weeks passed. He came to pay a call, and said that a sprain had prevented him from appearing sooner, and pressed my mother so earnestly to dine with him that she consented, after raising a crowd of objections. The only guests were the O'Connell family and myself. Our host urged Mr. O'Connell to come to him early the next day, and commissioned him to ask my hand in marriage. I was sixteen years of age. No one had ever paid me the smallest attention—at any rate, I had not noticed anything of the kind. The only passion in my heart was filial love. My mother was overwhelmed with fear that the feeble resources that supported our existence might fail. The Queen of Naples had been driven from her estates, and announced that she did not know if she could continue my mother's pension. Her lamentations touched my heart less than my father's silence and his face worn with sleeplessness.

Such were my impressions when Mr. O'Connell arrived, commissioned to offer me the hand of a husband who had an income of twenty thousand louis, who offered a dowry of three thousand louis, and hinted that as he had no relatives, and not a being dependent upon him in the world, nothing would be dearer to him than his young wife and her family. These proposals were announced to me. I asked for a day to consider my answer, although my mind was made up forthwith. I wrote a note to Mrs. O'Connell to ask her to invite me to lunch as she sometimes did, and to ask General de Boigne to meet me there. He was exactly punctual.

I then committed the grave, though generous, mistake of telling him that I did not care for him in the least, and probably never should, but that if he were willing to secure my parents' future independence, my gratitude would be so great that I could marry him without reluctance. If this feeling was enough for him, I would give my consent but if he asked for more I was too frank to promise him anything of the kind, either at the moment or hereafter. He assured me that he did not flatter himself with the possibility of inspiring any deeper feeling.

I insisted that an income of five hundred louis should be assured by contract to my parents, the deed to be signed at the same time as my marriage contract. Mr. O'Connell undertook to draft this document.

M. de Boigne then said that he could give me no more than two thousand five hundred louis as a dowry. I cut short the arguments which Mr. O'Connell was advancing by reminding him of the terms which he had proposed. I concluded all discussion, and went home entirely satisfied.

My mother was somewhat hurt that I had left her at a moment when my future was at stake. I told her what I had done; she and my father, though much touched, begged me to reflect carefully. I assured them that I was entirely content, and this was true at the moment. I was in the full flush of youthful heroism. I had quieted my conscience by telling my suitor that I never expected to love him. I felt certain that I could fulfill the duties of my position, and was in any case entirely absorbed by the happiness of extricating my parents from their difficulties. This was the only point I considered, and I did not understand that I was making any sacrifice. Probably at the age of twenty I should have been less courageous, but at sixteen one does not know that the rest of one's life is at stake. Twelve days later I was married.

General de Boigne was forty-nine years of age. From India he brought back an honourable reputation and an immense fortune, acquired in the services of the Mahratta Princes. His previous life was but little known, and he deceived me about his past, his name, his family, and his antecedents. I think that at that time he proposed to preserve the character that he had then assumed.

If a single thought of selfishness had entered my heart at that moment, or if the possibility of happiness had smiled on me for an instant, I doubt if I should have had the courage to support the lot which was mine. But I owe it to myself to say that, child as I was, no such feeling touched my mind, and I saw myself surrounded with luxury, without experiencing the smallest happiness.

M. de Boigne was neither so bad nor so good as his individual actions might lead one to believe. A member of the lower middle class by birth, he had been a soldier for many years. I do not know by what paths he had passed from an Irish legion in the French service to the back of an elephant, from which he commanded an army of thirty thousand sepoys which he organised in the service of Sindiah, the chief of the Mahratta Princes, who was enabled by this European organisation to become the dominant power in Northern India.

M. de Boigne must have used much skill and cleverness to leave the country with some small portion of the wealth which he possessed, and which nonetheless amounted to ten million pounds. The rapidity with which he had passed from the lowest rank to the position of Commander-in-Chief and from poverty to vast wealth had never permitted him to acquire any social polish, and the habits of polite society were entirely unknown to him. An illness from which he was recovering had forced him to make an immoderate use of opium, which had paralysed his moral and physical powers.

Years of life in India had added the full force of Oriental jealousy to that which would naturally arise in the mind of a man his age; in addition to this, he was endowed with the most disagreeable character that Providence ever granted to man. He wished to arouse dislike as others wished to please. He was anxious to make everyone feel the domination of his great wealth, and he thought that the only mode of making an impression was to hurt the feelings of other people. He insulted his servants, he offended his guests, and his wife was, *a fortiori*, a victim to this grievous fault of character. He was an honourable man, trustworthy in business, and his ill-breeding had even a certain kind of heartiness; but his disagreeable temperament, displayed with all the ostentation of wealth, the most repellent of all forms of outward show, made association with him so unpleasant a business that he was never able to secure the friendship of any individual in any class of society, notwithstanding his numerous benefactions.

At the time of my marriage he was somewhat stingy, but of luxurious tastes, and if I had wished I could have expended more of his fortune than I have done. We lived in great state constantly giving fine dinners and magnificent concerts at which I sang. M. de Boigne was glad from time to time to exhibit the beautiful and well-articulated machine that he had acquired. Then his Eastern jealousy resumed the upper hand; he was furious because I had been seen or heard, especially

if I had been admired or applauded, and told me so in the language of
the guardroom.

These concerts were then somewhat fashionable, and the most distinguished members of English and foreign society used to be present.
The Orléans* Princes often came and dined at my table, but always as
Princes. Their manners precluded any familiarity. I was too greatly influenced by Royalist hatred for their father, Philippe-Egalité,* who
had voted for the execution of Louis XVI, not to be somewhat preju-
diced against them; it was impossible, however, not to admire the dignity of their attitude. Of all our Princes, they alone received no help
from foreign powers.

In a little house at Twickenham, near London, the three of them
lived in the most modest, but entirely proper, style. M. de Montjoie
formed the whole of their court, and performed the functions of lord-
in-waiting upon the rare occasions when any form of etiquette was
necessary. In spite of my prejudices, I soon perceived that the Duc de
Montpensier was as amiable as he was cultivated and distinguished.
He was passionately fond of art and music. The Duc d'Orléans[3] en-
dured the music for his brother's sake. Nothing was more touching
than the friendship of the two Princes and their affection for the
Comte de Beaujolais.

The Duc de Montpensier was ugly, but was entirely graceful and
amiable, with manners so distinguished that his face was speedily forgotten. The Duc d'Orléans was comparatively handsome, but neither
his bearing nor his manners showed any distinction. He never seemed
entirely at his ease. His conversation, interesting as it even then was,
seemed somewhat pedantic for a man of his age. In any case, he did not
happen to attract me as much as his brother, with whom I should have
been very glad to talk more often if I had dared.

After ten months of a very stormy union, M. de Boigne had offered
to take me back to my parents. I accepted his offer and was received
with joy. This determination, however, did not please the rest of my

3. See Louis-Philippe in the *Dictionary of Characters.*

family or my society, who wished to use the millionaire for their own purposes and cared little if I paid for the privilege. It was at that moment that I became the victim and the spectator of the most hateful persecution. I must especially reproach him for the fact that before I was seventeen years of age he had shattered all the illusions with which I had entered the world ten months previously.

M. de Boigne had no sooner abandoned his prey than he regretted his action. Forthwith my relatives and all the most distinguished members of the *émigrés* entered his service. One undertook to spy upon my actions, another to question my servants. This one had interest at Rome, and could procure the annulment of my marriage. That one could find flaws in the contract, et cetera, et cetera. Meetings were held at his house, where my character was torn to pieces, and slanders were invented and expressed in prose and verse, which were sold for hard cash. In short, everyone proceeded to persecute a child of seventeen, though they had overwhelmed me with flattery but a moment before.

M. de Boigne himself was very speedily disgusted, and closed both his purse and his house. I afterwards saw in his possession various denunciations of my conduct and base offers of personal service. He had been careful to preserve the names of the individuals concerned, and the amounts which had been asked and paid. These names were sufficiently distinguished to please his plebeian pride, and he discovered a new form of teasing in showing them to me.

It was impossible to induce M. de Boigne to make any arrangement which would leave me in peace. He promised to reform, while I felt vexed by the injustice of public opinion, which, under the influence of his agents and his money, regarded me as to blame. I therefore decided to rejoin him at the end of three months.

I shall give no detailed description of our married life. It is enough to say that when we were separated he was in despair and thought he adored me, but when we were united he was wearied by my society, and conceived an antipathy to me, and on five or six occasions left me forever. All these separations were accompanied by scenes which poisoned my youth, a time so ill-spent that it had passed before I realised the fact, and I found that it had gone and I had not enjoyed it.

In the year 1800, we travelled to Germany. I spent a month at Hamburg, where *émigré* society was ruled by Mme. de Vaudémont. Ridiculously innocent as I then was, I was so startled by the scandals of this clique that I could not close my eyes to them, and was correspondingly disgusted. I was no less disgusted by the relaxation of Royalist principles. Altona was a kind of purgatory where people who proposed to return to France came to prepare themselves for the renunciation of their exclusive principles. Accustomed as I was to another language, all this seemed heresy to me. I often went to Munich, which was occupied by the remnants of the army of Condé,* and there I found exaggeration pushed to an extravagance which brought me to the opposite point of confusion. I then became accustomed to accept opinion as such, and invented a golden mean for my personal use.

I remember hearing men argue at Munich that they must never consent to return to France except upon the condition that their châteaus, including the furniture, should be restored in the condition in which they had left them. Upon the restoration of property rights and all claims not a doubt was expressed. Possibly the fulfillment of these desires would have brought some disappointment, for the *émigrés* were so accustomed to say that they had lost incomes of a hundred thousand francs that they had eventually persuaded themselves of the fact. Any country house, no matter how small, now assumed the dimensions of a château in their recollections.

I crossed Tyrol, which I thought, in the words of the Prince de Ligne, the finest corridor in Europe. We then made our way to Verona, to see the sisters of M. de Boigne, whose existence he had hitherto concealed from me, after which we returned to London, where I had the happiness of meeting my father and mother again, from whom I had been separated by this journey.

A short time after my return to London, M. de Boigne informed me that he had sold our house, and took me to a furnished residence. He announced his intention of leaving England and entrusting me to my parents. Though in my heart I approved of this arrangement, I had no wish to become a topic of public scandal for the third time. The preceding winter he had left me one day when we had invited some five hundred guests to a concert; the story had gone about, both in the newspapers and in every drawing-room. I could no longer venture to believe in the kindness of public feeling, and felt my position very difficult. I therefore offered to follow him at any cost to myself. To this he returned an absolute refusal, but on this occasion we parted without a quarrel, and continued to correspond. He left me in moderate circumstances, though I was able to live respectably in the society which I frequented. He was even good enough to permit me to draw upon his banker to any extent within limits which I was not to exceed, and which I have never passed.

This phase of my life lasted for two years, which are the most peaceful in my memory. I went into society to some extent; I had a pleasant home, where I was adored. My father was in the full vigour of health and strength, and devoted his time to my brother, Rainulphe,* and myself. We had resumed our reading and our studies, and led an intellectual life. My brother had a very fine voice, and we had a great deal of music.

Other amateurs often met at our house, among whom I should not omit to mention the Duc de Berry.* He had set up house in London, where he led a life unworthy of his rank and still more unworthy of his misfortunes. His favourite society was that of some Creole women who fully responded to the freedom of his behaviour. These familiarities at any rate were confined to members of the French nationality; but he was also infatuated by an English girl of bad character, whom he took to the races in his own carriage, or to the opera, where she had a seat by his side. Sometimes, when the crowd was excessive, he would be seized with sudden shame, and take refuge in my box or elsewhere. But as we went out we used to hear the girl calling out "Berry!" to summon their carriage. The Duc de Berry's actions were often ill-considered, and he was a victim to fits of passion, in which he lost entire control of himself. This was his bad side, and it is with great pleasure that I can point to the other side of the picture.

The Duc de Berry had much talent, and was cheerful, lively, and companionable. He was an excellent storyteller; his powers in this respect were unusual, and he was aware of them; notwithstanding his rank of Prince, he would wait for an opening, and never initiate it. He had a kindly disposition, was liberal and generous, yet economical. Though the income which he received from the English Government was very moderate, and his tastes were expensive, he never ran into debt. As long as he had money, his purse was open to the unfortunate as readily as to his own fancies; when his purse was empty he deprived himself of everything until the next payment of his income.

He never shared the political absurdities of the *émigrés*. I have seen him honestly indignant with the people who tried to excuse the attempt of assassination of the First Consul* by means of an infernal machine.[4] I remember a quarrel which he had with M. de Nantouillet, his first equerry, on this occasion.

In this respect he was very different from the other *émigrés*. The Comte de Vioménil, for instance, used to call upon my mother, with whom he had been intimate for a number of years. Because I had said that I thought an infernal machine was a horrible idea, the future marshal told all his friends that he could not run the risk of listening to such language, and his audience shared his indignation.

The Duc de Berry remained a true Frenchman. One evening we learnt in Lady Harrington's drawing-room, when the Prince of Wales was present, that a little French squadron had been victorious in the Indian Ocean. The Duc de Berry could not hide his joy, and I was obliged to scold him before he would restrain himself within bounds appropriate to our company. The next day he called upon us early, and said, "Well, governesses, I was quite good yesterday evening, but I wish to kiss you this morning as a token of my joy." He kissed my

4. A Royalist plot carried out against Bonaparte on Christmas Eve in 1800, using an explosive machine, that did not succeed.

mother and myself, and then began to dance and leap, singing, "They have been defeated, they have been defeated! We beat them on water as on land; they have been defeated! Governesses, now I can say it, as we are alone here."

It cannot be denied that there was some generosity in this joy at a success which was entirely opposed to his personal interests. He was, in fact, the only Prince of his dynasty who felt any real patriotism; he was, again, the only Prince who had any taste for art, and this he culti-vated with some success; in spite of his failings, he was an honourable man. I think he would have made a very dangerous monarch, but he was at any rate the only Prince of his family who was in any degree ca-pable of generosity. Sorry as I am to say it, I fear that he was not coura-geous. I can hardly understand the fact, for this quality seemed entirely suitable to him, but he was continually giving vent to expressions and sentiments which Henri IV would not have disavowed. If he displayed timidity, and the fact is hardly doubtful, it must be ascribed to the de-plorable education of our Princes. His brother, however, a less distin-guished man in every respect, escaped this flaw.

When the bill concerning debts contracted abroad had been passed, the Comte d'Artois returned to London, as both he and his retinue were growing weary of Edinburgh. There had been many changes in his personal attendants during his last stay in Scotland. For many years he had been closely attached to Mme. de Polastron.* She was passionately devoted to him, but not to his reputation, and it is to her influence that we must in some degree attribute the somewhat dis-honourable part which this Prince played during the course of the Revolution. She was an inmate of his household, and their connection was so openly acknowledged that it had ceased to cause any scandal.

After his arrival at Holyrood, the Comte d'Artois, who was any-thing but a religious man, was greatly troubled by the zeal with which the Scotch Catholics went to expense in order to procure him Masses and services. At some great festival their forethought obliged him to go twenty miles in order to spend five or six hours in the chapel of a neighbouring nobleman. Tired by this imposition, he wished to have an almoner. Mme. de Polastron wrote to Mme. de Laage, and asked her to find a priest to say Mass of a social standing sufficiently low to exclude him from the apartments. The Comte's intention was that he should take his meals with his *valets de chambre*. Mme. de Laage applied to M. de Sabran, who said, "I have just what you want, a priest who is the son of my caretaker. He is young, not bad-looking, in no way fastidious, and you will have no trouble with him." The proposal was explained to the Abbé Latil; he accepted joyfully, and was packed off by coach to Edinburgh, where he was installed upon the terms proposed.

Such was the household of the Prince when he reached London. Mme. de Polastron was suffering from some pulmonary disease, and her condition grew worse; she abandoned herself to all the extravagant fancies which are symptomatic of this disease. As the household income was insufficient, M. du Theil, the major-domo of the Comte d'Artois, invented a new manner of procuring money. Emissaries were constantly coming from France. One of the most specious projects was chosen, and an enterprise was announced for the near future in Vendée or in Brittany, and by this means some thousands of pounds were obtained from the English Government. Two or three hundred were given to some poor wretch who went to meet his death on the coast, and the rest was swallowed up by the caprices of Mme. de Polastron. I do not know if the Prince was a party to these swindles. At any rate, he tolerated them, and must have known of their execution, for when the manoeuvre had been repeated thrice within a single month, Mr. Wyndham found it out, and expressed himself in energetic terms. It was from Mr. Wyndham himself that I learnt of it, and in any case it was no secret. The *émigrés* in England were accustomed to regard English money as their legitimate prey to be secured by any means.

Mme. de Polastron gradually sank. The Comte d'Artois used to spend his days alone with her. Her London house was too small for them to live together, but they lived in the same street. Every day at noon his Captain of the Guards would accompany him to Mme. de Polastron's door, knock, and leave him when it was opened. The captain returned for him at half-past-five for dinner, and brought him back afterwards for a stay from seven o'clock to eleven o'clock. These long mornings and evenings were passed in conversation. Mme. de Polastron, who could not speak without exhaustion, would listen to the reading of religious books, at first by the Prince, who was afterwards relieved of this task, at her instance, by the Abbé Latil.

Comments were soon added to the reading of texts. The Comte d'Artois was too affected by grief to avoid lending a respectful ear to the words which relieved the sufferings of his friend, and she preached her faith with the fervour of love. He sympathised with her entirely, and she was so far convinced of his feelings that at the moment of her death she took the hand of the Prince, and placing it in that of the Abbé, she said to him, "My dear Abbé, here he is: I give him to you, take care of him. I recommend him to your care." And then addressing the Prince: "My friend, follow the Abbé's instructions, that you may be as calm as I am in the hour when you will come to meet me again."

There were several people in the room during this scene, among others the Chevalier de Puységur, who told me the story. She bade an affectionate farewell to everybody, gave advice to her servants, but said not a word of the scandal she had caused. She fell asleep, and the Prince and the Abbé remained alone with her. A short time afterwards she woke up, asked for a spoonful of liquid, and expired.

The Abbé did not lose a moment, but carried off the Comte d'Artois to the church in King Street, where he kept him for several hours, made him confess, and gave him Communion the next day. From that moment, his influence was such that with a mere glance at the Prince, he could make him change his conversation. He had ceased to take his meals with the *valets de chambre* after leaving Edinburgh, but only then did he join the Prince's table, where manners were completely changed. The former laxity was replaced by extreme austerity, and M. de Rivière, who was abstemious by principle, returned and became a leading member of the household. The Comte d'Artois, who was always somewhat embarrassed by this change of front, was infinitely obliged to him for thus preceding him and entering by the same gate upon a path which they followed with the same fervour.

Before the sickness of Mme. de Polastron entirely absorbed the attention of the Comte d'Artois, he often went into society. I used to see him there, especially at Lady Harrington's, where I spent most of my time. There he often met the Prince of Wales and, notwithstanding their different positions, the French Prince appeared to greater advantage. His grace, nobility and polish, and his distinguished manner naturally brought him to the forefront, and the Prince of Wales seemed nothing more than his caricature. In the absence of the Frenchman, the manners of the English Prince certainly seemed admirable, but they were manners which were in the Comte d'Artois second nature. Though his face was less handsome than that of the Englishman, he had greater grace and dignity, while his bearing, his dress, and his mode of entering and leaving a room were incomparable.

I remember that on one occasion when the Comte d'Artois had just arrived and was paying his respects to Lady Harrington, the Duc de Berry, who was standing by me, said: "What an excellent thing it is to be a handsome Prince like that; it is half the battle."

This was a jest, but founded upon truth. At that time, indeed, the Comte d'Artois was the ideal of a Prince, even more, perhaps, than in his early manhood. At that date he hardly went into French society. He invited men to his house from time to time, and gave some dinners. On New Year's Day, on the festivals of Saint Louis and Saint Charles, ladies called. He left cards upon everyone, and made personal visits to those whom he knew. In this way I have seen him three or four times at my mother's house, though not upon intimate terms. We did not call upon Mme. de Polastron, and this was an unpardonable omission.

I have spoken of the drawing-room of Lady Harrington. This was the only social centre where people could meet, if not without invitation, at any rate with greater intimacy than at an ordinary social gathering. Lady Harrington would pay thirty calls in a morning, leaving invitations at the door for ladies to go to her house in the evening. As she went she would cross Bond Street several times, and pick up men who were out walking. This manoeuvre was repeated three or four times a week, and ended in the formation of a special clique, as is always the case in society. My more sociable French instincts induced me to prefer her parties to the larger gatherings to be found in other houses. Lady Harrington overwhelmed me with kindness, and I enjoyed myself greatly at her house.

About this time I was one day in the house of Mme. du Dresnay. M. de Damas* (known as Damas *jeune*), who was attached to the Prince de Condé, began a most violent invective against the *émigrés* who were returning to France. Mme. du Dresnay, though she did not return until 1814, was too sensible to approve of this effrontery, and said to him very dryly: "M. de Damas, when a man is elegantly dressed, like yourself, with a carriage like that waiting for you at my door, when a man is boarded, lodged, and cared for as you are at Wanstead, he has not the right to call down destruction upon poor people who are going elsewhere to seek the bread which they cannot find here."

"But, Madame, that is their fault. Do you not know what the King has done for them?"

"No, indeed I do not."

"Well, Madame, he has allowed them to work without losing caste."

This I heard with my own ears.

I have forgotten to say that before my marriage I used to see a good deal of Pozzo* at my parents' house. After my marriage, the vast jealousy of M. de Boigne, which comprehended the whole universe, including my father and my dog, had entirely withdrawn me from any social intercourse, and I only caught occasional glimpses of the world. Pozzo, moreover, had been making a long stay at Vienna, whither he had accompanied Lord Minto, his patron and friend. This connection had been formed at the time when Lord Minto, then Sir Gilbert Eliot, had been Viceroy of Corsica, where Pozzo was his counsellor and Minister. He was afterwards very intimate with my uncle, Edouard Dillon,* who commanded an Irish regiment in the English service, which was in occupation at Corsica.

When the British forces evacuated the island, Pozzo was obliged to leave it, as the French party gained the upper hand. I doubt whether Pozzo attached any real preference to the French or English party at this time; he merely wished to espouse the cause which Bonaparte was not supporting. The two cousins had each taken the measure of the other. The intimate association of youth had been succeeded by a hatred based upon ambition. Their sole thought was to be supreme in their island, and they promptly discovered that this was only possible if one of them became the conqueror of the other. I feel quite certain that Pozzo called in the English only because Bonaparte declared himself a revolutionary. It is possible that Pozzo afterwards became a genuine absolutist, but at this time he was very liberal and of a republican tendency. I have heard him improvise pieces upon *la Patria et les Castagnes*, with which I was entirely in sympathy, but which had little resemblance to the principles of the Holy Alliance.

Pozzo was perfectly correct in regarding himself as a rival of Bonaparte at that time. But once this idea was fixed in his Corsican head, he could never get rid of it, and continued to regard himself as the rival of the conqueror of Italy, the First Consul, and even the Emperor Napoleon. He was too sensible to proclaim this idea in set terms, but it was working in his brain and found expression in the most energetic hatred. He would have gone to the bottom-most pit to find antagonists to Bonaparte, and invariably dogged his steps with a perseverance to which his distinction of character and his brilliant talents gave an importance hardly to be foreseen from his social position.

At this time he was continually at our house, passing alternately from the depths of discouragement and despair to wild extremes of hope and joyfulness; but he was always witty, interesting, amusing, and even eloquent. His conversational style was slightly foreign, and this, added to his constant use of simile, gave it a picturesque and unexpected colouring which seized upon the imagination, while the originality of his talk was emphasised by his foreign accent. He was a most companionable man. His inadequate knowledge of the world had not yet been modified by that self-assurance which success afterwards gave him. Moreover, it was less startling to see a little Corsican breaking the rules of polite society at that time than afterwards, when he displayed his unpolished manner amid the splendour of ambassadorial residences.

Edouard Dillon introduced him to the Comte d'Artois. Pozzo speedily appreciated the Prince, and while the latter thought he had gained an agent, Pozzo regarded him merely as an instrument to be used if possible in the furtherance of his ambition, especially of his hatred. The instrument, however, seemed to him entirely blunt, and he was accustomed to express himself with great bitterness in referring to the lack of account to which he had been able to turn it. Edouard Dillon, of whom I have just spoken, was my mother's brother, and was for a long time known as the "Handsome Dillon." A contemporary chronicler pointed to him as one of the lovers with whom slander provided the Queen, a story which was based upon the following foundation.

Edouard Dillon was very handsome, very self-satisfied, and very much in fashion. He was a member of the circle of Mme. de Polignac, and probably offered to the Queen some of those compliments which were her right as a pretty woman. One day he was rehearsing at her house the figures of a quadrille which was to be danced at the next ball. Suddenly he turned pale and fainted away. He was placed upon a sofa, and the Queen was so imprudent as to place her hand upon his heart to feel if it was beating. Edouard recovered consciousness and apologised for his foolishness, admitting that in order not to be late for his appointment with the Queen he had left Paris without break-fasting, and that in consequence of a long-standing wound, which he had received at the capture of Granada, fainting of this nature occasionally attacked him, especially when he was fasting. The Queen ordered him some soup, and the courtiers, jealous of this small success, insisted that he was intimate with her.

The rumour soon died away at court, but was confirmed in town when he was seen on Saint Hubert's Day crossing Paris in the Queen's coach and eight. He had fallen from his horse and broken his arm for

the second time while hunting. The Queen's carriage was the only vehicle on the spot, and she ordered it to take my uncle home, returning
as usual in the King's carriage, as her own was only called out as a matter of etiquette. It is very probable that many stories about the poor
Queen have had no more serious foundation than this.

My uncle fought a duel which made some stir. When he was at
supper at the Minister's house, a man from the provinces, whose name
I have forgotten, said to him across the table: "Monsieur Dillon, I
should like to ask you what is the flavour of these little puddings."

Edouard, who was talking to the lady next to him, answered
curtly, "Oats" (*à l'avoine*).

"Then I will send you back some straw," answered the man, who
did not know that *pots à l'avoine* were a dish in fashion at that moment.

Edouard did not interrupt his conversation, but after supper a
meeting was arranged for the next day at a somewhat late hour, as he
did not care to be disturbed in the morning. His antagonist arrived at
his house at the time arranged. My uncle had not finished dressing. He
apologised for the delay, finished his toilet with all possible care and
with the utmost imaginable delicacy. While thus occupied he said
to his opponent, "Sir, if you have no business to call you elsewhere,
I should suggest our going to the wood of Vincennes. I am dining at
Saint-Maur, and I see that I shall have barely time to keep my appointment."

"What, so you intend . . . ?"

"Certainly, sir; I intend to dine at Saint-Maur after I have killed
you, for I gave my promise yesterday to Mme. de ————."

This boundless self-assurance possibly staggered the poor man; at
any rate, he received a shrewd thrust and my uncle went to dinner at
Saint-Maur, where the duel and the conversation were not discovered
until the next day, and then from the talk of a third person. It must be
admitted that effrontery of this nature has some attractiveness.

In 1803, at the time of which I am speaking, Edouard had long
since laid aside all the airs of a young man, and had become entirely

natural and agreeable. When a lady asked him what had become of the person known as the "Handsome Dillon," he replied with extreme seriousness, "He has been guillotined."

At the Peace of Amiens,[5] M. de Boigne had returned to France, and urged me to meet him there. Apart from my own disinclination, I thought I had every reason to keep away from a country destined to further catastrophes. We knew that an upheaval was in preparation, and that Pichegru* was at the head of this intrigue. He, at any rate, committed no indiscretion, and his conduct was marked by prudence and skill. He used to live almost entirely alone, often going away for a short time to throw people off the scent; when idlers began to talk of his absence, he would suddenly reappear and show that he had been making a very ordinary journey, and one which was excellent evidence for his want of occupation.

One day he started definitely upon his dangerous expedition; unfortunately for him, he was to be followed by the members of the Polignac* family. They acted very differently. They paid a round of farewell visits, undertook messages for delivery in Paris, showed a list of persons who were awaiting them, and who had probably no idea that their names were thus in use. It was inconceivable that their journey, after this publicity, should seem to be of no importance; yet they asserted that they were going off in secret. This was their method of conducting a conspiracy.

The day before their departure I dined with them in the country at the house of Edouard Dillon. It was necessary to cross a small common on the return journey. The Polignacs were on horseback: they posted themselves on the common and amused themselves for an hour by stopping the carriages which came up; mine was one of the number. They demanded my money or my life, and then went off with roars of laughter, saying that it was a kind of foretaste of their future trade. The next day this whimsicality was the talk and the delight of their entire circle. This foolishness would not be worth the trouble of narration did

5. Peace treaty concluded between France and Great Britain on March 25, 1802.

it not throw some light upon the character of this Jules de Polignac, which was fatal to the throne and to himself. Though he was then quite young, the discredit of this conduct is entirely his. His brother Armand, who was as stupid as Jules was foolish, was entirely under the influence of the latter.

We soon heard of the arrest of these conspirators, and soon afterwards we learnt the sad fate of the Duc d'Enghien.* His father, it must be said, was crushed by the news, which he heard in a dreadful way. The Duc de Bourbon was supposed to inhabit Wanstead, a magnificent castle which the Prince de Condé had rented near London. During his military career in the army which went under his name, his Highness had not neglected his finances, and was incomparably the richest of the *émigré* Princes. His son could not endure the regular life of Wanstead and was generally to be found in London in a small suite of rooms with one valet, called Gui, who had attended him from his youth. As his breakfast was late, he rang for Gui three times with no result. He then went down into the little kitchen, and found Gui with his elbows on the table and his head in his hands, shedding tears, with the newspaper before him. At his approach he raised his head and attempted to hide the newspaper. This the Duc de Bourbon did not permit, and he then read the sad news of his son's assassination. Two hours afterwards the Prince de Condé arrived and found him still in this kitchen, from which Gui had been unable to remove him, and into which he would allow no one else to enter. The Prince de Condé took him back to Wanstead. The care of Mme. de Reuilly, his natural daughter, who was brought up by Mme. de Monaco, afterwards Princesse de Condé, helped to soothe his grief. This excessive grief, accompanied by fits of rage and cries for vengeance, is the best feature in the life of the Duc de Bourbon, and one which I am glad to commemorate.

As for *émigré* society in general, and the Princes in particular, the impression made by this event was strangely transitory. Out of respect for the Prince de Condé, the Comte d'Artois decided that mourning, which would have been customary for five days only, should be worn for nine, and thought he had made a great concession. The Prince de Condé thought so, too, for he went in person to London to thank the Comte d'Artois. The news arrived on Monday. The Duc de Berry was absent from the opera on Tuesday, but reappeared on Saturday at the next performance.

The Moreau case[6] had been finished, and peace had not been disturbed in France. I therefore decided to accede to the repeated invitations of M. de Boigne. I felt that I was in a false position. The importance of the quarrels which made my life unbearable was now diminished by distance, and I had no sufficient reasons to advance for refusing to obey the orders which M. de Boigne had the right to issue. He had just acquired a charming house, Beauregard,[7] at four leagues from Paris, and wished me to join him there. My parents promised to come and see me if I could secure the erasure of their names from the list of the *émigrés* and this decided my action.

6. The Royalist General Moreau had been implicated in the 1804 plot against Bonaparte. He was arrested and condemned to two years of prison. He obtained permission to emigrate to Spain and from there went to the United States.
7. Beauregard was actually a splendid château bought by M. de Boigne in 1802. Mme. de Boigne spent more than six months a year on the property.

CHAPTER THREE

Empire

1804–1814

I did not care to be present at the festivities of Napoleon's coronation, which took place on December 2, 1804. The ceremony would have outraged my Royalist leanings. Notwithstanding my prejudices, I was never able to suppress a very sincere admiration for the First Consul. I admired him as the conqueror and the writer of bulletins. No one had explained to me his vast merits as a legislator and a calmer of passions, and I was incapable of appreciating him by my own judgement. Had I lived in another atmosphere, I should, I believe, have been really enthusiastic about him.

In London my poor mother had often wept with vexation at my political principles, and insisted that I was turning my brother's head in favour of Bonaparte. It is certain that after a close view of our Princes, and a distant impression of the First Consul, all my interest was concentrated upon the latter; the death of the Duc d'Enghien had made an impression upon me as fleeting as upon those with whom I was then living. Notwithstanding this attraction for the Emperor, I was still bound by a thousand prejudices to what was known as the Ancien Régime. My English education also turned me instinctively in the direction which has since been called Liberal. As far as I can discover, this was the point at which I had arrived when I reached France. M. de Boigne, difficult as I find the fact to understand, was no revolutionary, and upon this one subject of politics we were almost in entire agreement.

At the end of December we set up house in Paris, where I spent the three most wearisome months of my life. Parisian society is so exclusive that there is no place for a newcomer, who is completely isolated until he or she has formed a circle apart. Moreover, my fear of scenes, which M. de Boigne would begin upon any or no occasion, obliged me to lead a retired life which was not conducive to social intercourse. From time to time I found an old woman who remembered seeing me as a baby at Versailles, or another who told me stories of my childhood at Bellevue, but these were not exciting distractions.

I was very kindly received by the Princesse de Guéméné; she was as useful and serviceable to me as anyone who was bedridden and saw very few people could be. The Duchesse de Châtillon, on the other hand, was unendurable: she would keep me for hours, lecturing me upon a multitude of subjects on which her advice was as useless as it was antiquated; she would always begin and end her sermons with these words:

"My little queen, as I have the honour to belong to you," which meant in straightforward language, "Consider yourself highly honoured that I am willing to recognise our relationship," an honour which I did not feel disposed to admit.

In her magnificent residence in the Rue du Bac she lived in a large room, which she called her study, furnished with much old-fashioned luxury, and provided with eight or ten clocks, no two of which kept the same time. A splendid gilded cage hung down like a chandelier, full of birds singing at the top of their voices. This clatter, added to the low and monotonous voice of the Duchesse, got upon my nerves and made visits to the house a real torture. I never left it without vowing never to return again—a vow I should certainly have kept if my letters from London had not constantly contained messages for Mme. de Châtillon.

This Duchesse de Châtillon was the daughter of the Duchesse de Lavallière, a rival of the wife of the Marshal of Luxembourg, both beautiful and fashionable women. These qualities were thus shared by the daughter. The frame of a looking-glass in this study where she de-livered her long homilies to myself was papered with the portraits of her lovers. Not knowing what to do with them, she had added them to the furniture. The number of these portraits was considerable, and they made a very pretty decoration. She had been a free-thinker, but was now a strict supporter of religion. The family of Lavallière became extinct with her, and her two daughters, the Duchesse de La Tré-moille and d'Uzès, the family of Coligny-Châtillon.

The Marquise de Laval, who had become the Duchesse de Laval, a former friend of my mother, and my godmother, treated me with motherly kindness. She was as simple as Mme. de Châtillon was pre-tentious and never advanced her family claims. I was therefore very glad to visit her in her cell in the convent of Saint-Joseph, where she lived in the practice of a devotion both meticulous and lax. She gave all that she had to the poor, and her poverty was so apparent in her dress that one day in church a man tapped her on the shoulder, wishing to pay her for his chair.

"You are mistaken, Sir," replied the Duchesse gently. "It is not I, but that other lady."

The word "lady" in this situation always struck me as touching.

The Duc de Laval was by no means pleased with his wife's posi-tion. He tried to experiment with giving her money, which speedily escaped from her purse; he then resolved to rent a decent room for her, to pay her moderate expenses and those of her dress, though in the lat-ter he effected but little improvement. If he had insisted upon dress conforming to her social position, he would have reduced her to de-spair; she wished to be able to walk alone on foot in the mud, and to visit churches and the poor without being observed. Although she was not pretty, she had been the most exquisite and magnificent woman at the court of France during her youth; her uncle, the Bishop of Metz, used to pay all her bills, and she used to spend forty thousand francs on her dress. Never had there been a greater change, and perhaps she would have done better to avoid these two extremes. As she was, her husband respected her deeply, and her children adored her. Her husband was a really eccentric character, a phenomenon rare in any country, yet rarer in France, and rarer still in the class to which he belonged. Since he entered society, he had always lived splendidly upon his profits at play without suffering any loss of reputation. He never seemed to frequent gaming houses any more than other men of his position. He never went about looking for pigeons to pluck, but he calculated upon an income of one hundred thousand crowns from cards as he would have calculated upon a revenue from ground rents. He was the finest and the fairest player that could possibly be met, and a decision of the Duc de Laval on any doubtful point would have been regarded as law throughout Europe.

He had been a good officer, and it was insisted that he had a soldier's eye. He had distinguished himself in the campaign of the Princes, where he had been so unfortunate as to see his second son, Achille, killed before his eyes, the only one of his children for whom he cared. When this army was disbanded, he displayed a paternal generosity to his own regiment, which found no imitators and earned him the highest esteem. In the ordinary course of life he professed a selfishness which ran to exaggeration. He met his daughter-in-law walking in the street one day when it was beginning to rain, pretended not to notice her, and said to her in the evening:

"Caroline, you must have got horribly wet this morning. I would have taken you into my carriage, but I was afraid of the damp if the door were opened."

A thousand stories of this kind might be quoted, but his children loved him, and everyone respected him. He paid a large number of calls, for calling was in his case a rule of conduct; he insisted that it was the best means to prevent gossip about oneself, as nobody cares to talk about a man who might walk in in the middle of the conversation.

His eldest son, Adrien, who afterwards became Duc de Laval, was a society man. His name rather than his merit raised him during the Restoration to positions in which he did not display adequate capacity, but his achievements were nonetheless high above the powers of a nonentity, as some people wished to regard him. The desire to prolong his youthful tastes beyond a reasonable age exposed him to some ridicule. He was so unfortunate as to lose his only son, the last member of the branch of Montmorency Laval. His brother Eugène was the most disagreeable character that could possibly be met, and concealed the most barefaced selfishness beneath a puerile and bigoted pietism.

I have heard the Comtesse de Vaudreuil speak of "we pretty women," but it was reserved for Eugène de Montmorency, I believe, to invent the expression "we saints," and I have heard it used.

The first time that I went to a ball in Paris was at the Hôtel de Luynes; I thought I was entering Calypso's Grotto. The ladies all seemed to me like nymphs. The beauty of their costumes and of their figures impressed me so strongly that only after several evenings of the kind did I discover that I had actually been accustomed to see in London a far greater profusion of beauties. I was much astonished afterwards to find these women, who were so excellently dressed in society, disgracefully slovenly at home, with untidy hair, dirty wrappers, negligent to the last degree. These bad habits have completely disappeared within the last few years, and Frenchwomen are as careful as the English in their domestic life and dress in the best possible taste.

I was curious to see Mme. Récamier.* I was informed that she was in the little drawing-room with five or six other women; I went in and saw a person whose face seemed to me highly remarkable, and when she went out for a few moments afterwards, I followed her. Someone asked me what I thought of Mme. Récamier:

"Charming. I am following her to see her dance."

"That girl? That is Mlle. de La Vauguyon; Mme. Récamier is sitting in the window there in that grey dress."

When she was pointed out to me I saw in fact that a face which had impressed me but little was wholly beautiful. It was the special characteristic of this beauty, which may be called famous, to appear to greater advantage every time she was seen. She will probably reappear in these memoirs, as our acquaintanceship began soon afterwards and is still intimate.

My uncle, the Bishop of Cominges, who had become Bishop of Nancy, was then at Paris. He was anxious for me to enter the household of the Empress Joséphine,* which was then being organised, and explained the freedom which a position at court would provide for me with reference to M. de Boigne. Apart from the fact that such a proposal was contrary to my opinions, my tastes have always been repugnant towards servitude of any kind, and I should not care to be attached to a Princess at any period or under any government. He returned to the charge several times without success. From his manner of discussing the question as one which merely awaited my consent, I am inclined to think that he was performing a commission, but I never experienced any disagreeable consequences. Whatever may be said, when a refusal was given with proper modesty and without undue emphasis, there were never any unpleasant results, nor was constraint ever exercised except upon people who wished to be constrained.

An opposition party is always badly informed. This fact I had every opportunity of learning, when I afterwards lived in intimacy with people engaged in business under the Imperial Government. They proved to me the absurdity of a number of things which I had piously believed for years, and therefore I claim credence only for such stories as I know to be true.

For instance, I was present at a strange scene at the house of one Mme. Dubourg, where the society of the Ancien Régime used frequently to meet at that time. The Comte d'Aubusson had just been appointed Chamberlain to the Emperor. These nominations were highly displeasing to us, and we expressed our objections with more or less acerbity. The Princesse de La Trémoille was pleased to treat M. d'Aubusson with great severity, although they had been intimate friends and she saw him constantly. He asked her what he had done to deserve this severity.

"I think you know, Sir."

"No, indeed, Madame; it is in vain for me to consult my memory, and yet my recollections go very far back, even to the time when I was obliged to turn you out of the barracks for attempting to seduce the soldiers of my regiment."

The Princesse was petrified for a moment, and her fury then became hysterical. In spite of the partiality of the audience, the laugh was against her. It was asserted that when she was the Princesse de Saint-Maurice and was an energetic patriot at the beginning of the Revolution, she had been turned out of the barracks, whither she had gone to preach insubordination to the soldiers.

Although we were extremely insolent, we were by no means brave. This scene caused some stir; Fouché* spoke of it, and Mme. de La Trémoille was obliged to answer for it to the police, after which we were generally most polite to the new chamberlains. Mme. de Chevreuse was almost the only person who ventured upon any indiscretion, but she was so eccentric and her whimsicalities so universal that action of this kind was merely regarded as an additional caprice. Though red-haired, she was extremely pretty, very attractive, full of wit, and spoiled beyond expression by her mother-in-law, while she had a social position of her own which she turned to advantage with extremely bad taste. The Duc de Laval used to call her the Lady Purveyor of the Faubourg Saint-Germain. He was right, for she had all the manners of the upstart, and abused the advantage of her position to extort respect and to display impertinence to anyone willing to bear it. At the same time, she could be very gracious when she pleased, and as she found my house very pleasant, she was always extremely polite to me.

In the early days of the Empire, opposition society in Paris was very agreeable. As soon as I was initiated and had formed a circle of my own, I found life quite delightful.

Everyone was beginning to experience some return of peace and comfort, and no one was anxious to risk these advantages, so that political opinion was comparatively peaceful. Two great parties were in existence, the members of the Government and those who were outside the Government. The latter, of whom I was one of the most hostile, confined themselves to epigrams and bad jokes when the doors were closed; we were careful to observe due bounds. Some display of severity from time to time in the case of more turbulent spirits kept everyone respectful, and increased courtesy of intercourse was the result.

Social distinctions were still somewhat vague; few people possessed establishments of their own, and those who could keep open house in town or country found no difficulty in gathering agreeable society about them. Such was my position during the second winter, and this state of things lasted three or four years. At the end of this time desertions became more numerous; the great majority of the nobility attached themselves to the Empire, and the marriage of the Archduchess[1] carried off the rest. After that, ladies who did not go to the court were few indeed, and if the Emperor's prosperity had continued a few months longer, there would have been none of them.

My uncle had easily secured the erasure of my father's name from the list of *émigrés* because he had no property to claim in France. He came to rejoin me, together with my mother and my brother Rainulphe, towards the middle of 1805. They established themselves in my house in Paris and at Beauregard. I was anxious that my brother, whose livelihood was by no means assured and who was dependent upon myself, should enter the court service. My mother objected, and my father remained neutral, as he knew that his decision would be adopted by his son, and he did not wish to influence him. He was presented to the Emperor, who showed him much condescension, and was warmly welcomed by the Empress Joséphine, who wished to have him for her equerry or at any rate to attach him to her son-in-law, Prince Louis, in a similar position.

My brother would have preferred to enter the army, but he would have been obliged to enlist. The households of the Princes provided an opportunity of securing a commission almost immediately. Young men

1. The Archduchess Marie-Louise, daughter of the Emperor of Austria, married Napoleon on April 1, 1810.

Eléonore Dillon, Marquise d'Osmond

FROM A MINIATURE BY ISABEY

thus attached first followed the Princes to war without holding any rank, and if they behaved respectably were speedily given a commission. My mother wept, my brother hesitated; some evasion was made, and the post was given elsewhere. In the following winter Rainulphe began a close friendship with the beautiful lady[2] who has since become almost a historical personage by reason of the adventures of Blaye. Madame d'Hautefort and her society were enthusiastic in their opposition to the Emperor. My brother adopted their ideas, and henceforward the project of court service was entirely abandoned.

I cannot refrain from narrating a trivial circumstance which confirms all that has been said about the futility and fickleness of the Empress Joséphine. Mme. Arthur Dillon, the second wife of a Dillon who had married Mlle. de Rothe, and who was killed when acting as General in the army, was a Creole of Martinique and a cousin of the Empress, who often saw her and was especially fond of her daughter, Fanny Dillon. We were very intimate with the whole of this family. Mme. Fitz-James, daughter of Mme. Dillon by another marriage, was my best friend. When Mme. Dillon was staying with me at Beauregard, she went to pay a visit to Saint-Cloud, and the Empress deluded her with the idea that she could enable Fanny to make a fine marriage; on her return she asked me if I would sacrifice a heron's plume to her: M. de Boigne had brought some of these from India and had given them to me.

The milliner Leroi had brought a very poor specimen of a plume to the Empress that morning. Mme. Dillon had said that I had much finer plumes, and her Majesty was immediately seized with an extreme desire to secure them. We were still at table when a man on horseback, in the Emperor's livery, came to ask if the plume had been given to Mme. Dillon. It was impossible to refuse. I gave it, and Mme. Dillon sent it off.

The next day came a second message and a note from the Empress. Leroi thought the feather was excellent, but it was mounted in Indian

2. Allusion to the Duchesse de Berry and the Vendée expedition in 1832. She failed to bring about an insurrection against Louis-Philippe.

style, and a second would be required to make a handsome plume. I therefore gave the second. The next day Mme. Dillon went to Saint-Cloud, and on her return she explained with some embarrassment that a third was required to complete the aigrette. I gave the third, announcing that I had no more to give. A third note arrived, containing a hymn of joy and gratitude.

Some days afterwards Mme. Dillon told me that the Empress had had an ornament made up of very beautiful cameos, which she wished to present to me. I begged her to spare me the presentation, explaining that the plumes had been given to her, Mme. Dillon, and had not been offered to the Empress. After another visit to Saint-Cloud she assured me that she had made vain efforts to perform my commission. The Empress had seemed so hurt that it was impossible to resist, and the ornament would be sent to me shortly.

The following Sunday, my brother went to pay his respects. The Empress asked after me, spoke with delight of the beauty and rarity of the plumes, and said to him: "I have nothing so precious to offer her, but I shall ask her to accept some stones which are valuable for their ancient workmanship."

My brother bowed. On returning to Beauregard, the first thing he did was to repeat this conversation, and we held a family council to consider how I should receive this favour. It was impossible to refuse, and in spite of our prejudices we admitted that the choice of the gift had been made in excellent taste. Should I write, or should I request an audience to offer my thanks? And would this latter entail the necessity of a presentation? I might easily have spared myself all this anxiety and agitation, for from that day to this I have never heard a word of plumes or stones or anything of the kind. Those who knew the Empress well thought that when the case of cameos was sent back to her she found the contents so beautiful that she had not courage to part with them at the first moment of her infatuation. A month afterwards she would have been very glad to give them, but it was then too late.

Mme. Récamier came to spend some days with me at Beauregard, where I had many visitors. I returned her visit at Clichy, where she was living in the full security of assured prosperity, when a few days afterwards her husband's bankruptcy was declared. Although she was little more than a social acquaintance, I had no thoughts of dropping her and hastened to call. Her calmness, nobility, and simplicity in this situation, and the loftiness of her character, stood so high above the habits of her life as to impress me greatly. From that moment dates the keen affection which I bear towards her, and which has only been confirmed by the various events through which we afterwards passed.

Many portraits have been drawn of Mme. Récamier, but none, in my opinion, have reproduced the essential features of her character, a failure the more excusable since her variety of expression was infinite. Mme. Récamier was a true type of womanhood as made by the Creator for the happiness of man. She had all the charm, the virtue, the inconsistency, and the weakness of the perfect woman. If she had been a mother her destiny would have been complete; the world would have heard less of her, and she would have been happier. As she had missed this natural vocation, she was obliged to find compensation in society. Mme. Récamier was the incarnation of coquetry; her talent in this respect amounted to genius, and she was the admirable leader of a detestable school. Every woman who attempted to imitate her has become an object of scandal or disgrace, whereas she always emerged unscathed from the furnace into which it was her delight to plunge. The fact is not to be explained by any coldness of heart, for her flirtations were actuated by kindness and not by vanity. She was much more anxious to be loved than to be admired, and this sentiment was so natural to her that she always had some affection and much sympathy to give her numerous adorers in exchange for the admiration which she strove to attract; hence her coquetry avoided the usual accompanying selfishness and was not absolutely barren, if I may use the term. She thus preserved the affection of almost all the men who fell in love with her. Nor have I known anyone who could more dexterously combine an attitude of exclusiveness with a bearing of general friendliness towards a numerous circle.

Everyone has praised her incomparable beauty, her energetic benevolence, and her gentle courtesy; many people have praised her lively wit. But very few were able to discover beneath the easy manners of her social intercourse the loftiness of her mind and the independence of her character, the impartiality of her judgement and the accuracy of her intuition. I have sometimes seen her dominated; I never knew her to be influenced. In her early youth Mme. Récamier had adopted a kind of affectation from the society in which she lived, and this detracted from both her beauty and her wit; she soon abandoned it when she found another circle in full consonance with her tastes. She became very intimate with Mme. de Staël,* and acquired in her company a taste for keen intellectual conversations, in which she took the part which a woman should take, that of intelligent curiosity, which she could excite around her because of her own obvious interest. This mode of amusement, the sole recreation which nothing can replace when once the taste has been acquired, is only to be found in France and in Paris. This Mme. de Staël said with perfect truth amid the bitter experiences of her exile.

The attraction which Mme. Récamier was able to exert upon famous men caused the beginning of her connection with M. de Chateaubriand.* She devoted herself to him for fifteen years. The delicacy of his behaviour made him worthy of this affection, but I should not like to assert that he deserved it by his depth of feeling. The fact remains that she was both agreeable and useful to him, and that all her faculties were concentrated upon the task of softening his violent conceit, calming the bitterness of his character, ministering to his vanity, and dissipating his boredom. I think that he loved her as much as he could love anything, for she gave him all she could.

In 1806 I was affected by a malady so strange that I feel bound to describe it. Every day a violent headache preceded a fit of shivering which was followed by a high temperature, slight perspiration, and finally a well-marked attack of fever. But during the height of the fever my pulse slowed to a remarkable extent instead of quickening, and only became normal when the fit had passed away. I could eat nothing of any kind and was getting visibly thinner.

Sea-bathing had done me good in England, and I wished to try it now, though the doctors did not greatly encourage the idea. I was obliged to make the journey in my carriage. It lasted five days, and I arrived at Dieppe in the last stage of exhaustion. A week afterwards I was walking on the seashore, having recovered my health with the rapidity of early youth.

For twenty-five years my carriage was the only one of its kind which had entered Dieppe, and we made a prodigious sensation. Every time we went out a crowd gathered to see us pass, and the harness in particular was examined with inconceivable curiosity. The poverty of the inhabitants was frightful. The Englishman, as they called the British fleet—and for them its presence was worse than that of the Devil—was cruising incessantly before their empty harbour. With much difficulty a boat was able to escape from time to time and go fishing, always at the risk of being captured by the foreigner or confiscated upon the return journey if the telescopes of the watchers had seen it approach a vessel.

As for the comforts arranged for the convenience of bathers which Dieppe has since organised, they were nonexistent at that time. My brother was able to find a little covered cart, and with great trouble and great expense, notwithstanding the universal poverty, a man was hired to lead the horses down to the sea, and two women to go into the sea with me. These preparations raised the public surprise and curiosity to such a pitch that my first baths were watched by a crowd on the shore. My servants were asked if I had been bitten by a mad dog. I aroused extreme pity as I went by, and it was thought that I was being taken to be drowned. An old gentleman called on my father to point out to him that he was assuming a great responsibility in permitting so rash an act.

It can hardly be imagined that the inhabitants of a seashore should be so afraid of the sea. But at that time the people of Dieppe were chiefly occupied in keeping out of sight of it and in protecting themselves from the disasters which they feared the sea might bring, so that it was for them nothing more than a means of annoyance and suffering. It is curious to think that ten years later bathers were arriving in the hundreds, that special arrangements were made for their convenience, and that sea-bathing of every kind went on without producing any astonishment in the neighbourhood. I have thus attempted to point out that the custom of sea-bathing, which is now so universal, is comparatively recent in France, for Dieppe was the first place where it began.

My life was so monotonous during the ten years of the Empire, and my participation in great events so scant, that I have practically no landmarks by which to guide my chronology. I shall confine myself to putting down at random, without reference to dates, such recollections of this period as deal with personages of some importance, or depict the manners of that society in which I lived exclusively.

M. de Boigne had begun to build a house in Savoy, where he had bought an estate. At first he had spent some weeks every summer there, but these soon became months. Finally, attracted by the vast importance which his unequalled wealth gave him in his own country, he settled there definitely, and became the benefactor of the place. Beauregard was then too large a house for the income which he had left me. It was put up for sale and bought by the Prince Aldobrandini Borghese, and I transported my goods and chattels to a little manor in the village of Châtenay, near Sceaux. The birth of Voltaire in this house gave it some pretensions to celebrity. My removal from Beauregard did not take place until 1812.

I often went to Savoy, and stopped at Lyons during my first journey thither. M. d'Herbouville was prefect of the town, which was one reason for staying there. I was staying at the Hôtel de l'Europe, and arrived late. The next morning the headwaiter informed me that Mme. de Staël was in the house, and asked if I would receive her.

"Certainly, I shall be delighted; but I will send her word."

Five minutes afterwards she entered my room escorted by Camille Jordan,* Benjamin Constant,* Mathieu de Montmorency,* Schlegel,* Elzéar de Sabran,* and Talma.* I was very young, and this great celebrity with her extraordinary escort overwhelmed me at first. Mme. de Staël soon put me entirely at my ease. I had intended to take some drives in order to see Lyons, but she assured me that I might spare myself the trouble, that Lyons was an exceedingly ugly town between two beautiful rivers, and that if I knew that fact I was as well informed as if I had spent a week in exploration. She spent the whole morning in my room, receiving callers and delighting me with her brilliant conversation. I forgot the prefect and his prefecture. I dined with her, and in the evening I went to see Talma in Manlius; he played for her rather than for the public, and was repaid by the delight which she felt and which she communicated to others.

On leaving the theatre she got into her carriage to return to Coppet. She had broken the conditions of her exile and risked many disagreeable results in order to be present at the performance of Talma.

Thus it was that this meteor appeared before my sight, and my head was completely turned. At first she seemed to me ugly and ridiculous. A big red face, a complexion by no means fresh, and her hair arranged in a manner which she called picturesque—in other words, badly done. No fichu, a white muslin blouse cut very low, arms and shoulders bare, no shawl, scarf, or veil of any kind—such was the strange apparition which appeared in a hotel room at midday. She held a small twig which she was constantly twiddling in her fingers, with the object, I think, of showing off a very beautiful hand, though it was but the finishing touch to the eccentricity of her costume. At the end of an hour I was entirely under her charm, and throughout her intellectual enjoyment of Talma's performance I watched the play of her features, and was surprised to find her almost beautiful. I do not know if she guessed my impressions, but she was always entirely kind, amiable, and charming to me. The next year I met her at Aix, in Savoy, where I was staying with Mme. Récamier. It was under pretext of going to see her that Mme. de Staël again broke the conditions of her exile at Coppet, and arrived at Aix.

I was almost an eyewitness to many deplorable scenes, when two geniuses, Mme. de Staël and Benjamin Constant, used finer intellects than God perhaps has given to any other mortals for the purpose of tormenting one another. The long-standing relations between Mme. de Staël and Constant are perfectly well-known. Mme. de Staël retained a liking for his intellect, but she had other temporary affections which frequently gained the upper hand. On these occasions Benjamin attempted to begin a quarrel; she then clung to him more completely than ever, and after fearful scenes they made their peace. In an attempt to describe this position, he said that he was tired of being always necessary and never adequate to her needs. For a long time he had cherished hopes of marrying Mme. de Staël. Vanity and interest were motives at least as powerful as his affection for her, but she persistently refused. She desired to keep him in harness to her own chariot, but not to submit herself to the yoke of Benjamin. Moreover, she attached too much importance to social distinctions to exchange the name of Staël-Holstein for that of Constant. There was no greater slave to the most foolish aristocratic ideas than Mme. de Staël, with all her liberalism.

In the course of a journey that Benjamin Constant made in Germany, he met one Countess of Magnoz, by birth the Countess of Hardenberg. It was by no means the story of Mlle. Necker over again. She fell violently in love with him and wished to marry him. I think that the desire to show Mme. de Staël that an important personage did not disdain his name carried much weight in the eventual consent which he gave.

Mme. de Staël learnt of this project, and her fury was such that he dared not openly accomplish it. However, he was secretly married, and his wife accompanied him to Lyons. There she took some small quantity of a drug which produced violent vomiting, and declared that she would poison herself once and for all if he did not cast off Mme. de Staël by proclaiming his marriage. On the other hand, the latter vowed that she would stab herself if he did anything of the kind.

Such was the state of affairs when Benjamin Constant and Mme. de Staël met at Aix under the mediation of Mme. Récamier. The mornings were spent in appalling scenes, in reproaches, imprecations, and hysterical attacks. These proceedings were not altogether genuine. We dined together, as usual, at watering-places. By degrees during the meal hostilities were suspended. One witty or brilliant observation would produce another. Their mutual pleasure in this intellectual sword-play became paramount, and the evening passed delightfully, while the morrow saw a renewal of yesterday morning's fury.

At length a treaty was signed under the following conditions: Mme. de Staël would write to Mme. Constant, thus recognising the marriage. But the marriage was not to be published until three months after her departure to America, whither she really intended to go at that time. This concession of affection to vanity never gave me a very agreeable impression. Though Benjamin yielded to outcry, he nonetheless felt hurt. In any case, Mme. de Staël did not start, and the marriage was recognised, though after a considerable interval. I think that Mme. de Staël was anxious to secure a continuance of that amusement and pleasure which she found in the mind of Benjamin Constant, and wished to take him to America. Perhaps she thought of the possibility of marrying him when they were once beyond the Atlantic, and his marriage with another woman touched her more keenly at that moment. There was a real bond of sympathy between them, and his treatment of her pretty child, who was so indiscreet as to reproduce his features, was entirely paternal.

I have a clear recollection of one of the days of that period. We all went to dinner with M. de Boigne at Buissonrond, near Chambéry. He had gathered the most distinguished society in the town, including the prefect; there were thirty of us. Mme. de Staël was by the side of the master of the house, and the prefect opposite to her, at my side. She asked him across the table what had become of a man whom she had known as a subprefect; he answered that the man was now a prefect, and much respected.

"I am very glad to hear it; he was a good fellow. In any case," she added carelessly, "I have generally found that class of servant very decent."

I saw the prefect turn both red and pale, and felt my heart in my mouth. Mme. de Staël did not seem to notice that she had been rude, nor had she intended to be. I quote the fact to point out a strange anomaly in this eminently sociable mind, namely, that she was entirely wanting in tact. Mme. de Staël never considered her audience in the least when she was talking, and, without the smallest intention of causing embarrassment or giving offence, she would often choose subjects of conversation and expressions most disagreeable to the persons to whom she spoke.

I return to the dinner at Buissonrond. We had reached the second course, which was proceeding like all wearisome dinners, to the great disgust of the provincial guests. Elzéar de Sabran, seeing their disappointment, addressed himself to Mme. de Staël from the end of the table, asking whether she thought that the constitutional laws of Romulus would have preserved their influence at Rome as long as they did, had it not been for the religious laws of Numa. She raised her head, understood the appeal, merely replied to the question by a joke, and then became as brilliant and amiable as I have ever seen her. We were all delighted, and no one more so than the prefect, M. Finot, an intellectual man. An urgent letter was handed to him; he read it and put it in his pocket. After dinner he showed it to me. It was an order that Mme. de Staël was to be sent back to Coppet by the police from post to post as soon as he had received the letter. I begged him not to cause a disturbance in my house, and he assured me that he had no intention of doing so, adding with some bitterness, "I should be sorry if she changed her opinion concerning servants of my class!"

I undertook to make her understand that it was time to go back to Coppet, and he confined himself to enjoining the postmaster to issue horses only for the direct route.

Life at Coppet was extraordinary. It seemed idle and irregular in the extreme, and no one knew whether he should be anywhere or do anything at any special time. There was no special place of meeting for any special hour of the day, and every room was always open. Tents were pitched wherever a conversation began, and there they stayed for hours or days, uninterrupted by any of the ordinary affairs of life. Talking seemed everybody's first duty. Yet almost all the persons composing this society were seriously occupied, as is proven by the large number of works from their pens. Mme. de Staël worked a great deal, but when she had nothing better to do, the most trivial social pleasure would absorb her time. She liked amateur theatricals, driving, walks, bringing people together, fetching them to her house, and above all things, talking.

She had no special writing room; a little writing-case of green morocco, which she put on her knees and carried about from room to room, contained both her works and her correspondence. Even the writing-case was often enough surrounded by several people, and, in a word, the only thing she feared was solitude, and boredom was the scourge of her life. It is astonishing how many powerful geniuses have been entirely dominated by this impression. Mme. de Staël, Lord Byron, and M. de Chateaubriand are striking examples, and with the object of escaping boredom they have spoiled their lives, and would have been willing to turn the world upside down.

It was at Coppet that the abuse of the word "talent" began, which has become so constant in doctrinaire cliques. Every member of the society was always full of his talent or thinking of the talent of others: "That does not harmonise with your talent"; "That is in accordance with your talent"; "You ought to devote your talent to it"; "I will try my talent," et cetera, et cetera, were phrases which recurred twenty times an hour in their conversation. The last time that I saw Mme. de Staël at Coppet, she had placed herself in a very false position. After edifying the town of Geneva with the deplorable scenes resulting from a passion which she had conceived for a handsome American, Mr. O'Brien, she had shut herself up at Coppet and mourned his departure.

A young subaltern named Rocca, the nephew of her doctor, Bouttigny, had returned from Spain severely wounded. Country air was desirable for his health, and Mme. de Staël told Bouttigny to send young Rocca to her house. He had been at school with her sons, and she showed him much kindness. He had an attractive face, and she made him tell her stories of Spain and its horrors, which he did with the frankness of a simple heart. She admired and flattered him; the young man was intoxicated with self-conceit, and became infatuated with her. The fact is certain that the passion was entirely on his side. Mme. de Staël felt nothing more than the gratitude of a woman of forty-five who is adored by a man of twenty-two. M. Rocca began to display his jealousy in public, and his triumph became complete. When I found her at Geneva, M. Rocca was in the full flush of success, and, it must be admitted, a ridiculous figure, and a constant source of embarrassment to Mme. de Staël.

Mme. de Staël, who did nothing by halves, was extremely delighted by my singing; probably she had scolded M. Rocca for his evident disregard of my performances. One evening, I had finished a song and was standing by the piano talking with some of the guests when M. Rocca, who still used a crutch, crossed the room and called loudly over the piano in his nasal drawl:

"Maadame, Maadame de Boigne, I didn't hear your voice. Maadame, it goes to the heart."

Thereupon he turned round and went off again upon his crutch. Mme. de Staël, who was sitting near me, sprang up and caught my arm.

"Ah!" she said, "human speech is not his language." The phrase always struck me as the outcry of a clever woman in love with a fool.

Mme. de Staël was even then complaining of her feeble health, and I think that the consequences of this connection greatly accelerated her death. Her condition caused her great pain, but she kept the secret admirably. Her children honestly and sincerely believed she was suffering from dropsy. Spied upon as she was by a police force of extraordinary energy, it is astonishing that her secret was not discovered. She was at home to visitors as usual, merely saying that she was ill; and immediately after her confinement she fled the spot where she had suffered so much, and which had become intolerable to her, leaving no trace of the event which had taken place.

In view of the Emperor's constant animosity towards Mme. de Staël, he would not have hesitated to announce the secret, had he entertained the smallest suspicion. But it was faithfully kept, and appearances were entirely saved, which proves, by the way, that cleverness can overcome any difficulty.

Doubtless she might have married M. Rocca, but that was the last resource of desperation. She yielded only upon her death-bed at the earnest supplication of her daughter Albertine, the Duchesse de Broglie, after she had revealed to her the existence of the little Rocca.

M. and Mme. de Broglie, as well as her son, Auguste de Staël, made as many efforts to give their mother another legitimate heir as less scrupulous people would have made to avoid this result. I am inclined to think that this incident in her mother's life contributed to direct Mme. de Broglie towards the Methodism which she later adopted.

M. Rocca followed Mme. de Staël everywhere and clung to her in embarrassments which only his passionate devotion could have tolerated, for she was wearied and harassed by his presence, though touched by his affection. He died of grief six months after her death, thus justifying the weakness she had shown by the depth of his devotion.

This, in any case, was the explanation of the intimacy given by Mme. de Staël herself. She was the more delighted to be able to inspire deep devotion at her age, as her lack of beauty had always been a cause of great vexation to her. Her mode of concession to this weakness was unusual: she never said that a woman was ugly or pretty, but merely that she possessed or lacked external advantages. This was her habitual phrase, and one could not say that a person was ugly in her presence without hurting her feelings.

I have related my intimacy with Mme. de Staël at some length. Whether I have added anything to what is known of her, I cannot say, but I have been able to recall recollections which I highly prize. No one who had ever met her could forget the charm of her society. I think her conversation was far more remarkable than her books. It would be an entire mistake to think of her as in the least pedantic or affected. She would talk dress with as much interest as constitutional law, and if, as she said, she had made conversation an art, she had become a perfect artist, for naturalness was the dominant feature of her talk.

She gave enough attention to her financial affairs to avoid any monetary loss. Notwithstanding the apparent carelessness of her habits, she was exact in matters of business, and her circumstances were rather improved than worsened. Her exile was terribly harassing to her spirit, and it must be said that under the Emperor Napoleon exile was accompanied by all those petty vexations which can make it intolerable; no one attempted any mitigation of its severity. It was the chief restraint upon that section of society since known as the Faubourg Saint-Germain. I have known several persons thus exiled, of various tastes, habits, fortunes, and positions, and all expressed a despair which became a salutary warning to others. Hence prudence during this period was both scrupulous and general.

Actually, exile was easy to avoid by means of an attitude of reserve. The sentence of exile, except in two or three cases occasioned by private vengeance, only fell upon persons whose hostility was noisy and truculent. I have often been asked at that time:

"How is it that you are not exiled?"

"It is because I do not go out of my way to seek exile," I used to reply, "and am not afraid of it."

My house, in fact, was one of those where opinion was most outspoken. I saw many members of every party, and was agreeable to them all. My opinions were known, but were not expressed with bitterness. Moreover, we did not intrigue with inferior conspirators, the paid agents of disturbance and disorder, for whom my father entertained a scorn which he had communicated to me. I saw a great deal of the diplomatic body; Count Tolstoi and Count Nesselrode were constant visitors, as also were the Semffts and Count Metternich.* When they were replaced by the Prince of Schwarzenberg, de Kourakan, et cetera, the new diplomatic body separated in a marked degree from the opposition and devoted itself to the imperial court.

The obsequious respect of foreigners for the new greatness often excited our laughter. I can remember that old Count Romanzov, Chancellor of Russia, excused himself one evening for reaching my house late, saying that he had been detained because Monseigneur the Archchancellor had done him the honour of requesting him to make up a game. Those of us who had never dreamt of calling this man anything but plain Cambacérès* were not a little astonished by this language. By degrees, however, these formalities became established; and if the Empire had lasted a few years longer, we should have adopted them in our turn, as we had already done in the case of the imperial family.

I was brought most directly into connection with the court through Fanny Dillon. The Emperor had undertaken to get her married, and she did not allow him to forget his promise, while her innocent manner of reminding him amused him greatly. However, he kept her waiting a terribly long time. The marriages of Mlles. de Beauharnais and de Tascher with the Grand Duke of Baden and the reigning Prince d'Arenberg had greatly raised her claims. She had, however, condescended to consent to marry Prince Alphonse Pignatelli, the younger son of the house of Egmont. I do not know if the marriage would have taken place, but death carried off the bridegroom. After that, the Empress Joséphine successively mentioned Prince Aldobrandini, who would be made King of Portugal, and the Duke of Medina Sidonia, while she had a moment's anxiety upon the subject of the Prince of Neuchâtel. Eventually, during the spring of 1808, she spoke to me of her fear that she might be forced to marry Prince Bernard of Saxe-Coburg, whom she thought somewhat too German.

In the middle of the summer her sister, Mme. de Fitz-James, expired in my arms after a long illness caused by her husband's philandering. He had begun to regret her bitterly, I believe, when it was too late to save her. Her last words were to recommend her mother to my care, and I carried her off to Beauregard with Fanny. The same day the Empress arrived from Marsac, and, in spite of her mourning, Fanny went off to Saint-Cloud two days afterwards. She came back in despair: the Empress had told her that General Bertrand* was the husband whom the Emperor destined for her. The disappointment was great, and she felt it deeply. She was in tears when the Emperor came into the apartments of the Empress. She ventured to reproach him for deceiving her hopes, and grew so excited that she actually said, "What, Sire! Bertrand? Bertrand? Why not the Pope's monkey?"

This remark sealed her fate, and the Emperor said dryly, "That will do, Fanny," and left the room.

The Empress undertook to persuade him otherwise, thinking herself that Bertrand was not sufficiently important to marry a relative who was under her special care. She promised to send an answer by the end of the week. Poor Fanny spent the interval in tears. She went back to Saint-Cloud, saying that she had decided to refuse Bertrand at whatever cost, and her mother greatly encouraged her. She came back having accepted him, entirely reconciled to her fate. The Empress had shown her a prospect of high position, and the name of Bertrand hidden beneath a dukedom. She spent the evening in choosing the title which would sound best, but which she never secured. I have always thought that this was a piece of spite on the Emperor's part in return for the remark about the Pope's monkey.

The interview took place at Beauregard: Mme. Dillon declined to be present, and I was left in charge. Never had a sulkier or more slovenly fiancée appeared before a future husband. The General, however, was not repelled, and precisely one month after the death of Mme. Fitz-James, Mme. Dillon accompanied her other daughter to the altar, with a repugnance which she did not attempt to hide. The civil marriage took place at my house in Paris, and the wedding at Saint-Leu, at the house of Joséphine's daughter, Hortense de Beauharnais,* the Queen of Holland. I had been invited, but found a pretext for refusal.

To do justice to Bertrand, for a man of limited ideas he was entirely upright. He was a good husband and son-in-law, and we have always been on the best of terms. He was said to possess much capacity in his own profession. The Emperor was a good judge, but I think that his true merit was blind and unlimited devotion.

Fanny Dillon used to go driving at Saint-Cloud with my horses and servants. One day when a household official was putting them in their place, my coachman said to him:

"Of course, I will go where you like. We never come here for our own pleasure, so I do not care."

This piece of effrontery delighted our foolish partisanship. It recalls to me the remark of a sentinel uttered some years later at a moment when the imperial court was full of sovereigns. This functionary addressed a cabman who had stopped in the court of the Tuileries, and called out to him:

"You, there! Be off! Unless your master is a king you cannot stand there."

The Emperor was much amused at this story, for there were real kings among those thus treated.

I have often seen the Emperor Napoleon at the theatre, or driving in a carriage, but only twice in a room. The town of Paris gave a ball on the occasion of the marriage of the Princess of Baden. The Emperor wished to return it, and tickets were sent out for a ball at the Tuileries to many persons who had not been presented at court. Some of us young women received tickets, though we had not been present at the municipal ball, and after discussing the matter, we agreed that it was our duty to go. Dancing went on in the Galerie de Diane and in the Salle des Maréchaux. The public were confined to these rooms according to the colour of their tickets, and mine took me to the Galerie de Diane. There was no communication between one room and the other, and the court passed into the rooms successively. The Empress, the Princesses, their ladies, and their chamberlains, all in full dress, entered in the train of the Emperor, and took up their position upon a platform prepared beforehand. After watching the performance of a kind of ballet, the Emperor came down alone and went round the room, speaking exclusively to the ladies. He wore his imperial dress (which he almost immediately afterwards abandoned): the waistcoat and white satin knee breeches, the white shoes with gold rosettes, a coat of red velvet cut straight in the style of Francis I, with gold embroidery upon all the seams, the sword sparkling with diamonds above the coat, orders and stars also of diamonds, and a cap with the feathers held up by a diamond buckle. The costume was well designed, but was utterly unsuited for him on account of his small size, his corpulence, and clumsiness of movement. Perhaps it was prejudice on my part, but the Emperor seemed to me frightful, and looked like a mock king. I was standing between two women unknown to me. He asked the first her name, and she replied that she was the daughter of Foacier.

"Ah!" he said, and passed on.

According to his custom, he also asked my name, which I told him.

"You live at Beauregard?"

"Yes, Sire."

"It is a beautiful spot, and your husband employs much labour there; I am grateful to him for the service he does to the country, as I am to all who employ workmen. He has been in the English army?"

I thought it shorter to answer "Yes," but he continued, "That is to say, not entirely. He is a Savoyard, is he not?"

"Yes, Sire."

"But you are French, entirely French, and we therefore claim you, for you are not one of those rights easily surrendered."

I bowed.

"How old are you?"

I told him.

"And frank into the bargain. You look much younger."

I bowed again. He stepped back half a pace, and then came up to me, speaking lower in a confidential tone:

"You have no children? I know that is not your fault, but you should make better arrangements. Believe me, I am giving you good advice."

I remained stupefied; he looked at me for a moment with a gracious smile, and went on to my neighbour: "Your name?"

"A daughter of Foacier."

"Another daughter of Foacier!" and he continued his promenade.

I cannot express the deep aristocratic disdain with which the phrase "another daughter of Foacier" left the imperial lips. Neither the name nor the persons have ever come before me since that time, but it has remained in my memory with the inflection of that voice which I then heard for the first and last time. After he had made his round, the Emperor returned to the Empress, and all the gilded troop went off without commingling in any way with the plebeian horde. At nine o'clock in the evening all was over: the guests might remain and dance, but the court had retired. I followed the example of the court, being strangely impressed by imperial manners. I had seen other monarchs, but none who treated the public in so cavalier a fashion.

Some years afterwards I was present as an onlooker at a ball given upon the occasion of the baptism of the King of Rome.[3] I think it was the last imperial festivity. It took place in the Tuileries, in the theatre room: the court alone was present, and persons who had not been presented were given tickets for the boxes. A dozen of us ladies who belonged to the Opposition went there, and we were forced to admit that the spectacle was magnificent. Uniforms were prohibited, and our old soldiers seemed ill at ease, but the young ones, especially M. de Flahaut, rivalled the grace of Archambault de Périgord. The women were elegantly and magnificently dressed. The Emperor, followed by his escort, crossed the room as he arrived to reach the platform which occupied the back. He walked first with such speed that almost everybody, not excepting the Empress, was almost obliged to run to keep up with him. Dignity and grace were thus out of the question, but this rustling of skirts and rapid pace seemed to symbolise a dominant power which suited him. It was magnificent, though not in our way.

He seemed, indeed, the master of all this magnificence. He was no longer in his imperial costume, and the simple uniform which he alone wore in the midst of all this full dress made him a yet more striking figure, and spoke more loudly to the imagination than all the gold lace in the world. He was anxious to be gracious and kind, and made a far

3. Title given to Napoleon's son, born in 1811.

better impression upon me than at the other ball. The Empress Marie-Louise was a fine woman, fresh in appearance, but somewhat too red. Notwithstanding her dress and her precious stones, she seemed very vulgar and entirely without distinction. A quadrille was performed, danced by the Princesses and the court ladies, several of whom were our friends. I saw there the Princess Borghese, Napoleon's sister, who seemed to me the most ravishing beauty that I had ever looked upon. To all her perfections was added the air of candid maidenhood as complete as any young girl could have, though if history is to be believed, no one ever had less right to it.

The Emperor was anxious that the women he had wished to attract to his court should have an opportunity of seeing its splendours. He cast obliging glances upon the boxes and remained for a long time beneath ours, evidently of set purpose. In any case, there were already too many of our party at court, and there was no need for him to worry about those who were left outside.

I can never remember without shame the unpatriotic wishes which we cherished, and the guilty joy with which our partisanship received the news of our military reverses. Since that date I have read the portrait drawn by Machiavelli of the *fuori inciti*, and I blush to think that I must admit a resemblance. The *émigrés* of all times and all countries should use it as their manual; it is a mirror which should make them shudder at the sight of their own faces. Doubtless our sentiments were not shared by the majority of the country, but I believe that the masses had become profoundly indifferent to military successes. When the cannon announced that some brilliant victory had been gained, a small number of persons grieved, a somewhat larger number rejoiced, but the general population remained almost unmoved. The people were sated with glory and knew that fresh success implied fresh efforts. A victory was the forerunner of a conscription, and the capture of Vienna was merely the prelude to a march upon Warsaw or Pressburg. Besides, the accuracy of the bulletins was doubted, and their appearance excited but little enthusiasm. The Emperor was always more coldly received in Paris than in any other town.

In strict truth I must, however, say that upon the day when the twenty-sixth cannon shot announced that the Empress had been confined of a boy, a long shout of joy went throughout the town, which resounded as though evoked by an electric shock. Everybody was at the windows or the doors. The silence was intense while the first twenty-five shots were counted, and the twenty-sixth produced an uproar. This event completed the Emperor's happiness, and completion is always admirable. I should not like to assert that even the fiercest antagonists did not feel some slight emotion at that moment.

We invented a story about this child, to the effect that the birth was fictitious. This was sheer nonsense. The Emperor was passionately fond of the child, and as soon as the little king could distinguish anybody, he showed a special preference for his father. Possibly paternal love might have induced the Emperor to be more careful of the lives of men. I have heard M. de Fontanes, the head of the University, say that one day when he was at lunch with the Emperor, the King of Rome was playing about the table, and his father followed him with tender glances, when the child fell and hurt himself slightly, and there was a great uproar. Peace was restored, and the Emperor fell into a gloomy reverie, and then said aloud, addressing no one in particular, "I have seen the same cannonball carry off twenty from one file."

He then resumed the business discussion with M. de Fontanes from which he had been distracted by reflections the course of which can easily be followed. In any case, his misgivings were beginning, and possibly contributed to his philanthropic tendencies.

Were I to try to relate all the stories of the Emperor, I should never end, but as these reached me only from Opposition sources, I am inclined to doubt them. If the glasses of the Opposition showed objects in false colours, they certainly magnified them. I have been astonished to find how men who must, we thought, be as great as the purpose for which Napoleon employed them became small and inconsiderable when his support was removed. One of his special talents was to discover with his eagle eye each man's special powers, to turn those powers to account, and thus to make the utmost possible use of them.

The only people for whom he had an invincible repugnance were the true liberals, those whom he called idealists. When once he had given this title to a man, there was nothing more to be said: he would willingly have sent his victim to the lunatic asylum, and regarded him as a social scourge. Alas, it seems that we shall be forced to admit that Bonaparte's genius for government inspired him correctly, and that these dreamers of the happiness of nations, estimable as they doubtless are, are of no special service, and serve only to excite the passions of the mob by flattering them, and thus to disorganise society. I did not think so at that time, and the Emperor's hatred for idealists whom I would willingly have made my oracles seemed to me a great error.

Among these idealists he classed M. de Chateaubriand. This was a mistake. M. de Chateaubriand cared nothing about the human race; he was entirely occupied with his own persona, and with the task of erecting a pedestal from which he could look down upon his age. This was a difficult place to assume, side by side with Napoleon, but he worked incessantly, and his memoirs will show the world with what toil, with what perseverance, and with what hopes of success. He succeeded so far in that he always made for himself a little atmosphere of his own, of which he was the sun. As soon as he left this environment the outer air affected him so painfully that he became unbearably morose. But while he was in his own atmosphere no one could be kinder or more amiable, or send forth his beams with more grace. For the Chateaubriand of this latter position I had much liking, but the other side of his character is hateful.

If he had confined himself to his work as an author, to which his eminently artistic character impelled him, he would have been known solely for his goodness and kindness, apart from some bitterness due to criticisms of his works. But he had an ambition to be a statesman, and this brought him into regions where his claims were ill-received; this failure produced a number of evil passions within him, and poured floods of bitterness into his style which will make most of his writ-

ings unreadable when time has brought forth impartial readers. M. de
Chateaubriand had an instinct for the feeling of the moment. He could
guess the public taste, and flatter it so admirably that though he was a
partisan writer, he nonetheless became popular. For this purpose he
was ready to change his views entirely; to praise that which he had
scorned, and to scorn that which he had praised. He had two or three
principles dressed up according to circumstance, so that they were not
always recognisable, but enabled him to avoid every difficulty and to
claim complete consistency. This was all the easier for him as his intellect, which was little short of genius, was never troubled by any consideration of morality which might have stopped him. He believed in
nothing in the world except in his own talent, and before this altar he
was continually prostrate. In speaking of the Restoration and of the
Revolution of 1830, if these notes should be continued to that point, I
shall often have an opportunity of meeting him on my road.

Under the Empire I thought him merely a conscientious man of genius, who was persecuted because he refused to blow the trumpet of
despotism, and because he had given in his resignation as the Minister
of Valais upon the occasion of the death of the Duc d'Enghien.

Le Génie du Christianisme, L'Itinéraire de Jérusalem, and the poem of
the *Martyrs,* recently published, justify our admiration. I thought indeed that the enthusiasm of some ladies was a trifle exaggerated, but I
joined in it up to a certain point. I can remember a reading of the *Aben-
cérages,* given at the house of Mme. de Ségur. He read with the most
touching and emotional voice, with that faith which he possessed for
every production of his own. He threw himself into the sentiments of
his characters so far that his tears fell upon the paper. We shared this
keen impression, and I was completely spellbound. When the reading
was over, tea was brought in.

"M. de Chateaubriand, will you have some tea?"

"I will ask you for a cup."

Immediately an echo went throughout the salon.

"My dear, he would like some tea."

"He is going to have some tea."

"Give him some tea."

"He wants some tea."

And ten ladies started up to serve the idol with tea. It was the first time that I had been present at such a spectacle, which seemed to me so ridiculous that I resolved never to take part in it. Hence, though my relations with M. de Chateaubriand have been somewhat continuous, I have never been enrolled in the company of his *Madames*, as Mme. de Chateaubriand used to call them, and I have never reached the point of intimacy to which he only admitted real adorers.

When we left Beauregard in 1812 to set up house at Châtenay, M. and Mme. de Chateaubriand were living at the Vallée aux Loups, a ten-minute walk from my house. He had made a charming home and was extremely fond of it. We were friendly neighbours, and often found him writing on a corner of the drawing-room table with a worn-out pen which would hardly pass through the mouth of the wretched bottle which contained his ink. He would utter a cry of joy when he saw us pass his window, thrust his papers under the cushion of an old easy-chair which served him as a portfolio and a desk, and rush out to join us with the gaiety of a schoolboy let out from his class. At that time he was entirely agreeable. I cannot say as much of Mme. de Chateaubriand. She had plenty of talent, but used it to extract bitter and disagreeable elements from every object. She did her husband much harm by continually irritating him and making his home unbearable. Though he was always most considerate towards her, he could never secure domestic peace.

I have said that she had some talent, and the fact is indisputable. At the same time (and only the sight of her would persuade one of the fact), her middle-class pride was wounded by the literary reputation of M. de Chateaubriand, which she considered derogatory. Under the Restoration she most passionately desired titles and positions at court, to compensate for this vulgar success. She loudly advertised the fact that she had never read a single line of her husband's publications. At the same time, however, she continually told him that a country which had the glory of possessing him and was not governed by him was in a wretched state. She proved the fact by certain passages from the Apocalypse, of which she had made a profound study, and he pardoned her scorn of his merits by reason of her devotion to his claims. The amount of money swallowed up by this household, though their life was far from ceremonious, is another proof among thousands of the inevitable results of want of system. In any case, M. de Chateaubriand admitted himself that nothing seemed to him so insipid as to live upon a regular income, from whatever source derived. He wanted to realise his capital, squander it, feel the pinch of poverty, get into debt, be appointed an Ambassador, expend upon caprice the salary intended to defray his household expenses, resign his post, and become more embarrassed and more deeply in debt than ever; he wished to abandon a position where he had twenty-five horses in his stables, and have the pleasure of refusing an invitation to dinner under the pretext that he could not afford a cab; in short, he wished to experience every variety of sensation in order to avoid boredom, for that upon the whole was the great object and secret of his life.

Notwithstanding this chaotic existence, in which M. de Chateaubriand associated without the smallest scruple those who were devoted to him, he was an agreeable and companionable acquaintance. If he could refrain from revolutionising one's life, he was inclined to make existence very pleasant. From time to time he even showed a desire to make some sacrifice to those who loved him, but this was a custom too contrary to his nature to be persistent. Thus, although wearied by her presence, he permitted Mme. de Beaumont to follow him to Rome, where he abandoned her, and she died in almost complete isolation. So again, after having changed his mode of life, he entered society to attract Mme. de Noailles. He saw her go mad without a single sigh of grief. Thus, again, he barely consented to write a very cold newspaper article in honour of the memory of Mme. de Duras, who lived only for his sake for twelve years.

I might add many names to this list, as M. de Chateaubriand always had the greatest facility in attracting attention, without considering the trouble that he might cause. Of his many intimacies, the one which held the largest place in his heart was, I think, that with Mme. Charles de Noailles, who became the Duchesse de Mouchy. The story of this poor woman is in consonance with that morality which existed before the Revolution, and which we have been asked but recently to regret.

Mademoiselle de Laborde was as charming and accomplished a young lady as can be imagined. She married in 1790, thanks to the immense fortune to which she was heiress, Charles de Noailles, the eldest son of the Prince de Poix. Though he did not possess his wife's distinguished talents, he was by no means devoid of capacity, and was very handsome and entirely in fashion. The young couple made quite a sensation when presented at the Tuileries, in spite of the serious nature of events at that period.

Soon the storms of the Revolution separated them. M. de Noailles emigrated; his wife remained with her family, whose misfortunes she shared. She accompanied them to prison, where she was the guardian angel of her relatives, and among others the old wife of Marshal de Noailles, her husband's grandmother. She served his grandmother as a daughter or as a servant, until the day when the scaffold cut short these cares. She saw her own father perish and consoled her mother; in short, she attracted the admiration and veneration of all who were imprisoned with her. As soon as the prisons were opened, her first desire was to rejoin her young husband, for whom she felt the tenderest affection. To leave France was not an easy matter; however, by dint of courage and skill she succeeded in securing a landing upon the shores of England. Her daughter, whom she had entrusted to an American captain, had preceded her by some hours, and with this child in her arms she hastened to her husband's door.

Charles de Noailles was then attached by fashion to the train of Mrs. Fitzherbert. She was at least forty-five years of age, but the pleasure of being a rival of the Prince of Wales, who did not disguise his jealousy, made her seem charming in the eyes of M. de Noailles, and he was somewhat annoyed by the arrival of his pretty wife. Under pretext of economy, he hastened to take her to a little cottage in the north of England. She did not complain as long as he stayed with her. But business soon called him to London, where his visits became more frequent, until he set up house there.

He was extremely intimate with M. Duluc de Vintimille, a young man far less handsome but much more amiable than he. Noailles showed him the sad letters of his young wife, complaining of the trouble that they caused him. M. Duluc reproached him for abandoning her, and added that he deserved misfortune.

"You call that misfortune. The happiest day of my life will be that which relieves me of her lamentations."

M. Duluc eventually proposed to Charles de Noailles that he should try to alienate the affection of his wife. This friendly offer was eagerly accepted. The two friends went down together to the cottage. A few days afterwards Noailles went away, leaving M. Duluc to spend the long winter days with a woman twenty years of age, who was weary and depressed. She was as attractive as she was pretty, full of talent and wit. M. Duluc's head was already turned by her letters; he fell passionately in love with her and found no difficulty in playing the part which he had undertaken. To the husband he regularly reported his progress, and announced his success at the end of several months. The latter then announced that he proposed to visit the lonely couple. Mme. de Noailles was awakened from the pleasant dreams which she had cherished by the impending arrival of the husband she had injured, and gave way to unbounded despair. M. Duluc made vain attempts to soothe her, and at length decided to reveal the immoral compact by means of which he had succeeded, and showed her the correspondence to confirm his statements.

Mme. de Noailles was a pure and noble woman: she was revolted by such hateful treachery, and remained crushed by this horrible revelation. The next day she set off to Yarmouth with her child, announcing her intention of finding refuge with her mother. Her husband was delighted to be rid of her. M. Duluc hastened after her, caught her up before she had embarked, made his peace, accompanied her, and was pardoned. But for her the illusion of love was destroyed. M. Duluc was punished for his guilt by the passion and depth of his feeling for her, which afterwards wrecked his life.

Mme. de Noailles, her mind sullied and her affections blunted by the conduct of two men whom she had loved, reached Paris amid the saturnalia of the Directory,[4] in which she took but too energetic a share. She has herself summed up the consequences in these few words:

"I am very unhappy: as soon as I love one, another appears who pleases me more." Her attachment to M. de Chateaubriand was almost a rehabilitation. This intimacy was at its height when M. de Chateaubriand started for the Holy Land; the lovers arranged to meet at the Fountain of Lions in the Alhambra. Mme. de Noailles had every intention of keeping so romantic an appointment, and was at the spot on the day arranged. During the absence of M. de Chateaubriand she had permitted Colonel L. to distract her uneasiness with his assiduous attentions. While she was in Granada, awaiting the return of the pilgrim from Jerusalem, she learned of the Colonel's death. Thus, when M. de Chateaubriand arrived, full of excuses for his delay and panegyrics upon the punctuality of his beloved, he found a woman in deepest mourning, bewailing with extreme despair the death of a rival who had been successful in his absence. The whole of their tour in Spain was spent in this manner, M. de Chateaubriand combining the functions of consoler and adorer. He dates the cooling of his affection for Mme. de Noailles from this period, though their intimacy lasted for a considerable time.

The publication of the *Itinéraire* added new lustre to the popularity of M. de Chateaubriand and increased the desire of several people to see him. He made use of this fact to improve the position of Mme. de Noailles, arranging that his acquaintance should only be made through her, and putting a stop to his exclusiveness. This must be counted to

4. The Government of the Directory, thus named because the Constitution had set up an executive of five *Directeurs*, lasted four years, from November 1795 to November 1799. It was a period of great social relaxation after the tension of the Terror. The *coup d'état* of 18 Brumaire put an end to it and gave power to Bonaparte.

his credit, as he acted solely in the interest of Mme. de Noailles. People paid her attention in order to attract M. de Chateaubriand. As she was a charming woman, she pleased by her own merits as soon as she was known.

For a short time she formed part of a coterie composed of Mmes. de Duras, de Bérenger, de Lévis, and others. But she soon wearied of them and withdrew to her own room, where her first-rate talent was employed upon serious occupations. Thus she lived until the Restoration. She then plunged into the vortex of society and was seen dancing at a great ball, decked in rose-coloured finery. Her husband, who had never lost sight of her, arranged for a reconciliation. She assumed the title of Duchesse de Mouchy. She was offered rooms at the residence of the Noailles. There was talk of a possible brother for the sister who had been married for some years. Then everyone noticed the strange manners of Mme. de Mouchy. The Hundred Days[5] arrived; terror seized her and her strangeness of manner increased. For some months attempts were made to hide the fact, but at length it was necessary to place her under restraint. She has now been confined for twenty years, and has never recovered her reason. Such was the fate of a person endowed by nature with the highest gifts. I cannot but think that she deserved a better fate than the life which she led. Had it not been for that fatal journey from England, which brought her, wounded and disillusioned, to the disturbances in Paris under the Directory, she would probably have followed a better line of conduct. I have reason to believe that her husband regretted his behaviour more than once, together with the sacrifice which he had made to the false god of gallantry, which was paramount at the time when he entered society. He cannot have failed to recognise that he was primarily responsible for his wife's wrongdoing. M. de Chateaubriand had certainly intended to rehabilitate her in her own esteem and in the eyes of the world. But he was incapable of any sustained attention to the affairs of another person, and was too entirely absorbed by consideration for himself.

5. The period of time between Napoleon's escape from Elba and his second abdication.

It was at the time that Mme. de Noailles began her retirement that the society of the *Madames* was definitely formed. The chief members were the Duchesses de Duras, de Lévis, and Mme. de Bérenger; the other members are too unimportant to mention. These three ladies had each of them their special hour when M. de Chateaubriand was received, and they were at home to no one else; and goodness only knows what he had to suffer if he gave one of them some minutes that belonged to another. They were so proud of their success that their porters had orders to inform visitors that they were not at home because it was M. de Chateaubriand's hour, and it is said that the announcement was often prolonged beyond the due time, to make the greater impression. The scenes which these ladies made by their mutual reproaches became a source of general amusement. But every evening all recovered their good temper, and went off to pay the most assiduous attention to Mme. de Chateaubriand, whom they overwhelmed with care and kindness. One day, when she had caught a slight cold, she asserted that she had received five possets in one morning, accompanied by the most charming notes, which she displayed with amusing sarcasms upon these ladies. At bottom, however, she was by no means displeased by this homage from the great.

It is said that the success of Mme. de Lévis was tolerably complete; Mme. de Duras was consumed with jealousy, while Mme. de Bérenger resigned herself to other modes of displaying her power. The *Madames* of the second rank did not raise such high claims. Those who had been admitted to the friendship of Mme. de Lévis thought her both pleasant and pretty. To me, she seemed ugly and surly when seen at a distance which I never felt tempted to cross.

Mme. de Duras was a daughter of M. de Kersaint, of the Convention. She and her mother had spent the years of revolutionary uproar on their plantations at Martinique. When Mme. de Kersaint brought to London her stalwart daughter of twenty-two, who was by no means pretty, she found that her daughter's marriage with the Duc de Duras had been arranged almost beforehand. He was reduced to a state of poverty which made him dependent to an irksome degree upon the

Prince de Poix, his uncle. Though the fortune of Mlle. de Kersaint was not very considerable, it was quite satisfactory for M. de Duras. She had hardly disembarked when he married her, and for a long time she adored him.

M. de Duras was First Gentleman of the King's Chamber; these officials came on duty for successive years, and when the emigration began, those entitled to serve did not fail to appear. M. de Duras had already performed his year of service upon one occasion, in waiting upon Louis XVIII,* and his turn came round once more a short time after his marriage. He left London with his wife to go to Mitau. When he reached Hamburg he received an official communication, stating that the King would consent to receive M. de Duras in view of his position, notwithstanding his marriage, but that the daughter of a Conventionist could not expect to be received by the Duchesse d'Angoulême.* Mme. de Duras was formally excluded from Mitau.

M. de Duras was a man of honour, notwithstanding certain ridiculous points: he did not hesitate to take his wife back to London and to stay there with her. Mme. de Duras felt extremely hurt, and I have always imagined that this insult was the origin of that independent feeling which eventually proved an honour to her character. After a stay of some years in England, the Duras household returned to France with two little girls, the only children that they had.

Mme. de Duras soon perceived her superiority over her husband, and made him realise the fact with a frankness which led to discord. At the time of her infatuation for M. de Chateaubriand, which was as innocent as it was extravagant, she was looking for some distraction from her domestic annoyances. In her youth Mme. de Duras had no very attractive qualities, but she had a lively spirit, a lofty heart, and true distinction of character. The higher the scene in which she was called to play a part, the more obvious her true worth became; this fact I had long before discovered.

Among the women who adored M. de Chateaubriand was Mme. Octave de Ségur, though she could not claim his affection. Her story is so romantic that I propose to relate it, though I may be anticipating in some degree. Mlle. d'Aguesseau married for love her first cousin Octave de Ségur. Under the Directory the young couple enjoyed complete happiness. They lived with their parents, and provided for their personal expenses by translating English novels. They had three sons, whose education was becoming a concern, when Octave was ap-pointed a subprefect by the First Consul. His wife followed him to Soissons. The Comte de Ségur, their father, joined the Government, which had become imperial, and was appointed Grand Master of the Ceremonies, while Mme. Octave was made lady-in-waiting to the Empress Joséphine. Domestic happiness was forthwith disturbed; the long absence necessitated by the duties of Mme. de Ségur developed a jealousy in Octave, which his passionate heart cherished unknown to himself. Etienne de Choiseul became the object of his anxieties, it is said, without the smallest reason. He was like Orosmane, "cruelly wounded, but too proud to complain."

Mme. Octave accompanied the Empress to Plombières, and her husband obtained leave to spend some days with her. He arrived upon a magnificent moonlit evening. Mme. Octave was not expecting him. She had gone out, and her husband followed her; she was walking with Etienne de Choiseul. Octave did not reveal himself, left Plom-bières without a word to anyone, and did not return to Soissons. A search was made in every direction in vain; nothing could be heard of him. At the end of a year Mme. Octave received by post a note which bore the Boulogne postmark and these words: "I am, dear Féli-cité, about to brave an element less agitated than this heart, which will never beat except for you." This note was closed by a seal which she had given him, and which bore the words: "Friendship, esteem, and eternal love."

Philippe de Ségur started immediately for Boulogne, but could find no trace of his brother. He was, however, on board one of the pinnaces where Philippe looked for him, but he played his part of soldier so per-fectly that none of his comrades suspected his disguise. He followed Napoleon's *Grande Armée* to Germany. Several years elapsed, and a sec-ond note was handed to Mme. de Ségur which merely bore the words engraved on the seal, in the handwriting of Octave. This was the only sign of his existence, and after a period of despair Mme. Octave eventually consoled herself.

Her three sons were her first interest, and she watched over them with most thoughtful care. Octave had been made a prisoner, and had been taken to a little town in the depths of Hungary; it was not until long afterwards that he learnt of the death of Etienne de Choiseul, who was killed at the battle of Wagram. He then desired to see his country once more. The steps which he took to obtain his liberty were unsuccessful and were outstripped by events. Peace at length liberated him, and he returned to France in 1814.

His wife was reduced to despair by his return. Whether it was that Octave had been warned of the fact upon his arrival, or could not trust himself, he wished to remain upon a footing of simple friendship with his wife, reserving his first affection for his sons. He treated her with a grave politeness which never changed. Mme. Octave, piqued by this attitude, felt reviving within her that passion which her husband experienced in secret, and employed all her powers to attract him.

"Take care, Félicité!" he would say to her sometimes; "it is with my life that you are playing."

At length he gave way and indulged in those feelings which had always reigned exclusively in his heart. Some months of happiness recompensed him for long years of suffering. Mme. Octave followed her husband and her eldest son to the garrison, where both were serving in the same regiment. Octave secured an exchange, and wished his wife to leave the garrison. Under the pretext that her son was remaining, she wished to spend the winter there; Octave objected, and an angry scene took place. For the first and last time he reproached her with arguments based upon the trouble which she had taken to bring him back to her side.

He went back to Paris alone, hired a lodging of the kind which would best suit him, and spent his time arranging it in full conformity with his taste. He asked her several times to join him, but she persistently refused. At length he wrote that if she were not in Paris before six o'clock upon a certain day, she would repent it all her life. She did not come, and at nine o'clock Octave jumped into the Seine. He was discovered with his hands firmly clasped. He was an excellent swimmer, but having resolved to perish, his will had overpowered the instincts of self-preservation.

Mme. Octave was overwhelmed with grief and remorse, and retired to a convent. I have seen her in her cell, a very touching spectacle. The arguments of her sons, who were devoted to her, notwithstanding their deep affection for their father, brought her back to the world, where she leads a somewhat retired life—a life, however, less striking to the imagination than that of her convent cell.

At an age when disinterested affection was so rare, the passion of Octave is certainly remarkable. He was a handsome man, and very companionable when he could overcome the timidity and embarrassment which the strange character of his first adventure always caused him. Though his wife was not entirely pretty, she was extremely attractive and was able to win affection. Notwithstanding the cruel events of her sad life, she preserved devoted friends among women whose conduct was above reproach.

I have no more to say of the disastrous retreat from Moscow than of the glorious campaigns which preceded it. Upon all of these events my information is only general. I am not writing history, but merely putting down my knowledge of certain details. When public affairs come under my special cognisance, I shall treat them with the same exactitude that I have used in dealing with social anecdotes.

The fall of the Empire was approaching, and we were foolish enough not to be afraid: the truth is that the strong and clever hand of the great man had, so to speak, stifled anarchical passion. Who, in any case, could have foreseen the calamities which were to accompany the fall of this Colossus? Every man of common sense must have trembled, but we rejoiced with the carelessness of partisans. At the same time, it is only right that excuses should be made for us. The yoke of Bonaparte was becoming intolerable, and his head had been finally turned by his alliance with the House of Austria. He listened only to flatterers, and would not bear any contradiction. He had reached the point when he could no longer endure the truth, not even the truth of facts and figures.

The Government officials were completely disorganised. I sometimes went to the house of Mme. Bertrand; her husband was Grand Marshal of the Palace. One morning, I saw an officer coming from the Emperor's army, then another sent by Marshal Soult, then an envoy from Marshal Suchet, all bringing news of the most disastrous events. Poor Fanny was on thorns. At length, by way of culmination, an Illyrian official appeared. He proceeded to tell us how he had been tracked throughout Italy, and with what difficulty he had reached the French frontier. She could no longer hold out, and said to them, with extreme vivacity:

"Gentlemen, you are all wrong. Last night excellent news came from every quarter, and the Emperor is entirely pleased with all that is going on."

Each man looked at his fellow in astonishment, and it was clear to me that this remark was intended for myself. I smiled, and left the field entirely free for their lamentations, which were probably deep and loud as soon as they were alone.

If their side was under illusions, ours was no less absurd. We imagined that the foreign powers were working in the interests of our passions, and anyone who might have attempted to enlighten us in this respect would certainly have been regarded as a traitor. We had concluded that the Prince of Sweden, Bernadotte,* was the most active agent in forwarding the Bourbon restoration. We had assumed that he was in Brussels, surrounded by French princes, and we would not abandon the idea.

One evening M. de Saint-Chamans came to tell us that Colonel de Saint-Chamans, his brother, had just arrived from Brussels, and assured him that neither Bernadotte, nor our princes, nor a single foreign soldier was in Belgium, and that the Swedes were somewhere or other behind the Rhine. Not only did we refuse to believe him, not only did we suspect the veracity of the Colonel, but we were so angry with M. de Saint-Chamans that we almost looked upon him as a traitor. He was treated with marked coldness as a suspicious character.

Such is the honesty and justice of parties. There is no doubting our good faith, and when I remember that I shared these unreasonable impressions, I am entirely indulgent towards the illusions and the unreason of party members. I am only astonished that the knowledge of these faults in themselves or in others does not induce them to amend their ways, and I can hardly understand intolerance in the case of those who have passed through a series of revolutions as we had done. It must, however, be recognised by way of excuse for our foolishness that we were obliged to guess the truth from the official accounts, which almost always disguised it.

The Emperor had grown to think that the country had no right to inquire into the affairs of the Empire; that these were his personal business, and that he owed no account to anyone. The battle of Trafalgar, for instance, was never officially reported in France, so no newspaper mentioned it, and we only learnt of it by secret intelligence. When such pieces of news are passed over, malcontents have every right to invent fables like that of the Swedish and Bourbon army which we had imagined as ready in Belgium.

Events were proceeding, and the enemy was afraid to march on Paris; it was frightened by the very thought. We, who should have feared this intention, welcomed it with our prayers. The disorganisation of the Government became obvious. Unfortunate conscripts filled the streets, and no preparation had been made for their reception. They were perishing with hunger on the sidewalk, and we used to take them into our houses and give them rest and food. Before disorganisation made arrangements impossible, they were cared for, clothed, and sent off to the army within twenty-four hours. The poor boys reached the army only to perish, having no powers of self-defence.

I have heard Marshal Marmont* relate that at the battle of Montmirail, in the hottest of the fire, he saw a conscript standing calmly at ease.

"What are you doing there? Why are you not firing?"

"I would fire as well as anybody," replied the young man, "if I knew how to load my gun."

The Marshal had tears in his eyes as he repeated these words of the brave young man who thus remained exposed to bullets which he could not return.

As the tide of war approached, it became more difficult to conceal the truth concerning the futility of the enormous efforts made by Napoleon and his admirable army; the result was inevitable. I must ask pardon of that generation that has since grown up in admiration of the Emperor's liberal principles; but at that moment friends and enemies alike were suffocating beneath his iron hand and felt a desire to rise against him with equal force. To speak frankly, he was detested; everyone regarded him as the obstacle to peace, and peace was the first necessity for everyone.

"*Abbiamo la pancia piena di libertà*," a postillion said to me one day at Verona, refusing a crown struck with the effigy of liberty. France in 1814 would gladly have said in its turn, *Abbiamo la pancia piena di gloria*, and of glory she wished no more. The allies were not mistaken upon this point, and were quite able to regard this weariness as the mainspring of their success, but they feared that it was not yet sufficiently complete for their own security. In order to revive the public spirits, a courier was sent with orders to hand over, in the middle of a parade at which the Empress was present, the flags and swords of the Russian Generals who had been made prisoners at the battle of Montmirail. The time for these pretences had gone by, and the courier was not sufficiently dust-stained to reassure the Parisians.

On Sunday, March 25, we saw after the parade a magnificent regiment of cuirassiers starting off; they had arrived from the Spanish army and were about to join the Emperor's army, for which purpose they were proceeding along the boulevard at about three o'clock. I have seen few troops by whose appearance I have been more greatly impressed. On the morning of the next day scattered members of them appeared at the barriers of Paris making their way to the hospitals; they and their horses were more or less wounded, and their long white cloaks were stained and covered with blood. It was evident that fighting was proceeding quite close to us. I met several of them when I went for a walk in the Jardin des Plantes, and the contrast with their appearance the evening before went to my heart. After two hours, my mother and I again passed along the boulevards. Even in this short time their aspect had been entirely changed; they were now thronged with the population of the outskirts of Paris, walking onwards, mixed with cows, sheep, and their poor little possessions. The people wept and lamented, relating their losses and their terrors, and naturally venting their anger upon anyone who seemed more fortunate. It was impossible to proceed except at a walk; our carriage came in for its share of abuse, though that was not necessary to make me understand the ugliness of war when seen at close quarters.

We reached home without difficulty, but we were somewhat frightened and deeply moved. The distant boom of cannon was soon heard, and we learnt that in the ministerial offices and in the households of the Princes of the imperial family preparations were made for departure. At nightfall the courts of the Tuileries were filled with wagons, and it was said that the Empress was leaving the city, though no one would believe it. We spent the whole of that Monday in the greatest anxiety and in the midst of the most contradictory rumours; everyone had a certain piece of news, which entirely overthrew a no less certain piece of information brought by someone else. The next day, at five o'clock in the morning, everybody was instantly and loudly informed by musketry fire and a cannonade that Paris was being vigorously attacked on three sides. At the same time we learnt that the Empress, the court, and the Imperial Government had departed.

We were living in a house in the street Neuve des Mathurins. Our highest windows gave us a full view of Montmartre, and towards the end of the morning we watched the capture of this position. Shells passed over our heads. Some fell upon the boulevards and put to flight the fine ladies in feathers and furbelows who were walking about among the wounded brought back from the barriers and the reinforcements of arms, men, and supplies, which were being sent thither. Many people left Paris. I had no wish to go away, and as my father felt that the roads in such confusion would be more dangerous than the town, he authorised us to stay.

Eugène d'Argout, my cousin, who was wounded at the battle of Leipzig, and had not been able to take part in the French campaign, undertook to provide for our safety. He began by getting in provisions and buying supplies of flour, rice, several hams, and in fact everything that was necessary for spending a few days in confinement. He then put out all the fires, closed all the shutters, and made the house look as deserted as possible. He also dragged a large hay-cart which had come in from the country that morning under the archway, intending to place it against the large door if the town was captured. He then told everybody that anyone who was outside would not come in until peace was restored.

Eugène had taken part in all the wars of the last ten years, and had seen the capture of many towns. He said that the smallest obstacles were enough to stop a soldier, always in a hurry, fearing that he might be forbidden to plunder by his officers.

People came from time to time to tell what news could be learnt in the suburbs. When the cannonade was silent on one side it began upon another. Sometimes the noise approached and sometimes became distant, as positions were captured or fresh attacks were made. What we chiefly feared was the arrival of the Emperor, as we did not know where he was.

Alexandre de La Touche, the son of Mme. Dillon, was living in the Tuileries with his sister, Mme. Bertrand. He came in the morning to beg me to leave Paris, and I refused absolutely. Soon afterwards we learnt that hostilities had been suspended and negotiations for a capitulation begun. He came back, and positively went down upon his knees before my mother and myself to induce us to depart, beseeching us to let him put in our horses. We told him that it was hardly the right time for departing, as the danger had passed. "It has not, it has not! If I could only tell you what I know! But I have given my word. Start, I beg of you, start!"

We refused, and he went away, weeping, to rejoin his mother and sister, who were waiting for him with the carriage. This persistence on the part of M. de La Touche returned to my mind when I was told some days later that the Emperor had given orders to blow up the powder magazines. He certainly believed that he was in possession of a secret which would be revealed with disastrous effect.

I shall never forget the night which followed this exciting day. The weather was magnificent, the moonlight splendid, the town entirely calm, and my mother and I stood at the window. Our attention was attracted by the noise of a very small dog gnawing a bone at some distance. From time to time the silence was broken only by the challenges of the sentinels of the allied army, who answered one another as they went their rounds upon the heights which overlooked us. It was these foreign accents which first made me feel that my heart was French. They impressed me very painfully. But we were too afraid of the Emperor's return for this impression to last.

The square and streets were full of the French army, bivouacking on the pavement in sadness and silence. Its attitude was most admirable; it neither exacted, demanded, nor even expected anything. It seemed as if these poor soldiers felt that they had no claim upon the inhabitants whom they had not been able to defend. However, eight thousand men under the command of the Duc de Raguse* had been engaged for ten hours against forty-five thousand foreigners, and had left them thirteen thousand dead to collect. Thus the allies could not believe how few troops defended Paris in the following days. History will do justice to the foolish malignity which has accused Marshal Marmont of betraying the town, and will restore the brilliant action of Belleville to the place which it should occupy in our military annals.

I am about to begin my story of the Restoration. As my position brought me into the intimacy of most influential people, I have seen events close at hand from this time. I cannot say if I shall be able to re-late them with impartiality; this is a quality which everybody boasts of, and which no one really possesses. People are more or less influ-enced, entirely unconsciously, by position and environment. At any rate, I shall speak independently, and will tell the truth as I believe it. More than this I cannot promise.

CHAPTER FOUR

First Restoration

1814

*My opinions in 1814 ~ Entrance of the Allies in Paris ~
Performance at the Opera ~ Emperor Alexander ~ Entry of
Monsieur ~ The King starts from England ~ Meeting of the
sovereigns in Compiègne ~ Declaration of Saint-Ouen ~ Court
dress and etiquette during the Restoration ~ My father refuses the
Vienna Embassy ~ He accepts the ambassadorship to Turin ~
The Duc d'Orléans ~ Mme. de Talleyrand*

My personal opinions in 1814 are doubtless of little interest to anyone but myself. It is, however, a task which amuses me, thus to take stock of myself at different periods of my life, and to observe the variations which have marked them.

My Anglomania had for the most part disappeared, and I had become once more entirely French, socially, if not politically. As I have already said, the challenge of the enemy sentinels affected me more than the noise of their cannons. I had experienced a sensation of patriotism, fleeting as it was. By position, by tradition, by recollections, by environment, and by conviction I was a Royalist and a Legitimist.[1] But I was more an anti-Bonapartist than a Bourbon partisan; I detested the tyranny of the Emperor when I saw it in operation. I had no great opinion of those of our Princes whom I had seen face to face. I was assured that Louis XVIII held different principles. The extreme animosity which existed between his little court and that of the Comte d'Artois gave reason to hope for the truth of this statement.

I had left England before the vicissitudes of exile had brought the King there, and I lent a ready ear to my mother's praises of him, which

1. The Legitimists was the name given after the Revolution of 1830 to the supporters of Charles X and his descendants who refused to recognize Louis-Philippe.

were given in spite of the fact that, in her eyes, he laboured under the disadvantage of having been part of the Assembly of 1789. It was upon this same disadvantage that my hopes were founded, for upon careful consideration I found that I was invariably as liberal as my aristocratic prejudices would allow, prejudices which I fear will accompany me to the grave.

The organisation of political life in England has always seemed to me the most perfect in the world. On one hand there is the complete and real equality before the law, which guarantees individual independence and therefore inspires the individual with self-respect; on the other hand are the great social distinctions, which create defenders of public liberties, making these patricians the natural leaders of the people, who return in homage what they receive by way of protection. This is what I have wished for my own country, for I can only conceive of liberty, apart from licence, as based upon a strong aristocracy. This is a fact which nobody in France understood—neither the lower classes, nor the middle classes, nor the nobility, nor the King himself. Equality among us is a disease engendered by vanity. Under pretext of this equality, everyone claims the right to superiority and domination, and fails to recognise that if anyone is to be inferior, the existence of superiors must be readily admitted.

On Wednesday, March 31, 1814, my mother and I were at a window on the first floor when we saw in the distance a Russian officer followed by several Cossacks. When he had nearly reached our house he asked where Mme. de Boigne lived; at the same moment he raised his head, and I recognised Prince Nikita Wolkonski, an old acquaintance. He saw me at the same moment, dismounted, and came into the house; his escort took up a position in the courtyard, and two Cossacks stood as sentinels before the archway door, which remained open. I have always considered that the terror of the people inspired by the Imperial Government was shown by the fact that their fears overcame the Parisian love of sightseeing. Notwithstanding the curiosity which these Cossacks must have aroused, the first that appeared in Paris, during the hour that Prince Wolkonski visited us there was no crowd before the door, and the passers-by did not even stop for a moment. Had they been more religious, they would readily have crossed themselves to avert the danger of merely beholding a spectacle which seemed to them to be compromising.

Prince Wolkonski, as may be believed, was welcomed effusively. He told me at once that Count Nesselrode, the Russian Minister of Foreign Affairs, had ordered him to come to us, to assure us of entire safety and protection, and then to ask my father what the reasonable and possible hopes of our party were, as the Emperor Alexander* was arriving before any decision had been taken. We sent to fetch my father from the house of the Duc de Laval.

Prince Wolkonski afterwards told me that, having passed through the streets to the barrier, he had met on the way nothing but demonstrations of grief and anxiety, and not a sign of joy and hope. I think that he gave a full report, for the Emperor Alexander entered Paris no less undecided than he had been in the morning.

My mother and I went to take our places in the rooms of Mme. Récamier. She was then at Naples, but M. Récamier retained her house in the Rue Basse du Rempart. We found ourselves in a first-floor apartment, on a level with the boulevard, in the narrowest part of the street. My father, on thus installing us, made us promise to give no signs which might be interpreted as an expression of opinion, and to receive no visitors who might arouse attention. He thought that such consideration was owed to the hospitality and the very moderate sentiments of M. Récamier.

We soon saw on the pavement of the boulevard a number of young men walking past, wearing the white cockade, waving their handkerchiefs, and shouting "Vive le Roi!" but there were very few of them. I recognised my brother among them. My mother and I exchanged mournful and anxious glances; we still hoped that the band would increase. They dared not advance beyond the Rue Napoleon, which is now the Rue de La Paix; thence proceeding to the Madeleine, they retraced their steps. We saw the band pass five times, but were unable to cheat ourselves with the hope that it had grown larger. Our anxiety became greater and greater.

It was certain that if this demonstration remained ineffectual, all who had joined in it would be lost, and this idea was fundamentally correct. It was a feeling seen clearly in the eyes of all who observed these poor young men with their white cockades going by. They drew forth neither anger nor hatred, and much less enthusiasm. They were looked at with the kind of pity inspired by madmen and devoted victims. Several passers-by displayed their astonishment, but no one opposed their action or molested them in any way.

Eventually at twelve o'clock the allied army began to march past our window. The apprehensions which I had experienced throughout the morning were too real for my patriotism to become prominent, and I admit that I felt nothing but relief. As the head of the column approached, some white cockades were bashfully brought out of pockets and displayed on the sidewalks. But they were by no means numerous, though the white handkerchief which the foreigners all wore upon their arms as a sign of alliance had been immediately interpreted by the population as a demonstration in favour of the Bourbons. Our faithful escort of young men surrounded the sovereigns,[2] shouting at the top of their voices and making themselves appear as numerous as possible by dint of zeal and activity. The women did not spare themselves; white handkerchiefs were waved, and cheers were given from windows as well. Just as the sovereigns had found Paris gloomy, silent, and almost deserted until they reached the head of the Place Vendôme, so they found it animated and excited from that point to the Champs Elysées.

Must I admit that the antinational faction had concentrated in this spot to welcome the foreigners, and that this faction was chiefly composed of the nobility? Was it right or was it wrong? I cannot now decide, but at that moment our conduct seemed to me sublime. For the

2. Mme. de Boigne means the Emperor of Russia and the King of Prussia.

most part it was entirely disinterested, if party spirit can ever be considered so, and it was ennobled in every case by personal danger.

I have forgotten to say that Count Nesselrode had informed me through Prince Nikita that he was going to ask me to give him dinner that day. I had asked the Prince to come also. We were all assembled when Prince Wolkonski and one of his comrades, Michel Orloff, arrived, bringing a note from Count Nesselrode. He sent his excuses for not coming, and with them a paper which he said would easily secure his pardon until he could retrieve it in person that evening. It was the declaration which was to be posted, and which announced the intention of the Allies not to deal with the Emperor or with any member of his family. It was the result of a conference held at the house of M. de Talleyrand* upon Emperor Alexander's arrival. Emperor Alexander had begun the discussion with these words:

"Well, here we are at last in the famous Paris. It is you who brought us, M. de Talleyrand. Now, there are three things that we can do: we can deal with the Emperor Napoleon, we can establish a regency, or recall the Bourbons."

"The Emperor is wrong," replied M. de Talleyrand. "There are not three things we can do; there is only one, and that is the last that he has mentioned. All-powerful as he is, he is not powerful enough to choose. If he were to hesitate, France, which expects this reward for the grief and humiliation which consumes it at this moment, will rise in a body against the invasion. And your Imperial Majesty knows full well that the finest armies melt away before the anger of a nation."

"Very well," replied the Emperor, "Now, what is to be done to attain your object? Remember that I do not wish to impose commands, but merely to yield to the wishes expressed by the country."

"No doubt, Sire; we have but to give the country a chance of making its wishes heard."

This dialogue was reported to me the very next day by one who was present at the council.

In the evening Count Nesselrode came, and the warmth of his reception I can leave to be imagined. We had so often exposed anti-

Bonapartist opinions—I will not say with him,[3] for he was too great a diplomat, but in his presence—that he had no need to inquire into our feelings at that moment. He talked a long time with my father concerning affairs and people. Among other things, he asked him if he thought it advisable to leave M. Pasquier* in charge of the police. My father answered that the office could not be in cleverer or more honest hands, and that if he consented to retain his post, his help might be regarded as a piece of good fortune and that his word could be trusted entirely.

I cannot remember if it was this evening or the next day that a Royalist meeting took place at the house of M. de Mortefontaine. The meeting sent a deputation to the Emperor Alexander expressing its wishes. I can only remember my father came back wearied, disgusted, and despairing: all the folly of the *émigré* party and the most foolish opposition had appeared in triumph. The discussion turned only upon victory, persecution, and vengeance on fellow-countrymen, at a moment when the country was at the feet of a foreign monarch.

At the beginning of the spring of 1814 the weather was magnificent, and all Paris was out-of-doors. No event in this town, no battle, foreign occupation, revolt or disturbance of any kind, could influence or restrain women's fashions. On Tuesday they walked in all their finery upon the boulevards amidst the wounded, braving the shells. On Wednesday they came to see the allied army march past. On Thursday they wore their elegant costumes to visit the bivouac of the Cossacks in the Champs Elysées.

The spectacle of these inhabitants of the Don peacefully pursuing their habits and customs in the middle of Paris was indeed a strange sight. They had no tents or shelter of any kind; three or four horses were tied up to each tree, and the riders, sitting near them on the ground, talked together in quiet and harmonious accents. Most of them were sewing, mending their clothes, cutting out and preparing

3. Count Nesselrode had been posted in Paris during the Empire.

new garments, repairing their shoes or the harness of their horses, or altering for their own use their share in the pillage of the preceding days. These, however, were the regular Cossacks of the Guard, and as they rarely went on scouting duty, their plundering was less successful than that of their brethren, the irregular Cossacks.

Their uniforms were very handsome. Wide blue trousers, a long tunic also blue, standing out across the chest and fastened tightly round the waist by a large belt of black varnished leather, with buckles and harness of shining copper, to which their weapons were slung. This half-Oriental costume and their strange horsemanship—since the elevation of their saddles puts them in a standing position and prevents any bending of the knee—made them an object of great curiosity to the Parisians. They readily allowed people to approach them, especially women and children, holding the latter upon their shoulders.

I have seen women take their work in their hands to examine more closely their mode of sewing. From time to time they amused themselves by uttering a kind of growl, which made the curious women recoil in fright. They uttered cries of joy and burst into roars of laughter, shared by those whom they had alarmed. They did not allow men to approach as closely, but sent them away with just a calm, quiet gesture and a word which probably approximates the "stand back" of our sentinels. Obviously, no one ventured to disregard this order. However, if a man came up with women and children they paid no attention to him.

They had every reason for remaining by their horses, for never under any pretext would they take a step. When they were not sitting on the ground they were on horseback. To go round the bivouac from group to group, they would mount their horses. They were also to be seen holding their lances in one hand and a jug, or plate, or even a glass in the other as they went about the business of their little households. I say a glass, because I have seen one of them quietly get up, mount his horse, take his lance, bend to the ground to take up a gourd, then ride thirty paces away to get water from a tub which was surrounded by a guard, drink the water, return to his position with his empty bottle, get off his horse, replace his lance in the general bundle, and resume his work.

These nomadic customs seemed to us so strange that they excited our curiosity, which we satisfied the more readily as we were persuaded that our affairs were proceeding excellently. Partisan success disguised the bitterness of a foreign bivouac in the Champs Elysées. I will do my father the justice to say that he did not share this impression, and that I could never induce him to go and see this spectacle, which he always insisted was more sad than curious.

The foreigners were very much more uneasy and very much more astonished by their stay in Paris than we were. They were neither blinded by party spirit nor disillusioned with regard to the prestige which the name of the Emperor Napoleon inspired. The marvels of the French campaign prevented them from believing in such a complete and real destruction of the army, and they expected to see it rise up from underground at any moment. This sentiment was evident from all that they said, and they had the good sense not to be greatly reassured by us, for they could judge of our futility on many points.

At all events, we were right when we assured them that the country was so disgusted, so wearied, so eager for tranquillity, and so surfeited with glory, that it had completely seceded from the Emperor, and asked for nothing but security. There had never been a time when the patriotic sentiment had less force in France; the Emperor had perhaps weakened it by his immense conquests, whilst thinking to increase it. We scarcely recognised a compatriot in a Frenchman of Rome or of Hamburg. Perhaps, too, and to this idea I am more inclined, the system of deception which he had adopted had disgusted the greater part of the country. The bulletins never spoke of anything but our triumphs; the French army was always victorious, the enemy's army was always beaten, yet successive defeats had brought it from the banks of the Moskowa to those of the Seine.

No one believed the official news. People exhausted themselves trying to discover the key to the enigma, and the masses ceased to take much interest in events on which they could only speculate. Affairs were no longer public, with no exact information to be obtained, and inquiries forbidden. The Emperor had worked so hard to establish the fact that it was his business and not ours, and finally we took him at his word. And whatever may have been thought and said in later years, it is certain that in 1814 everyone, including his army and the public functionaries, was so tired that their only desire was to be relieved of duties no longer dictated by a wise and reasonable will. Absolute power had intoxicated and blinded him; it is perhaps not given to a man to withstand the weight of such power.

As nations, even more than individuals, are ungrateful, France forgot the immense benefits that she owed to Napoleon, and overwhelmed him with her reproaches. Posterity in its turn will forget the aberrations and weaknesses of his sublime genius. It will see the poetic side of his stay at Fontainebleau;[4] it will avoid all mention of the obstinate haggling by which he strove, after his heroic farewells to the eagles of his old battalions, to get a little more furniture to take with him into exile and in this posterity will be right. When a figure like Bonaparte appears amid the ages, we ought not to remember the few shadows which might darken some of its splendour. But we must explain how it was that contemporaries, who had all been dazzled by him, found his splendour no longer a source of life, but rather of pain and grief.

Early on Friday Count Nesselrode sent us word that the sovereigns were going to the Opera. Our domestics went off at once on a campaign to get us boxes, so that we might be there in full force. The florists were in demand, and requested to supply us with lilies, which we wore in our hair, in bouquets, and in garlands. The men wore the white cockade in their hats. So far all was as it should be, but as a Frenchwoman I blush to tell of our behaviour at this performance.

In the first place, we began by applauding the Emperor Alexander and the King of Prussia with enthusiasm. Next, the doors of our boxes

4. Napoleon signed his abdication at the château of Fontainebleau.

were left open, and the greater the throng of foreign officers who entered, the more delighted we were. There was not a single Russian or Prussian subaltern who had not the right and also some desire to join the crowd. Two or three foreign Generals who were in my box considered this familiarity less charming than I did and turned them out, to my great disappointment. I was somewhat consoled, however, by the presence of the Generals, and by the visit of the Russian Ministers and of Prince Augustus of Prussia, whom I had known for a long time.

Just before the arrival of the sovereigns in the imperial box, some young Frenchmen of our party went in and covered the eagle which surmounted the draperies of this box with a white handkerchief. At the end of the performance these same young men shattered the eagle with hammers, amidst our enthusiastic applause. I took part in all this with the rest of my party. I cannot say that it was in accordance with my conscience, for I felt some misgivings which I could not entirely define. These demonstrations, no doubt, had an implied meaning— the fall of Bonaparte and the presumed return of our Princes. It was that which we were really inaugurating, but our purpose was insufficiently plain.

Political parties are too easily persuaded of their universality. Only a short time previously we might have been convinced that we were merely a very trifling fraction of the nation, and yet we now gaily proceeded to affront the honourable sentiments of the country while cruelly wounding the feelings of the army. We seemed to be offering up the same eagle which the army had borne victoriously in all the capitals of Europe as a holocaust to the inhabitants of those same capitals, who perhaps scarcely respected us for this display of antinational feeling.

Undoubtedly this was not our object, any more than it was our idea, but it certainly did not require a great amount of malevolence to explain it in this way. The fallen party may honestly have believed this, and it is not surprising that such conduct should engender those long hatreds which die out with such difficulty. It is with great regret that I admit it, but the Royalist party is that which least loves its country for the country's sake; the quarrel which sprang up between the various classes has made the nobility hostile to the land where its privileges are not recognised. And I fear that the nobility is therefore more in sympathy with high-born foreigners than with the French bourgeoisie. Common interests attacked have established affinities between classes and broken up nationalities.

On this Friday, the day of the Opera, we were at dinner, when the door of the dining-room opened noisily and a Russian General suddenly burst in. He waltzed round the table, singing, "Oh, my friends, my dear, dear friends!" Our first idea was that he was mad, and then my brother exclaimed, "Why, it's Pozzo!"

And indeed it was he. Communication was so difficult under the Imperial Government that, in spite of the intimacy between us, we did not even know that he was in the Russian service. He had not known where to find us until a few minutes before his arrival in such delight. He went with us to the Opera, and from then on hardly a day went by without my seeing him at least once. It was partly through him that I was initiated into current events. Not that I interfered, but he found me dependable, always interested and discreet, and he liked to *sfogarsi*,[5] as he used to say with me. I was all the more ready for this, as I have always liked taking part in politics as an amateur.

In France the name of Napoleon was powerless and aroused no sympathy. It was in vain that Napoleon had called the Normans and the Bretons to the help of the Burgundians and the inhabitants of Champagne, thus reviving the old names of the provinces. These phantasmagorias, in which he had been as lucky as he was skillful, had now lost their prestige, along with that of victory. The Breton felt himself no more electrified than the inhabitant of Finistère. Either the Allies were ignorant of this, or they feared a reawakening, but it is certain that it was not without continual apprehension, and calling in reinforcements, that the foreigners remained in the capital of France.

The news that negotiations had been opened between Prince

5. To unburden himself.

Schwarzenberg and Marshal Marmont postponed the departure of the Emperor of Russia. It cannot be denied that the wise, moderate, and generous behaviour of this sovereign justified our enthusiasm for him. He was then thirty-seven years of age, but looked much younger. A handsome face and a still better figure, an expression that was both gentle and imposing, predisposed everyone in his favour. The confidence which he had in the Parisians, going about as he did without any escort and almost alone, won all hearts.

He was simply adored by his subjects. I remember, a few weeks later, arriving one night at the theatre just as he was entering his box. The door of it was guarded by two great giants of his army, who observed so strictly military an attitude that they did not dare move to wipe their faces, which were bathed in tears. I asked a Russian officer what had happened for them to be in such a state.

"Oh," he answered carelessly, "the Emperor has just passed by, and probably they have managed to touch him."

Such a piece of good fortune was so highly valued that they could only express their happiness by tears. I had often seen the Emperor, I had even had the honour of dancing the polonaise with him, without weeping for joy like his guards. But I was sufficiently struck by his superiority to regret keenly that our Princes resembled him so little. It was not until some years later that mysticism developed in him a tendency towards suspicion, which eventually became a madness. All contemporary memoirs see two totally different men in the Emperor, according to the epoch of which they speak, and the year 1814 was the zenith of his glory.

M. de Chateaubriand's pamphlet, *Bonaparte and the Bourbons*, printed at a rate not nearly quick enough for us in our impatience, made its appearance. I remember reading it in a perfect transport of admiration and with torrents of tears, and was much ashamed of my emotion when it came into my hands again some few years later.

Foreigners, less blinded than we were, realised all that the pamphlet meant, and the Emperor Alexander took offence at it. He had not forgotten that he had lived in deference of the man so violently attacked. M. de Chateaubriand already fancied himself a statesman, but no one else had thought of such a thing. Yet M. de Chateaubriand went to a great deal of trouble in order to obtain a private audience with Alexander.

I was deputed to speak to Count Nesselrode about it, and my wish was granted. The Emperor only knew M. de Chateaubriand as an author, and he was left waiting in a room with M. Etienne, the author of a play which the Emperor had seen the previous evening. Passing through this room, on his way out, the Emperor found the two men waiting there. He first spoke to Etienne about his play, and then he said a few words to M. de Chateaubriand with regard to the pamphlet, which he professed not to have had time yet to read. He preached to the two authors of peace between literary men, and assured them that they ought to make it their business to amuse the public, and not to interfere with politics. He then moved on, without giving M. de Chateaubriand the chance to utter a word. The latter threw a very bellicose glance at Etienne, and went away furious.

Count Nesselrode, although annoyed at the incident, could not help laughing when he gave us the details of this interview. I have never been able to make out whether the association of M. de Chateaubriand with Etienne was the Emperor's cleverness or his mistake. M. de Chateaubriand, though, had taken precautions to avoid any such mistake. From the very day following the arrival of the Allies he had arrayed himself in a fancy uniform; over this he wore a thick cord of red silk as a shoulder-belt, to which was attached an immense Turkish sword, which he dragged across every floor with a fearful clatter. He certainly looked much more like a pirate captain than a peaceable writer. The costume seemed a trifle ridiculous even to his most devoted admirers.

I have not attempted to dissemble the small amount of esteem I had for Monsieur's[6] character from all that I saw and knew of him, but enthusi-

6. The Comte d'Artois was known as Monsieur during the reign of his brother, Louis XVIII. See Bourbon in the *Dictionary of Characters*.

asm is so contagious that upon the day of his entrance into Paris I was quite under the influence of it. My heart beat fast; my tears flowed, and I felt the keenest joy and the most profound emotion.

Monsieur possessed to perfection the outward forms and the language capable of inspiring enthusiasm. He was gracious, courtly, debonair, obliging, anxious to please and good-natured, but at the same time dignified. I have never known anyone who had acquired to such perfection the attitude, the forms, the bearing, and the court language desirable in a prince. Add to this a great courtesy of manner which made him charming at home and beloved by all who came in contact with him. He was more capable of familiarity than affection, and had many intimate friends, whom he did not care for in the least.

The evening before his entrance into Livry, Monsieur had slept at a little house belonging to the Comte de Damas. It was there that the newly improvised mounted National Guard awaited him. He exerted all his attraction to fascinate his new Guard, no very difficult task, considering the mental attitude of these young men. He distributed several pieces of white ribbon, which the members of the Guard then wore in their buttonholes. This is the origin of the Order of the Lys, which was promptly rendered ridiculous by the prodigality with which it was bestowed. But at first, and accompanied by all Monsieur's cajoleries, the young men were charmed by it. They brought back their Prince in the midst of their squadron, and were beside themselves with joy, royalism, and love of their leader.

Monsieur, on his side, was so visibly delighted and appeared so full of the present moment and so completely oblivious of any hostile or painful memories, that his appearance must have inspired confidence in the lovely formula made up for him by M. Beugnot in the account given in the *Moniteur*:

"Nothing is changed; there is merely one Frenchman the more."

History will tell, only too accurately, all the mistakes committed by Monsieur during the period when, as Lieutenant-General[7] of the

7. A *lieutenant-général du royaume* is a personnage who has been invested with the supreme authority for a limited period of time.

kingdom, he exasperated all hatreds, stirred up every kind of discontent, and most especially showed a lack of patriotism which scandalised even foreigners.

Count Nesselrode gave me an idea of it upon the day when Monsieur showed such liberality in giving up French strongholds that the Emperor Alexander was obliged to check his anti-French generosity. Pozzo groaned and exclaimed every now and then:

"If things go on like this, the work that we have accomplished with such difficulty will last no time."

The Emperor Alexander was very anxious to bring about a reconciliation between Caulaincourt,* the Duc de Vicence and the former French Ambassador to Russia, whom he liked very much, and the royal family. The share which public opinion, wrongly as I believe, attributed to the Duc de Vicence in the murder of the Duc d'Enghien made him odious to the Princes. Monsieur refused to receive him at his house. The Emperor, vexed at this resistance, determined to arrange a meeting. He invited Monsieur to dinner, and not only was the Duc de Vicence present, but the Emperor took a great deal of notice of him, and made a point of trying to bring him nearer Monsieur.

The dinner party was cold and stiff. Monsieur felt hurt, and went away directly afterwards, leaving the Emperor furious. He walked up and down in the room, among his more familiar friends, inveighing against the ingratitude of people for whom others had conquered a kingdom at the risk of their lives, whilst certain people had not cared to risk theirs, and would not now yield on a simple question of etiquette. When he had calmed down, it was pointed out to him that Monsieur was perhaps the more susceptible precisely because he felt that he was under such great obligations; that it was not a question of etiquette, but of sentiment, for he believed that the Duc de Vicence was guilty with regard to the Ettenheim[8] affair.

"I have told him that he was not," said the Emperor.

No doubt this assertion ought to have had great weight with Mon-

8. The Duc d'Enghien had been seized at Ettenheim. See Enghien in the *Dictionary of Characters.*

sieur, but the public was not then enlightened about the matter, and it was very easy to understand his repugnance on remembering that the Duc d'Enghien was a near relative of his.

The Emperor continued walking up and down.

"A relative, a relative," he muttered, "his repugnance!" and then, suddenly stopping short and facing his interlocutors, he added:

"I dine constantly with Ouvaroff!"

If a bomb had fallen in the middle of the room it could not have produced a greater shock. The Emperor continued his promenade; there was a moment of bewilderment, and then he spoke of other things. He had just revealed the motive of his anger. Everyone then understood his persistence during the last five days in wishing Monsieur to admit the Duc de Vicence.

It was said that General Ouvaroff had strangled the Emperor Paul with his enormous thumbs, which certainly were of a remarkable size. Alexander was shocked to see our Princes refuse to sacrifice their private susceptibilities for the sake of politics, when he himself sacrificed so much more.

It will easily be understood that all argument on this subject ceased, and Pozzo went to Monsieur and told him that he must receive the Duc de Vicence. The latter did not take advantage of the situation; he went once to the house of the Lieutenant-General, and never presented himself there again.

This discussion, which bitter memories served to make extremely personal for the Emperor Alexander, separated him from the Tuileries and brought him nearer to the Bonapartist grandees. With an assiduity prompted by a generous mind and misguided reasoning, he had already hurried off to Malmaison and met with Empress Joséphine, offering affectionate rather than helpful words. After this scene at dinner he went to Saint-Leu, the residence of Queen Hortense, and the welcome that he received from those that he was dethroning touched him all the more deeply when he compared it with what he called the ingratitude of the others. The visit to the château of Compiègne completed this impression, but we shall come to that subject later.

* * *

Monsieur received women. Anyone who wanted to appeared at his house, even Mlle. Montansier, an old theatre director for whom the Prince had had a fancy as a young man. The sincere joy of most of us, however, covered this lack of etiquette.

In the salons of the Tuileries persons hitherto separated by the most opposite opinions now met. We showed great affability to the ladies of the Empire. They were hurt at our advances in a place where they were accustomed to reign exclusively, and they considered us impertinent. As soon as they felt themselves no longer alone, they considered themselves paramount, an excusable impression. We meant very well; we were too well satisfied not to feel sincerely kind. But there is a certain ease, a certain freedom in the manner of women of good society, which gives them the appearance of being at home everywhere and of doing the honours wherever they may be. Women of the other class are often shocked at this; consequently the pettinesses and the little jealousies of the bourgeoises were stirred beneath the jewels which adorned their breasts.

Monsieur succeeded better than we did. He was charming to everyone, said the right thing to each person, managed this heterogeneous court with wonderful tact, appeared dignified but good-natured, and enchanted everyone by his graceful manners. There was a gala performance at the Opera, at which all the Allied Sovereigns were present. All three of them, for the Emperor Francis arrived before Monsieur, went into a large box at the back of the house. Monsieur occupied the King's box, over which the French arms now replaced the eagle that had been so roughly torn down. He went to pay a visit to the foreign sovereigns during the first interval; they returned it during the second.

There was nothing very remarkable that evening except the admirable behaviour of the public, the tact with which it comprehended all the allusions on the stage and took part in all that went on in the house. For instance, when Monsieur went to see the sovereigns, everyone arose and was perfectly silent. But when they returned his visit, there was wild applause, as though to thank them for this homage to our Prince. Parisians in a body are singularly tactful.

As public affairs progressed the King was the more impatiently awaited. Every day those who surrounded the Lieutenant-General steadily urged him to adopt the attitude of a party chief; and if the Emperor Alexander had not been there to moderate this tendency, we should have seen all the talk of Coblentz put into action.

The old officers of the army of Condé, those who had escaped from Vendée, came out of their retirement, fully persuaded that they were conquerors and wishing to adopt a triumphant attitude. This claim was quite natural. Accustomed for the last twenty-five years to consider their cause associated with that of the Bourbons, on seeing their throne restored they persuaded themselves that they had triumphed. On the other side, the servitors of the Empire, accustomed to domination, could not easily accommodate themselves to these untimely claims.

A man who had won his epaulettes by helping to win a hundred battles was rebellious on seeing another man, who had come from a tobacco or a lottery *bureau* wearing the same epaulettes, wishing to lord it over him, given precedence at the Tuileries which had formerly belonged to Napoleon's soldiers, and in his turn addressed as *Mon vieux brave* by the new people in authority there.

Great skill and impartiality were needed to be able to respect these transitions, and Monsieur had neither. Besides, it was almost impossible to satisfy such natural and incongruous requirements.

Finally the King's gout allowed him to leave Hartwell. His journey through England was accompanied by every imaginable rejoicing. The Prince Regent received him in London with extreme magnificence. Pozzo was sent by the Emperor Alexander to pay court. He found him on board the English yacht. Here the King received him as a man to whom he owed the greatest obligations. He accompanied him to Compiègne, and, continuing on his way, went to report his mission to the Emperor.

The Emperor started at once to pay a visit to Louis XVIII, intending to spend twenty-four hours at Compiègne. He was received there with the coldest formality. The King had ransacked his vast memory for details of all that had taken place in interviews between foreign sovereigns and the Kings of France, and intended to be faithful to tradition.

The Emperor, finding neither informality nor cordiality, instead of remaining to talk familiarly, as he had intended to do, asked after a few minutes to retire to his apartments. He was conducted through three or four magnificently furnished suites on the same floor of the château. He was told that these were destined for Monsieur, the Duc d'Angoulême,* and the Duc de Berry, all of whom were absent. Then, after a portentous journey through corridors and up hidden staircases, he arrived at a small door which led into a very modest suite of rooms. It was that of the Governor of the château, and was quite outside the grand apartments. This was the suite destined for him.

Pozzo, who accompanied his imperial master, was suffering tortures, for at every turn in the corridors he saw that the Emperor's very reasonable annoyance was increasing. The latter, however, made no observation about the matter; he merely said very briefly:

"I shall return to Paris this evening. Let my carriages be ready after dinner."

Pozzo managed to bring the conversation round to this extraordinary lodging, and to attribute it to the helplessness of the King.

The Emperor answered that the Duchesse d'Angoulême looked sufficiently like a housekeeper to have been able to attend to it. This little spice of malice, of which Pozzo made the most, relieved his mind, and he returned to the drawing-room rather less vexed. But the dinner did not repair the harm done by the lodging.

When the King was told that dinner was served, he asked the Emperor to take his niece in, and then passed before him with the slow waddle to which the gout had reduced him. On arriving in the dining-room only one armchair was placed at the table, and this was for the King. He was served first, all the honours were rendered to him with affection, and he only distinguished the Emperor by treating him with a kind of familiarity and paternal kindliness. The Emperor Alexander said himself afterwards that the King adopted the attitude with which Louis XIV would have received Philip V[9] at Versailles had he been expelled from Spain.

Almost as soon as dinner was over the Emperor went to his carriage. He was then alone with Pozzo. For a long time he remained perfectly silent, after which he spoke of other things, and then finally with bitterness about this strange reception. There had been no question whatsoever of business, and not a word of thanks or of confidence had been uttered either by the King or by Madame. He had not even heard one pleasant sentence. From that time on, therefore, the friendly intercourse for which he had been prepared was impossible.

The Emperor paid and returned visits of etiquette, and gave orders through his ministers, but all marks of friendship, all forms of intimacy, were exclusively reserved for the Bonaparte family.

This conduct of the Emperor Alexander contributed more than a little to facilitate the return of the Emperor Napoleon in the following year. Many people believe, and appearances authorise the opinion, that Alexander regretted what he had done and was attached to the new dynasty. He delighted in saying, over and over again, that all the royal families in Europe had spilled their blood in helping the Bourbons recover three thrones, while none of them had risked a single scratch.

This visit to Compiègne, upon the details of which I can have no doubt, proved to what a degree the truth may sometimes appear improbable. Certainly King Louis XVIII was intelligent; he had common sense, and was not swayed by passion or timidity; he delighted in talking, and had a gift for saying clever things. How is it that he did not realise all that he might have obtained from these advantages in his position with the Emperor? I will not attempt to explain the difficulty. As to Madame, she lacked the good breeding which would have

9. Philip V was Louis XIV's grandson.

shown her that in this circumstance the most friendly reception would have been most suitable.

Nearly all those about the King's person found themselves observing etiquette for the first time. They had the zeal of neophytes, and, in spite of their feudal names, all had the pride and insolence of upstarts.

The Emperor Alexander was not the only person who returned dissatisfied by his visit to Compiègne. M. de Talleyrand, to whom the King owed the throne, was received coldly by him and very badly by Madame. And the King avoided any mention of business with such affectation that after a stay of a few hours he started back, like a courtier who had paid his respects at Versailles, very much embarrassed in his position as Minister and party chief at having no message to take back to his colleagues and his associates.

The marshals of the Empire were better received. The King was able to say a few appropriate words, to the effect that he was aware of the occasions on which they had especially distinguished themselves. He indicated, too, that he did not separate his interests from those of France. This was very wise and clever.

All the favours were reserved for a few old women of the former court who had hastened to Compiègne. In spite of their age, they were somewhat scared at Madame's costume, for she was dressed in English style.

The long separation between the British Isles and the Continent had produced great differences of dress. With much difficulty they persuaded Madame to give up this foreign costume for the day of her entry into Paris. She persisted in wearing it until then, and indeed for a long time afterwards when she was not on ceremony. This was again her pride, and was misunderstood. The poor Princess had so much dignity in misfortune that she ought to be forgiven a few mistakes in her prosperity. My mother and I were called into the feminine council as to what toilette should be sent to her at Saint-Ouen.

The King stayed there two days and received all the notables. My father was among their number, and he was well received by the King.

Madame, in spite of the familiar kindliness with which she had seen him treated by her mother, Queen Marie-Antoinette, did not appear to recognise him.

My father came back very well satisfied with his visit personally, but vexed to see the bevy of intriguers hovering around this new court. Some of them based their claims on the fact that they had done everything, and the others on the fact that they had done nothing, for the last twenty years.

I have no definite idea how the Declaration was elaborated which is known as the Declaration of Saint-Ouen,[10] so different from that of Hartwell, whose authenticity we always denied, but which was only too real. All that I know is that M. de Vitrolles drew it up, and it filled me with satisfaction. I saw that my dream was about to be realised. My country was to enjoy a representative and truly liberal government, and legitimacy would give it the seal of permanence and security. As I have said, I was rather a Liberal than a Bourbonist. I had proof of this then, for in spite of the fits of contagious enthusiasm to which I had for some time abandoned myself, the Declaration of Saint-Ouen gave me joy of quite another kind.

Many people began to agitate immediately for a modification of that Declaration. I will not venture to say of all of them that this was retrogression as far as ideas were concerned, and there was perhaps wisdom in treating the Declaration as too advanced at that time. Perhaps the concessions of power were really beyond the actual needs of the country. It was not yet educated enough for a Constitution, and was too accustomed to the iron hand of the administrative government. Undue relaxation involved the risk that this unbroken steed might bolt. Experience has since taught me to appreciate fears of this

10. Saint-Ouen was a village a few miles north of Paris where, before he entered Paris, Louis XVIII signed a proclamation on May 2, 1814 that was the basis of the Constitutional Charter he bestowed on his subjects. It established a constitutional monarchy. The King was the head of the executive branch, he named the Ministers and the functionaries, and he was the head of the army and had the right to impose whatever ordinance he deemed necessary to the safety of the state. The Parliament was made up of two entities, the Chamber of the Peers and the Chamber of the Deputies.

kind; but at the time of the Declaration of Saint-Ouen, I was too young to conceive such ideas, and my satisfaction was full of confidence.

We went to watch the entry of the King from a house in the Rue Saint-Denis. The crowd was enormous, and most of the windows were decorated with festoons, mottoes, fleurs de lys, and white flags.

The foreigners had had the good grace to confine their troops to barracks, as they had for the entrance of Monsieur. The city was given over to the National Guard, which from that day began the honourable career of patriotic service which it has since well continued. It had already won the esteem of the Allies and the confidence of its fellow-citizens.

The absence of foreign uniforms was a restful sight. General Sacken, the Russian Governor of Paris, was the only officer to be seen in the city. He was very well liked, and we felt that he was watching to see that the orders given to his own troops were kept.

The procession was escorted by the old Imperial Guard. Others will tell of the misguided treatment of the Guard both before and after that day; all that I have to say is that its aspect was imposing, but that it froze us. It marched quickly, silent and gloomy, full of remembrances of the past. The Imperial Guard stopped, by one look, our outbursts of affection for those who were arriving—the shouts of "Long live the King!" died on our lips as it rode by. Here and there were heard shouts of "Long live the Guard! Long live the Old Guard!" but it did not welcome these, and appeared to accept them in derision. As it passed by the silence became general, and soon nothing could be heard but the monotonous tramp of the quick step striking our very hearts. The consternation increased, and the contagious sadness of these old warriors gave to the whole ceremony the appearance of the Emperor's funeral rather than that of the King's accession.

It was time for this to end. The group of Princes appeared. We had been ill-prepared for their arrival, but they were greeted warmly, although without the enthusiasm which had accompanied Monsieur's entrance into Paris. Were our impressions already somewhat exhausted? Were people dissatisfied with the Lieutenant-General's brief administration, or had the sight of the Imperial Guard chilled enthusiasm? I cannot tell, but certainly the gloom was very noticeable.

Monsieur was on horseback, escorted by the marshals, the Officers-General of the Empire, those of the King's household, and of the line. The King was in an open carriage, with Madame at his side. In front were the Prince de Condé and his son, the Duc de Bourbon. Madame wore the feather toque and the dress with the silver thread that had been sent to her at Saint-Ouen, but she had managed to give a foreign touch to this Parisian costume. The King wore a plain blue coat with very large epaulettes, and the blue order and badge of the Saint-Esprit. He had a handsome face, which was expressionless when he meant to be gracious. He presented Madame to the people with an affected and theatrical gesture. She took no part in these demonstrations, but remained impassive, and in her way was the counterpart of the Imperial Guard. Her red eyes, though, gave the impression that she was crying. Her silent sorrow was respected, and everyone sympathised with her, so that if her coldness had only lasted that day, no one would have dreamed of reproaching her for it.

The Prince de Condé, already almost in his dotage, and his son did not seem to take any part in the proceedings. They only figured there as images in the ceremony. Monsieur alone appeared there to advantage. He had a frank, contented expression on his face, identified himself with the populace, bowed in a friendly and familiar way, like a man who finds himself at home and among his own people. The procession ended with another battalion of the Guard, which reproduced the impression of the first detachment.

I must own that, as far as I was concerned, the morning had been very painful in every way. The people in the open carriage did not correspond to the hopes I had formulated. I was told that Madame, on arriving at Notre-Dame, sank down on her prie-Dieu in a way that was most graceful, noble, and touching. There was such resignation, and at the same time such gratitude, in this action that tears of sympathy had flowed from all eyes. I was also told that on arriving at the Tuileries she was as cold, awkward, and sullen as she had been beautiful and noble in the church.

At that time, the Duchesse d'Angoulême was the only person of the royal family whom people remembered in France. The young generation knew nothing of our Princes. I remember one of my cousins asking me just then whether the Duc d'Angoulême were a son of Louis XVIII and how many children he had. But everyone knew that Louis XVI, the Queen, and Madame Elisabeth had perished on the scaffold. For everyone Madame was the orphan of the Temple, and all the interest aroused by such frightful catastrophes was felt for her. The blood that had been shed baptized her as the country's child.

Much, indeed, was owing to her, but she should have accepted these regrets with greater readiness. Madame did not rise to the delicate situation; she expected these regrets haughtily, and accepted them stiffly. In reality she was full of virtues and kindness, a French Princess at heart, but she managed to make people think that she was disagreeable, cruel, and hostile to her country. The French believed that she detested them, and in the end they detested her. She did not deserve this, and certainly people were not thus inclined at first. It was the effect of a fatal misunderstanding and of false pride. With a little grain of intelligence added to her noble nature, Madame would have been the idol of her country and the paradigm of her race.

The King first received the ladies who had formerly been presented, and he received us the next day. He treated me with special kindness, called me his little Adèle, talked to me of Bellevue, and said all kinds of nice things. He always took special notice of me whenever I went to court, although I went very little to the Tuileries.

On arriving at Madame's, her maid of honour, Mme. de Sérent, asked me my name. As she was very deaf, she asked me to repeat it, but Madame said in her quick, dry way:

"Why, it is Adèle!"

I was much flattered by this sort of recognition, but it went no further. She then asked me one of those idle questions, after the manner of royalties, which did not presuppose that there had ever been anything between us before. My intercourse with Madame was never on any other footing.

That same day, I believe, when Marshal Ney's* wife came to pay her court, Madame called her Aglaé. She was very much horrified at this. She saw in it a reminiscence of the time when she was admitted to Madame's presence, as her mother was chambermaid to Queen Marie-Antoinette. I am convinced that Madame meant, on the contrary, to show her great politeness, just as she did to me when she referred to me by the name of Adèle. Her tone, though, was so unpleasant, her speech so curt, her gestures so brusque, and her expression so cold, that it did not ever seem as though her words could be kindly meant. People have told me that, when one knew her intimately, these surly ways disappeared, but I never had the honour of being admitted into her intimacy.

After these first receptions, attention was given to the regulation of court dress and etiquette. Madame made a very serious business of this. Such strict attention given at such a time to the length of lappets and the size of mantillas appeared to me to be a triviality unworthy of the situation. A court costume had to be chosen, and Madame would have liked to return to hoops, as at Versailles, but the rebellion against this was so general that she gave way. But to the imperial costume all the "paraphernalia" of the former style of dress was added, and this was singularly incongruous. To our Grecian style of hairdressing, for instance, these ridiculous lappets were added, and the elegant cherusque, which completed a garb copied from Van Dyck, was replaced by a heavy mantilla and a kind of pleated plastron. At first Madame was very particular that all this should be strictly observed. The model given to her tradespeople had to be copied exactly, and she was very much displeased with anyone who attempted any modification. Later on, the Duchesse de Berry* emancipated herself from this servitude, and others followed her example. The lappets were then worn very wide, and as they looked like a veil, they were not without a certain grace. The mantilla, on the other hand, was so scanty that it no longer crushed the dress.

When all this was settled, the next thing was to determine the etiquette of precedents, and this matter was the King's affair. It was chiefly with the help of the Duc de Duras that this task was accomplished, and the honours of the throne-room were established in place of the honours of the Louvre. M. de Duras, who was more Duc than the late M. de Saint-Simon, was extremely anxious that the distinctions attached to this title should be marked as definitively as possible, and he invented the procedure adopted. Monsieur and Madame disapproved strongly of it, and the separation between the ladies was never enforced at their receptions.

The new etiquette delighted the duchesses and aroused the anger of the others, particularly the elderly ladies of the former court. It must be admitted that precautions had been taken to make the distinction as offensive as it could be to those who attached any importance to it. The arrival was through the Marshals' Hall, which then served as the guards' room and led to the staircase. The blue drawing-room, which was only dimly lighted, had then to be crossed. We all stayed in the Salon de la Paix, which was almost as dark. The duchesses continued their way and entered the throne-room, which alone was brilliantly lighted. One of the folding doors leading into it remained closed, and an official stood there to refuse admittance to anyone who had not the right to enter. The faces of the former court ladies were worth seeing each time that one of the fortunate women of the new regime crossed the Salon de la Paix, as it were over their bodies. Indignation was constantly renewed, and the subject was the everyday text of outbursts which frequently entertained me. The poor duchesses were exposed to sarcasm of all kinds, and all that was said of those of the Empire can easily be imagined.

The closing of the door announced the entrance of the King in the throne-room. He went around, saying a few words to the duchesses or to the titled persons, as they alone were called. After this he placed himself in front of the chimney-piece, with his attendants around him, and either remained standing or sat down, according to the state of his gout. The door was then opened once more and we entered in procession, turning short to the right, passing by the throne and arriving in front of him, where we stopped to make a deep curtsey.

When he did not speak to us, and this was the case for nine out of ten women, we continued to file along, and went out by the door that led into the drawing-room just before the Galerie de Diane, which was styled the council room. When the King spoke, and the most highly favoured were granted no more than two or three phrases, he closed his audience by a slight inclination of the head. We replied by another deep curtsey, and then followed those who had preceded us out of the room.

We crossed the Galerie de Diane, and on descending the staircase arrived at Madame's reception room. As she said much more than the King, and spoke to everyone, there was always a block at her door. With a little diplomacy, however, and a great deal of pushing, we contrived to get inside the room. She was standing not far from the door, her maid of honour by her, and the rest of her suite at the end of the room.

She alone, although elaborately dressed, wore no court mantle. After a very short time she recognised everyone, without any help from her maid of honour. We stopped in front of her, and she said the right thing to everyone. Her manner alone was lacking, for with her words and a little more affability she would have held her court very well. When her little bow signified to us that the conversation, which was of a much more uncertain length than the King's, was over, we again made our curtsey and went on to the Duc d'Angoulême.

He was always taken unawares, for with his clumsy fussiness he could not stay long in one place. His words were as awkward as he was himself, and he was a great trial to those who were interested in the family. It is nonetheless probable that if this Prince had succeeded his uncle immediately, the Restoration would have lasted and there would have been tranquillity. I shall frequently have to speak of him.

On leaving the Duc d'Angoulême we were in the vestibule of the

Pavillon de Flore—that is, in the street, for in those days it was paved and had neither doors nor windows, so that it was entirely exposed to the inclemencies of the weather. We were not allowed to go back through the rooms of the palace, so the only alternative was to go down into the basement, along the open passage where the kitchens were, or to cross to the Pavillon de Marsan in our carriages. In the first instance we had to go our way with neither shawl nor cloak, as etiquette did not permit either within the Château.[11] In the second we had to go as far as the square for our domestics, as they were not allowed to approach any nearer. The courtiers who had been entrusted to regulate all these forms and ceremonies had shown no consideration for the comfort of the persons for whom they were intended.

On arriving at the Pavillon de Marsan we went upstairs and found Monsieur there, always perfectly gracious and obliging. He possessed the art of appearing to hold his court for his own enjoyment and diversion. We then went down again to the ground floor, where the Duc de Berry, with neither grace nor dignity, received us with perfect ease of manner and with witty good humour. I cannot really judge his attitude as a Prince, for he had always treated me familiarly. His father and he had brought with them from England the custom of shaking hands. The Duc de Berry kept it up for his old acquaintances, and I fancy that Monsieur, too, never quite relinquished it until he mounted the throne. After the first few days, though, he did not honour me anymore with this distinction, which became unusual.

The reception was certainly very badly organised, for we never came away from it without feeling bored, tired, and discontented. I was among those who were well treated, and yet I never went willingly, and as rarely as possible. It was a real infliction, for we had to change our dinner-hour, array ourselves in a most uncomfortable costume which we could never wear elsewhere, be at the Tuileries at seven o'clock, wait there an hour for the sake of seeing the duchesses go by, as we used to say, struggle before Madame's door, catch cold in the

11. The Tuileries was called the Château during the entire period of the Restoration.

outer corridors, in spite of our precaution of wrapping the trains of our dresses around our head and shoulders, thus making ourselves look incredibly strange, and then again have difficulty at the Pavillon de Marsan in finding our servants. Unless they were very intelligent, we were apt to lose them frequently in these peregrinations. As no man was admitted to these receptions, the poor women in full dress were to be seen running after their carriages to the middle of the square. To all these annoyances must be added that of our standing for three hours. It was at this price that we obtained the honour of being ten seconds before the King, a minute before Madame, and about the same time with the Princes. It was out of all proportion.

The persons entrusted with court ceremonies ought to have taken care to make them convenient. The Restoration and its servitors never took any trouble upon that point. They wanted to reestablish the old conditions, and they never considered that the place and the customs had changed. For instance, a lady at Versailles was always followed by two lackeys, often by three, and by a sedan chair which took her directly to the antechambers. These customs removed any difficulties of communication. Our mothers never failed to remind us of this fact, after a diatribe about the way in which the duchesses trampled upon them, as they expressed it. They could not reconcile themselves to this, and they told us that at Versailles one never noticed the privileges allowed to titled women. Duchesses had then no other prerogatives than that of being seated at the King's dinner and this rarely happened, because it would have been necessary to be present at the whole meal, and it was more convenient for them only to put in an appearance and go away.

They certainly were seated when there was a state dinner, but as untitled ladies were not then present, the difference of treatment was never marked. These ladies forgot, in their annoyance, that the carriages of the duchesses used to enter a reserved court, that their sedan chairs, followed by three lackeys instead of two, and covered with red velvet, used to enter the second antechamber, and that there were other prerogatives attached to their position which nearly resembled the custom of awaiting the arrival of the King in the reception room, but which the force of habit made less disagreeable to our mothers.

The only reason I envied the ladies of the throne-room was the advantage they had in being able to get through the tiresome drudgery of these receptions more quickly than we could. The King's reception was every week, but the Princes only received once a month.

I will now return to 1814. We very quickly saw that the great services rendered by M. de Talleyrand offended M. de Blacas.* He alone governed the King, and he did not care to admit anyone to share his predominance. The prejudices of the royal family, justified perhaps by the earlier behaviour of the Prince de Talleyrand, but which recent events ought to have effaced, fed into the plans of the favourites only too well. Everyone soon saw what M. de Talleyrand had himself recognised from the time of his visit to Compiègne. Obligations too public to be denied annoyed the King, and M. de Talleyrand had no influence and no strength to hope for except outside the Tuileries. He did not attempt to make himself the representative of France, for he was too unpopular with the country, but he did try to make himself indispensably necessary through his influence with the foreigners.

In his desire to free himself from the control of M. de Talleyrand, M. de Blacas would have liked to make friends with the distinguished people in the country. More moderate and less exclusive than the other political *émigrés* who had returned with the King, he was far from blaming my father for his refusal to adopt the prejudices of the *émigrés*, and realised all the value of a Royalist who was devoted, wise, and who knew and judged with sanity the state of mind in France, to which he had returned ten years ago. He would have liked to attach him to his fortunes, but my father, incapable of entering into any cabals, had thrown in his lot with M. de Talleyrand ever since his conduct during the entrance of the Allies, and he received M. de Blacas's advances very coldly.

It was during the time of these ostensible flatteries from the favourite that the nomination of my father to some ministry was announced to me every day. I did not feel greatly disturbed, as I was persuaded that he would not consent to lose his liberty for any position. I cannot describe the astonishment I felt when he told us one day that the Embassy of Vienna had been offered to him, and pointed out the many reasons for accepting it. He found my mother and myself so reluctant about the matter that he eventually conceded that the only ambassadorship he would not refuse was that of London.

From the moment that it became clear to me that there was a position he would not refuse, I understood that he would accept any post, and that he would perhaps finally solicit one. I said to my mother that we no longer ought to try to exercise an influence which would only embarrass my father, and she was all the more easily persuaded as she herself was not averse to an important embassy.

After the public had received the Declaration of Saint-Ouen, the next thing was to formulate a Charter, but either because the period of reflection had begun, or because people were ready to adopt the concessions suggested, opinion grew that these concessions were too extensive.

M. de Talleyrand, in his speech to the King, had very neatly observed that barriers were supports; the court feared that they were obstacles. Whilst supposing that it was wise not to flood with excessive liberty a country which for a long time had been under severe constraint, it was a great mistake to nominate three men to draw up the Charter who professed most energetically their dislike for representative government, namely, Chancellor Dambray, M. Ferrand, and the Abbé de Montesquiou.

They then boasted, and have since admitted, that the Charter was only, in their eyes, a transition to the Ancien Régime, or rather to absolute monarchy. Institutions which had been created by time, manners, and customs, and which formed insurmountable obstacles to arbitrary power, had been swept away by the revolutionary torrent. Whatever may have been their intentions, France took their work seriously, as she has since proved.

In spite of my dislike for ceremonies, I wished to be present at the royal session where the Charter was to be promulgated. My liberalism was shocked at the way in which the Saint-Ouen conditions had been modified. The Charter seemed to me to be a mystification. This impression was by no means general; everyone was busy trying to find the article in it which he could utilise for his own benefit. I was little edified by my compatriots on this occasion. The King was wonderfully well received. The ceremony was very fine, but it lacked that seriousness and that religious feeling with which a great nation should receive the tables of the law. Attention was chiefly directed to the new costumes, the new faces, and to old customs which had become new again after long disuse.

When the King ended his speech, which was well composed and delivered in an imposing voice, with the words, "My Chancellor will tell you the rest," an almost audible smile went round the house. After the reading of the Charter, M. Dambray read the list of peers. He commenced with the ducs and peers of the Ancien Régime, and then went on to those of the new one. On arriving at the senatorial peers he read among others the names of Comte Cornet and Comte Cornudet in so perfectly impertinent and disdainful a tone that I was scandalised, and could not help saying to my neighbours:

"A strange way certainly to make partisans! These people, to whom a considerable favour has been granted, are by that very tone of voice relieved of all obligation."

Only six new peers were made, among whom was Comte Charles de Damas, who has already been mentioned as commanding one of the red regiments of the King's household. Consequently, a few days later, Comtesse Charles de Damas, who since then has belonged to the extreme opposition, said to me:

"I meet people who blame these proceedings. For my part, as I am convinced that the King has much more intelligence and judgement than I have, and that he is in a better position for knowing what is wise, as soon as he utters a wish I fall in with it without a moment's hesitation." I remember this phrase, because I was delighted to repeat it to her word for word in 1815, when she was furious that all the Bonapartists should not be put to death because of mere hue and cry.

Once the Charter was promulgated the foreign sovereigns went away. Meanwhile, M. de Talleyrand was as considerate as possible to my father on every occasion. Their acquaintance dated from early youth; and, although they had followed very different lines, and their intercourse had been interrupted for twenty-five years, he always made much of the capacity and loyalty of my excellent father. My premonitions about the change that had come over my father's inclinations were very soon justified, for, after refusing to go to Vienna, he accepted the Turin ambassadorship. In spite of his superior reason and judgement, in the midst of this general place-hunting, he could not avoid some touch of ambition.

M. de Talleyrand spoke to him of Turin as leading promptly to London, considering that M. de La Châtre was incapable of holding out there; even more influential was his observation that Turin, being regarded as a family ambassadorship, ensured the right to the Cordon Bleu.[12] Now my father had always wished for this decoration above everything else, so true is it that the ideas of early life leave strong traces in the most elevated minds! To be a knight of this order seemed to him the finest thing in the world. If M. de Talleyrand had been Minister, my father would have been included in the first promotion.

When the question of the ambassadorship of Turin came up, things did not go quite smoothly. My mother was furious, I was grieved, my brother annoyed, and finally my father decided to yield to our wishes. He went to the King and told him that, having refused the ambassadorship of Vienna, he would be inconsistent in accepting that of Turin.

The King answered that the cases were quite different—he understood his refusal of Vienna, but that the King of Sardinia was his

12. The ornament worn by the Knight of the Order of the Holy Ghost. The order, created by Henri III, had been suppressed in 1791 and reestablished by Louis XVIII. It was the highest of the decorations of the monarchy.

brother-in-law. And this strange argument appeared conclusive to my father. The King, who was anxious to persuade him, told him that he was inclined to grant him anything that might be agreeable as a favour and a mark of content and satisfaction. My father invented a request for the right of entry to his private study, which meant permission to pay his court on days of reception in one room rather than another. It was after obtaining these two results, at the end of a long conversation, that my father returned home very much delighted, informing us that he had not been able to resist the King's orders any longer. It was not until later, and after he had accepted, that M. de Talleyrand promised London and the Cordon Bleu.

I cannot sufficiently repeat that my father was the most straightforward of men and the least capable of any pettiness I have ever met, and yet he yielded then to seductions which would not have exerted any influence upon him twenty-five years previously. As for me, I passed from one amazement to another without making any progress in the courtier's arts.

This appointment brought us back from the country, where we had gone to rest after so agitating a winter and a spring. My mother had had a fall which prevented her from moving, so that all the worries of the preparations for the departure fell upon me. These cares, together with the sorrow that I felt at leaving my friends and changing my habits and customs, absorbed me so entirely that I had little time for the consideration of public affairs; consequently these are now less clear in my mind.

Monsieur fell dangerously ill, and his condition caused intense anxiety to all those who called themselves Royalists. I shared this anxiety very sincerely. Our prayers for his recovery were answered, but alas! neither for his happiness nor for ours! He spent his convalescence at Saint-Cloud. We went there from Châtenay to pay our court to him, and he was very gracious and very talkative. He showed us all the splendours of Saint-Cloud with great satisfaction. He said laughingly that no one could accuse Bonaparte of having spoilt the furniture. Long deprivation of these royal magnificences made him appreciate them all the more. At Saint-Cloud I met the Chevalier de Puységur. I had left him a few years before in London the most amiable, agreeable, and sociable of men. We were great friends, and I was delighted to see him. I found a cold, affected, disobliging, silent personage; I could not understand such a metamorphosis. I went away embarrassed because my own advances had not been reciprocated.

I heard a few days later that, besides the Anglomania which had made him dislike everything French, he was annoyed by his aged appearance. He had lost all his teeth, and had hitherto failed in his attempts to replace them. A more skilful dentist afterwards helped him to be rather more sociable, but he never recovered his former graciousness, and remained surly and morose. He did not come to my house, but I frequently saw him at my uncle Edouard Dillon's.

One day when Lord Westmeath, who was interested in agriculture, had been to Saint-Germain in the morning, he asked us how cattle were fed in the suburbs of Paris. He had thought there was only a little land for pasture. We felt it our duty to explain to him that he would find more on other routes, but the Chevalier cut us short.

"You are right, my lord," he said; "there is no pasture; the horrible cows eat thistles in the ditches and besides, you would never be able to discover our meadows in France, as the grass is not green."

"What do you mean? The grass is not green? What colour is it, then?"

"It is brown."

"When it is scorched by the sun."

"No, always."

I could not help laughing and saying:

"What strange information for a Frenchman to give to a foreigner!"

The Chevalier replied sharply:

"I am not a Frenchman, Madame; I am of the Pavilion de Marsan."[13]

Alas! he spoke truly, and in this sarcastic outburst may be found the

13. The Pavillon de Marsan was the part of the Tuileries palace occupied by Monsieur. To be of the Pavillon de Marsan implied extreme political views.

text of the whole conduct of the Restoration, of all its faults and of all its misfortunes.

Many years later, and beyond the point where I intend to close these memoirs, in April 1832, during the worst of the disastrous cholera epidemic, I called one morning upon the Duchesse de Laval: the Duc de Luxembourg, her brother, and the Duc de Duras were there. I had just heard from Baron Pasquier, who had witnessed it, an account of the death of M. Cuvier,* who had fallen victim to the scourge which was ravaging the capital. He had given proof at that supreme instant of all the sublimity of his immense intellectual distinction, and a strength of mind which continued up to his very last breath, while he retained all his tender-heartedness. M. Pasquier had been deeply touched by this, and had made me share his impression.

I arrived at the house of the Duchesse full of my subject, and I repeated the details that I had just heard. The two Ducs listened in an indifferent way. M. de Luxembourg then turned towards M. de Duras and asked him in a low voice:

"Who is this M. Cuvier?"

"He is one of the gentlemen of the King's garden," answered the other.

The illustrious Cuvier one of the gentlemen of the King's garden! I was stupefied. Alas! Alas! I said to myself, such words from the lips of the captains, the guards, the gentlemen of the chamber, the confidants of the King of France, explain sadly the Cherbourg journey.[14] Europe was envying us the glory of possessing Cuvier, and the court of the Tuileries was ignorant of even his existence. The two Ducs were of the Pavillon de Flore, just as M. de Puységur was of the Pavillon de Marsan.

Around this time, the Duc d'Orléans arrived in Paris. He was married to Princesse Amélie de Naples. She had first been destined for the Duc de Berry. This alliance was about to be concluded in Vienna, during

14. Cherbourg is the port from which Charles X left France after the Revolution of 1830.

the Queen of Naples's visit to that city with her two daughters. The Duc de Berry, who was then in love with one of the de Montbois-sier girls, made some unseemly joke in public about the few charms he found in the young Princess. His remarks reached the ears of the Queen. She wrote him a dignified, noble, and yet kindly letter, in which she took back her word and broke off all engagements as far as her daughter was concerned. She sent a copy of this letter to my mother, and I read it several times.

The Duchesse d'Orléans was good enough to remember our inter-course as children, and she welcomed me with a kindliness which re-vived my affection for her, an affection which increased each day when I saw her exercising all the virtues, in addition to all the graces which can accompany them.

The Duchesse d'Orléans was not pretty. She was even ugly: tall and thin, with a red complexion, small eyes, and irregular teeth. But she had a long neck, her head was well set, and she had a very distin-guished air. She was admirable in full dress, was very gracious, and at the same time extremely dignified. Then, too, in her little eyes there was such expression, an emanation from her pure, great, noble soul, and her glance was so changeable, so full of feeling, so kindly, so en-couraging, so stimulating, so grateful, that it fully compensated for any sacrifice on my part. I am convinced that the Duchesse d'Orléans owed part of the fascination she exercised over the most hostile people to the influence of that look.

She was very well received at the court of the Tuileries, the Duc d'Orléans less so, and Mademoiselle, her sister-in-law, Adélaïde,* with great coldness. I do not think there ever was a reconciliation with her, not even by letter, and the Duchesse d'Angoulême could not dis-simulate the repugnance she felt for the brother and sister.

I heard my uncle, Edouard Dillon, say that he was at Hartwell when the Duc d'Orléans paid his first visit there. The visit had been under discussion for a long time, and Madame had only consented with difficulty. The Duc arrived earlier than he was expected one Sun-day, as everyone was returning from Mass. Madame met him as she was crossing the hall, followed by all those who lived in the castle. On seeing the Prince she turned extremely pale, her legs trembled, and words died away on her lips. He advanced to support her, but she repulsed him. She was obliged to sit down, as she was very faint. Everyone gathered around her, and she was led away to her apartments.

The Duc d'Orléans was deeply hurt, grieved, and annoyed. He was left alone with my uncle, and, as it was impossible to keep up any pretence, he spoke to him bitterly of this scene, and expressed a wish to go away at once. Edouard proved to him how desirable it was to avoid a scandal, and offered to go to the King on his behalf and take his orders. The King was with his niece, and he sent word to the Prince that Madame was subject to this kind of indisposition, that she was better again, and that by dinner-time there would be no further sign of it.

A few minutes later he received the Duc d'Orléans in his study. I do not know what passed between them. Madame made the best of it at dinner, and even spoke to the Duc d'Orléans of this palpitation to which she was subject. There was no truth, however, in this, and the Prince was very glad, as can be imagined, to get into his carriage and drive away directly after the meal. Scenes of this kind leave traces which are not forgotten on either side.

Madame's ostensible repugnance to the Duc d'Orléans decreased as time went on, but she could neither conquer nor dissimulate the disgust which Mademoiselle inspired in her. However, a sincere and mutual friendship sprang up between her and the Duchesse d'Orléans. Madame usually called her "my real cousin," as their mothers had been sisters.

My father would have liked my brother to be attached to the House of Orléans, as his name gave him old family rights there. The kindness of the Duchesse d'Orléans to me allowed me to speak of this to her. Although she was in deep mourning for her mother, she used to receive me often, and she promised to attend to this matter. A few days later she told me that the Duc d'Orléans had made so many promises already that he was not likely to have any posts that he could dispose of. That was not exactly the truth, which was as follows:

The Duc d'Orléans was already surrounded by a few persons belonging to what was still called the Ancien Régime. Instead of wishing to increase the number, he wanted to complete his household with those of another order, who belonged to the revolutionary interest. He was keen-sighted enough to realise that it was greatly in his interest to deal cautiously with them, and his policy was always directed to secure this amalgamation. It would have been a very clever idea for the Princes of the royal family, but I should be sorry to assert that it was entirely simple for a Prince of the blood thus to dissociate himself from the Bourbon policy.

It is certain that from the very first day the Duc d'Orléans, though I am sure that he did not conspire against them, avoided any association with their proceedings, and his whole attitude was that of a man very glad to be thought as the Opposition.

M. de Talleyrand very nearly followed the same line of conduct. If he had been as respected in the country as he was important, he would not have hesitated, but the Restoration was too much work for him to venture to separate himself from it on account of private animosities. Disgusted with all the rebuffs which were showered upon him at the Château, he wanted to go away, and he proposed that he attend the Vienna Congress,[15] the importance of the negociations and the presence of the sovereigns justifying that of the Minister of Foreign Affairs.

M. de Talleyrand's salon was very amusing. The doors did not open till after midnight, but all Europe crowded there, and in spite of the strict etiquette of the reception and the impossibility of moving one of the heavy seats occupied by the women, one could always find a way of spending a few moments there which were entertaining, or interesting at any rate, for a spectator.

15. The Congress of Vienna was the assembly that reorganized Europe after the Napoleonic era. It began in September 1814 and completed its Final Act in June 1815 just before the end of the Hundred Days. The settlement, based on the principle of the balance of power, lasted for over forty years.

Mme. de Talleyrand, seated at the end of the two rows of armchairs, tranquilly did the honours. The remains of her great beauty adorned her stupidity with a fair amount of dignity. I cannot refrain from telling a somewhat indecorous story characteristic of this courtesan, then such a *grande dame*. Edouard Dillon, who, as I have mentioned previously, was known as "Handsome Dillon," had had all the successes that such a nickname suggests. Mme. de Talleyrand, then Mme. Grant, had been attracted by him, but as his time was occupied elsewhere, he did not pay much attention to her. The rupture of a liaison which greatly affected him made him decide to leave Paris and undertake a journey to the East. This was an event in those days, and the mere idea of it added that curiosity to his other fascinations.

Mme. Grant redoubled her attentions, and finally, the evening before his departure, Edouard agreed to return home with her for supper after the opera. He found a very charming flat, with the table set for two persons, and all the studied refinements which belonged to Mme. Grant's profession. She had the most beautiful hair imaginable and Edouard admired it. She told him that he did not yet know what it was like, and, after retiring into her dressing-room, she came back with her hair loose, covering her like a veil. She was a second Eve, before any clothing had been invented, and, with less innocence than her ancestress, naked and not ashamed. The supper was finished in this primitive costume.

Edouard started for Egypt the following day, in the year 1787. In 1814 this same Edouard, on his return from exile, was driving with me to call on the Princesse de Talleyrand, to whom I was to introduce him.

"The contrast," he said to me, "is so amusing between this visit and the one I paid formerly to Mme. de Talleyrand, that I cannot resist telling you of my last and only interview with her."

He then told me the preceding story. We were both much amused, and curious as to what her attitude would be towards him. She received him wonderfully well, and in a very simple way. But after a few minutes she spoke of my head-dress, admired my hair, wondered how long it was, and then, suddenly turning to my uncle, who was just behind my chair, she said:

"Monsieur Dillon, you like beautiful hair, do you not?" Fortunately our eyes did not meet, as it would have been impossible for us to have kept serious.

Mme. de Talleyrand did not keep her naive remarks solely for her own use; she had some to spare for M. de Talleyrand. She never failed to remember that such-and-such a person (another of my uncles, for instance, Arthur Dillon) was one of his fellow-students at the Seminary. She would address him from the other side of the drawing-room, and call upon him to affirm that the ornament he liked best was a pastoral cross of diamonds which she was wearing.

When someone advised her to have larger pendants to her pearl earrings she answered:

"Do you imagine I have married the Pope?"

There are too many of these absurdities to quote. M. de Talleyrand met them all with his imperturbable calm, but I am convinced that he must often have wondered how he could have married this woman.

I was at Mme. de Talleyrand's on the day of M. de Talleyrand's departure, and I saw her when she was told that Mme. de Dino, then Comtesse Edmond de Périgord, was accompanying her uncle to Vienna. The meeting place had been arranged at a country house near Paris. An indiscreet person told her this in a very innocent way. Mme. de Talleyrand made no mistake about the importance of this meeting, which had been arranged so secretly. She could not conceal her anxiety nor yet recover from it. She was not mistaken in her premonition, for from that day forth she never saw M. de Talleyrand again, and she was soon after banished from his house.

For some years, we had frequently seen the Princesse de Carignan, niece of the King of Saxony. She had married the Prince de Carignan at the commencement of the Revolution. He was then far removed from the crown but recognised as a prince of the blood. She had adopted revolutionary ideas and had won over her husband to them. He was absolutely devoid of the most ordinary intelligence. After his death, she secretly married a M. de Montléard. She had several children by him, whom she had carefully concealed from the time of their birth. She only acknowledged the two Carignans, a girl and a boy.

The boy, whose childhood had been so neglected that he had run about Paris with all the small boys of the neighbourhood, had been in a pension at Geneva for a few months at this time; the King of Sardinia sent for him and established him in Turin. He now became an important personage. As the King had only daughters and his brother no children, the Prince de Carignan* was heir presumptive to the throne.

The Duc de Modène, brother to the Queen of Sardinia, and married to her eldest daughter, would have considered it simpler to change the order of succession. Austria supported his claims. The revolutionary opinions of the parents and the conduct of the Princesse de Carignan militated against the young Prince de Carignan; but he was from the House of Savoy, and that was a great point in his favour in the King's eyes. To secure his recognition and the public proclamation of his rights was one of the most important features of the mission confided to my father. It was in the greatest interests of France that Austria should not add Piedmont to the states it governed in Italy.

CHAPTER FIVE

Turin and the Hundred Days

1814–1815

King Victor Emmanuel ~ His government ~ The Opera
~ Social customs ~ Appearance of the city of Turin ~
Lodgings ~ Journey to Genoa ~ Napoleon flees from Elba
~ He disembarks in France ~ The Princess of Wales ~
Anxiety for my brother ~ Return to Turin ~ Napoleon
reaches Paris ~ General Bubna ~ Expulsion of the
French residing in Piedmont ~ I leave Turin for Paris

We started at the beginning of October 1814, and we reached Turin at a moment when society was utterly disorganised. The King, Victor Emmanuel I,* had come back from Cagliari with only one idea, to which he clung with the obstinacy of dotage; he wished to reestablish everything as it had been in *Novant-ott*. This was his way of expressing 1798 in his Piedmont patois, at which date he had been driven from his estates by the French armies.

Ridiculous consequences were the result: for instance, his former pages resumed their duties side-by-side with new appointments, so that some were fifteen years old and others forty. Similar confusion prevailed everywhere else. Officers who had risen to higher rank could only remain in the army by becoming subalterns once more. The same principle was pursued in the judiciary and the civil service, et cetera, and the confusion was indescribable. There was one exception to the law of *Novant-ott*, on which matter the good King showed himself wholly pliable; this concerned the levying of taxation. Taxes had been trebled since the French occupation, and to this change his Sardinian majesty adapted himself very readily.

The King had brought back all the courtiers who had followed him to Cagliari during his exile. Not one of them was capable of performing the work of government for a single day. Moreover, the Emperor Napoleon had, as usual, skimmed off the most distinguished characters from Piedmont for employment in the service of the Empire, for which reason they were regarded by the King as unable to serve in his Government. The consequent difficulties were great.

An attempt was made to bring back to public life a man who had retired from politics but was not without capacity; this was the Count di Valese, who for many years had lived in seclusion in his castle in the Val d'Aosta. He had retained many aristocratic prejudices and ideas opposed to revolutionary principles, but he might be regarded as a Liberal in comparison with the new arrivals from Sardinia. He was obliged to treat them gently, and I think that he must often have blushed for the concessions which he was forced to make to their ignorance.

In his passion for restoring the system of Novant-ott, the King wished to destroy all that the French had created, including several scientific collections. He was asked one day to spare the ornithological collection which he had visited the evening before and with which he had seemed delighted. He flew into a passion and said that all these innovations were works of Satan; that these collections did not exist in Novant-ott; that they got along very well without them; that there was no need to be cleverer than one's ancestors.

His anger being exhausted, he added that he would make an exception only for the birds, as they pleased him, and he wished that great care should be taken of them. The Sardinian party in the council approved the King's resolution. Count Valese and Count Balbe lowered their eyes and were silent; the destruction of the ornithological collection and the preservation of the collection of birds was adopted by an immense majority.

Absurdities of this kind, though I give but one example, were a daily occurrence, and exposed the Government to ridicule; upon our arrival in Turin it had fallen into the lowest disrepute. Afterwards the great geniality of the King had secured him a kind of popularity, and necessity had obliged him to moderate the absurd ideas which he had brought back from Cagliari. He was obliged to turn to people whose merits were known and appreciated by the country, even though they had not passed twenty-five years of their lives in idleness.

Count Valese did not find association with men to whom he had been hostile for so long an easy task. Perhaps he feared that once the objections to their employment were completely overcome, intellects superior to his own might be found among the Emperor's former servants. As, however, he was a man of honour and desired the welfare of the state, he advised the King to entrust important posts to those who were able to fill them adequately, and each day brought some improvement to the original absurdities.

The absence of the Queen, who had remained in Sardinia, made the King more amenable to reasonable advice. She had, however, delegated her influence to a certain Count Roburent, a chief equerry and a kind of favourite, whose importance at court was outstanding. He represented the old system of the exiled party, with all the extravagance which might be expected in a man of limited views and profound ignorance. I remember that one day at my father's house the conversation turned upon the ceremonies of initiation which sailors undergo when crossing the Equator: my father said that he had undergone this ceremony, and Count Roburent observed with a gracious smile, "So your excellency has crossed the line. I suppose, then, that you have been Ambassador at Constantinople?"

There were then three legal codes in force in Piedmont—the old civil code, the military code (which was able to claim jurisdiction in every case), and the Napoleonic code. A *biglietto regio*, or royal edict, enjoined the use of that code favourable to the party protected by the authorities, a procedure renewed in every instance. If this precaution had been insufficient, a second *biglietto regio* quashed the decision and decided in a contrary sense without any right of appeal, though it must be admitted that this process was only possible in the case of people in high favour.

One incident during our stay caused much stir. Two provincial nobles at Piedmont had been to court, and the case was decided at Casal.

The man who lost rode to Turin, made his way to Count Roburent, and pointed out to him that the judgement was unjust in view of the fact that he was his cousin. Count Roburent understood the force of this argument, and easily obtained a *biglietto regio* in favour of his cousin. Three days afterwards the other litigant arrived, bringing with him a full genealogy, and supported by documentary evidence, which proved that he, too, was a cousin of Count Roburent and one degree nearer than his opponent. The Count examined the genealogy with great care, admitted that he had been guilty of injustice, went to the King, and brought back a second *biglietto regio* which reestablished the original decision. All this was done quite openly, and the only point where concealment was practised was that of our own amusement, a necessary precaution in an official position such as ours.

Intolerance was carried to such a degree that the French embassy was regarded as a centre of wickedness. Our King was not to be pardoned for the grant of the charter; still less was my father for his approval of the grant and for his open assertion that it was a salutary measure rendered indispensable by public feeling in France. These subversive doctrines proved so repugnant to the spirit of the Sardinian Government that the Piedmontese received strong hints to avoid listening to theories which the Government could not prevent the Ambassador from professing.

The intolerant were little inclined to visit the embassy; those who had acquired some tinge of Liberalism from service in France were afraid of compromising themselves, and thus we hardly saw the natives of the country except upon formal visits, nor was the fact much to be regretted.

Turin society, like that of almost every town in Italy, offers but few of those honourable people who compose society in other countries. A few scholars and some highly distinguished people, perhaps a little more numerous here than elsewhere, lead a secluded life full of intellectual interest. To break this charmed circle or to attract any of the members composing it is an exceedingly difficult task, though success would amply repay any trouble expended for these purposes. On the other hand, the rank and file who go to balls and call upon one another are incredibly stupid and ignorant.

It is said that in the south of Italy natural intelligence is to be found. The native of Piedmont is a northerner by intelligence and a southerner by education. Generally speaking, the country has been unfortunate. Its climate is colder than that of France in the winter and more stormy and suffocatingly hot than the rest of Italy in summer, while the fine arts have not crossed the Apennines to enter this province. They would be appalled at the frightful jargon spoken there, which would inform them that they were not in their own country.

Throughout the period of my stay at Turin, during the so-called early evening when my father received callers, I daily and regularly heard a discussion of the question which I propose conscientiously to explain from every point of view.

Prince Borghese,* the Governor of Piedmont under the Emperor, had placed a chandelier in the hall of the great theatre. This was, it must be said, an innovation. He offered to give it, to sell it, to take it away at his own expense, to spread a report that he had sold it, but to take no money, to accept anything that the King would care to give for it, and finally to say nothing more about it. I would willingly have fallen in with this last proposition. When I left Turin, at the end of ten months, the question was still undecided and society was shaken by violent views upon the subject of the chandelier; they were awaiting the arrival of the Queen to settle the matter.

The distribution of the boxes had for a time provided some distraction from this former occupation. I was so unprepared for these customs that I cannot describe the astonishment with which I learnt that as the carnival approached, the King had gone to the theatre with his confessor to decide to whom the boxes should be given. The Loyalists received the best treatment, though the first-floor boxes could only be obtained every day by those of high birth in addition to sound political opinions. The second-rate nobility were admitted to the second tier, and the minor nobles struggled with the upper commercial classes for the remaining boxes. At the same time, to get the third or the fourth of a box in the third tier, some aristocratic connection was indispensable.

While this list was being composed, the confessor was the centre of an infinite number of intrigues, and the publication of the list gave rise to complaints no less numerous. This fact will be understood if it is remembered that individual jealousies and their interaction were thus published every evening for six weeks. Therefore, the fury and the anger of people who for twenty years had lived on an equal par with the nobility, and who suddenly found themselves degraded to membership of a class excluded from the only pleasure of the country, may be understood.

I was surprised at the fact that a woman of noble birth who had married a commoner received better consideration in the distribution of the boxes than the wife of a noble who was herself a commoner. I suppose the regulation was made in the interest of girls of high birth who have no kind of fortune in Piedmont, and am the more inclined to believe it, as I have heard the statement that a girl brought the right to half a box as one of her advantages in a proposed marriage.

When the list had been revised, discussed, and corrected, it was confirmed, and a magnificent official letter was despatched, signed by the King and sealed with his arms, informing the recipient that a certain box, in part or in its entirety, was assigned to him, and that he could send for the key. To get the key it was then necessary to pay a sum quite as large as that charged by any other theatre in Europe. It was necessary, moreover, to have the box furnished, to paper it and put in curtains and chairs, for the key merely provided admission to an empty kennel with dirty walls. Thus there was a fine windfall for the King's upholsterer.

After this expense a further payment was made at the doors for entrance into the theatre. However, the rate was comparatively moderate; hence a stranger invited to be present at a performance was obliged to pay for his ticket. In spite, or perhaps in consequence, of all these formalities, the opening of the grand Opera was an event of the utmost importance. On the morning of the day the whole population was in a ferment, and in the evening the doors were thronged by so huge a crowd that, notwithstanding all our ambassadorial privileges, my mother and I were almost crushed upon our arrival.

The theatre itself was sufficiently handsome: the chandelier had been left in place provisionally and provided adequate illumination, though the enthusiasts of the Ancien Régime objected that it tarnished the splendour of the "crown." By the "crown" was meant the King's box. This was a little drawing-room at the back of the theatre. Two rows of boxes high, with the width of nearly five boxes, it was highly decorated with hangings and gold fringe, and brilliantly lighted by clusters of candles. Before the innovation of a chandelier the theatre had depended upon the royal box for its light.

The box of the French Ambassador was always opposite that of the Prince of Carignan, in the best possible place. An attempt would have been made to take it from the Ambassador of a constitutional king, but no effort of the kind was ventured, as my father himself had intimated that he would be forced to regard deprivation as an affront. Nor could he act otherwise, in view of the importance popularly attached to this privilege.

The performance was as it is everywhere in Italy: two good singers were surrounded by detestable supernumeraries, so that there was no kind of uniformity in the performance. It was, however, quite satisfactory to people who only went to the theatre for purposes of conversation. They listened to two or three pieces, and chattered the rest of the time as if they were in the street; the pit, where people stood, became a promenade when there was room. A detestable ballet aroused transports of admiration, and the scenery was little better than the dancing.

Young married women await the opening of the Opera with great interest, as they generally live with their mothers-in-law, and therefore are unable to receive callers in their own home. At the theatre their box becomes their home, and they can admit whom they will. Men of the lower nobility can converse with the ladies of the upper nobility, who would not be able to see them in their townhouses. One often hears the phrase, "So-and-so is one of my theatre friends," and Mr. So-and-So appears quite happy with this connection, which is said to become intimate at times and never claims to pass the threshold of the lady's house. The custom of "attendant cavaliers" has fallen into disuse. If any of the fraternity are left, they refuse to be as disinterested as they used to be, and except for the fact that they are more public, these intimacies are no more innocent than elsewhere.

The custom in Piedmont is to marry children without giving them any fortune. The girls have a dowry so small that it can barely suffice for their personal expenditure; moreover, it is always paid to the father-in-law, who defrays the expenses of the young household, but provides no income.

I have seen Count Tancred di Barolo, the only son of a father who had an income of twenty thousand pounds, obliged to go to him to settle the expenses of a carriage to take his wife to the waters. The Marquis di Barolo went into long calculations as to the amount necessary for the journey, and the proposed visit, after which he readily provided the funds. If his daughter-in-law expressed a desire to see her apartments refurnished, architects and upholsterers came in and repairs were completed in magnificent style. But she would not have been able to buy a seven-and-sixpenny table which might have struck her fancy. She had full permission to import all the Paris fashions and the bills were always met without the slightest protestations. In a word, the Marquis di Barolo refused nothing to his children except their independence. I learnt these details because the lady was a Frenchwoman, Mlle. de Colbert, and was somewhat vexed by this custom, which was, however, general. As long as the parents were alive, the children remained members of the family in the full sense of the term, though attempts were made to satisfy their desires as far as existing fortunes would allow.

The Marquis di Barolo, of whom I have just spoken, was a senator and an assiduous courtier of the Emperor. While the latter was staying at Turin, the Marquis made vigorous remonstrances to him about the fact that he was paying extraordinary taxes to the extent of five thousand louis.

"Dear me," said the Emperor, "are you really paying five thousand louis?"

"Yes, Sire, not a halfpenny less, as I can prove to your Majesty. Here are the papers."

"No, no, that is quite unnecessary; I believe you, and I compliment you warmly upon the fact."

The Marquis di Barolo was obliged to be content with these words.

The ladies of Piedmont take such delight in the theatre that their attendance is regular, though no longer obligatory, as before the Revolution. When a woman was away from the Opera for two consecutive days the King used to send to inquire the reasons for her absence, and if her excuse was thought inadequate she was reprimanded.

Nothing upon the whole was so despotic as this so-called paternal Government, especially as regarded the nobility. The nobility were, indeed, often permitted to repudiate debts which they had contracted with commoners, which fact, by the way, so raised the rate of interest upon loans that many families were ruined in consequence; on the other hand, the Government decided in what way a man's revenue should be expended. Some were told to build a castle, others to found a chapel, another to give concerts, another to give balls, etc.

The Government fixed the residence of every man in such province or town as might be found convenient. To go abroad, it was necessary to ask the special permission of the King, which was never immediately given, and only for a very limited time. A stay of greater or less length in the fortress of Fenestrelle would have been the result of the slightest disobedience, while if absence abroad were prolonged beyond the limits imposed, the property of the absentee might be confiscated without further ado.

The Marquis del Borgo, one of the richest lords of Piedmont, so greatly suffered from rheumatism that he had established himself at

Pisa, being unable to bear the climate of Turin. When King Victor Amedée built the square of Saint-Charles, a *biglietto regio* ordered the Marquis to buy one of the sides of the square and construct an arcade. Shortly afterwards a new *biglietto regio* ordered the construction of a magnificent residence, plans of which were provided; then came orders to decorate it, and then to furnish it with royal magnificence, room by room. Eventually a final *biglietto regio* intimated that the owner of so fine a residence ought to live in it, and permission to remain abroad was withdrawn. The Marquis returned to Turin in a fury, and established himself in a servant's room at the end of his magnificent reception room, which he refused ever to see, but which was crossed morning and evening by the she-goat who provided him with milk; and this was the only female that ever went up the grand staircase as long as the old Marquis was alive. His children had been left in the old family residence.

I have visited his daughter-in-law when she was settled in this residence in the square of Saint-Charles; it was a remarkably fine house. She was a strong opponent of the formalities of the Sardinian sovereigns, for the reason that when she was very young, and was present at a court ball, Queen Clotilde had sent a maid of honour across the room with a pin to fasten her fichu, which the Queen thought was too wide open.

The Marchioness del Borgo, sister of the Marquis de Saint-Marsan, was witty, sarcastic, and cynical, but amusing and amiable. She was, however, of little use to us, as she had every reason to fear the result of any familiarity with us.

The conduct of the ladies of Piedmont is as a rule very far from strict. It is possible, however, that foreigners exaggerate their wrong-doing, for they proclaim their intimacies with that careless effrontery of Italian manners which we find so objectionable. The husbands seem to raise no obstacle, and to trouble themselves but little in such matters. This marital philosophy is common to all classes beyond the Alps. I remember a story told by Ménageot, the painter. When he was director of costumes at the Paris Opera, he went in one day to old Vestris

and found him trying to console a young dancer and fellow country-
man, whose wife, a pretty and lively member of the ballet, was giving
him great anxiety. After the commonplace phrases appropriate to calm
the fury of the stage Othello, Vestris added in his half-Italian jargon:

"Well, you see, my friend, in our profession growing horns is like
cutting teeth: it's the devil of a business to cut them, but one gets used
to them by degrees, and eventually one eats with them."

Vestris asserted that this advice had speedily proved efficacious.

As long as the Opera season lasts calls are neither given nor returned.
This is a greater advantage for the reason that at Turin social custom
permits only evening calls. The mansions are not provided with door-
keepers nor the staircases with lights. The servant who follows you
holds a lantern with which he escorts you to the first, second, or third
floor of a vast house in which the titled proprietor occupies a small corner, the remainder being let, often to financial grandees. It is necessary
to appear at his door in person. To sit in one's carriage and send to inquire if the occupant is at home is regarded as rude.

Ladies, however, are rarely at home to visitors in Turin. The style
of dress in which they are to be found and the arrangement both of
their rooms and of their persons show that they are not ready to receive
society. An exception must be made in the case of some houses which
were always open, those, for instance, of del Borgo, Barolo, Bins,
Masin, et cetera.

We were not very regular attendants at the theatre and often spent
many quiet evenings at home. Our greatest resource was Count and
Countess Balbe. The Count was one of those distinguished men to
whom I have referred above. His deep learning in every department did
not prevent him from being a witty, amiable, and lively companion in
the ordinary intercourse of life. The Emperor had placed him at the
head of the University. Public confidence had appointed him chief of
the provisional government which had been formed between the departure of the French and the arrival of the King. He had so entirely secured popular favour that no attempt was made to enforce his complete

retirement, and he had remained director of public education with a seat on the council, to which, however, he was only summoned for special reasons or discussions, for instance, upon ornithological museums! He was far removed from any childish fear of the consequence of any kindness shown by him to us, and we saw him daily. His wife was a Frenchwoman, kind, lively, and amusing; she was a cousin of M. de Maurepas and had known my parents at Versailles, and her intimacy with us soon became established.

The Cavour family also numbered among our intimate friends. They were too deeply compromised already to have any reason for prudence; the mother had been a lady of honour to the Princess Borghese, and the son marshal of the palace and the Prince's friend. His wife's sister had married a Frenchman who had certainly solved a great problem. M. d'Auzers, director of the police during the French administration, not only gave entire satisfaction to his superiors, but had become so popular throughout the country that protests were universal when the King wished to drive him out with the other French officials in Piedmont. He remained at Turin on excellent terms with everybody, and eventually acquired great influence in the Government, and since my departure I have heard that he became one of its leading members.

We also knew, though less intimately, the Countess Masin, a highly distinguished intellect: she had been brought up by her uncle the Abbé Caluso, the celebrated astronomer, whose name is familiar to every learned man in Europe. These names, together with the diplomatic body, formed the basis of our social circle.

The Prince de Carignan was delighted when his tutor brought him to our house. Hardly had he escaped from a boarding-school at Geneva, where he enjoyed a schoolboy's freedom, when he was subjected to the stricter life of a Prince of Piedmont, though the authorities hesitated to proclaim him heir to the Crown. To secure this recognition formed part of my father's instructions; he worked zealously to this end, and the young Prince regarded him as his protector and used to tell him all his vexations.

Of these, one of the chief irritants was the exaggerated precautions which were taken to preserve his life and personal safety, and the constraint which this care imposed upon him. For instance, he was only allowed to ride a horse in his garden between two equerries and under the eye of his doctor and his confessor.

This confessor dogged his every footstep, was with him when he went to bed and when he rose, and at every meal made him say his prayers; in short, he did his best to exorcise the demon which had presumably entered into the soul of the Prince during his stay in those two accursed places, Paris and Geneva. However, instead of securing the confidence of the Prince, he had merely succeeded in persuading him that he was a spy and reported his every action to the King's confessor, who had placed him in attendance upon the Prince.

While sympathising with his misfortunes, my father urged patience and prudence. He understood that a young man of sixteen who had hitherto been brought up in the enjoyment of almost exaggerated liberty, for his mother troubled herself very little about him, must feel the irksomeness of so complete a change in his life. M. de Saluces, his tutor, was greatly attached to the Prince, who trusted him and also Count Balbe, one of his guardians. When he found himself at my father's house, with only these men and ourselves about him, his happiness was inexpressible. He was already very tall for his age, with a handsome face. He lived all alone in the immense palace of Carignan, which had been given up to him. He had not yet gained possession of his property, so that he lived uncomfortably, with much privation, and indeed it was difficult to meet the very small expenses of his establishment.

The King was very little better off. The palace had been left furnished, but the necessary utensils belonging to Prince Borghese had been taken away by him, so that the King found nothing upon his arrival. For a long time he used china, linen, crockery, horses, and carriages borrowed from the nobles of Piedmont. I do not know how expenses were paid.

Negotiations to secure the recognition of the Prince de Carignan had been concluded, but the influence of Austria and the intrigues of the Duke of Modena, the King's son-in-law, still prevented any announcement of the fact. One day when there was a court reception my father's carriage happened by arrangement to cross that of the Prince de Carignan; my father pulled the check string, and gave the Prince the right of way. The French Ambassador had right of precedence over the Prince de Carignan. This concession therefore announced the Prince as heir to the Crown, and forced the declaration which the King personally desired. The gratitude of the Prince was extreme.

The diplomatic body included Mr. Hill for England, a pleasant companion, though gloomy and a hypochondriac; he rarely emerged from a seclusion which made his position somewhat equivocal. There was also Prince Koslovski for Russia, an intelligent and well-informed man, but so unprincipled as to be useless for social purposes. The other embassies were still unoccupied, though Austria was represented by Count Bubna, a General of the army of occupation which had been left in Piedmont. His position was thus both diplomatic and military. It is harder to imagine a man of greater intelligence or one able to tell a story with greater wit and attraction. He had recently married a young German of Jewish birth, who was not received in Vienna society. Hence he desired to remain abroad. His wife was a pretty and by no means unintelligent woman, and the best company in the world. She spent her time at our house. She was greatly bored in Turin, though at the time she was much in love with her husband, who treated her like a child and gave her a ball once a week at the expense of the town of Turin. His military position implied full indemnity for all diplomatic expenses, and he denied himself nothing.

Upon several occasions he had been sent to negotiate with the Emperor Napoleon when the Austrian monarchy was in its most critical condition, and he used to give very amusing accounts of the details of these dealings. I much regret that I cannot recall them with sufficient exactitude to narrate them here. He used to speak of the Emperor with extreme admiration, and to say it was easy to deal with him as man to man, though difficult when it became a question of Empire to Empire.

The truth is that Napoleon appreciated and was fond of Bubna, and had given him several marks of his esteem. Approbation thus highly prized was a great means of seduction. In any case, the fact remains that I have often sat up until one o'clock in the morning listening to Bubna's stories of Bonaparte.

Bubna also had a reputation as an expert pillager, an idea by no means refuted by the dexterity with which he tapped the resources of the town of Turin, though peace had been long established; hence he desired to maintain the military occupation as long as possible. My father, on the contrary, supported the Sardinian authorities, who were anxious to be relieved of this occupation. This business opposition never altered our social relations, as the General was too sensible not to keep business in its proper place. We always remained upon intimate and friendly terms. At length the Austrian troops were withdrawn and Count Bubna remained as Minister, pending the arrival of Prince Stahrenberg, who was to take his place.

I may be doing the people of Piedmont an injustice when I assert that the town of Turin is the gloomiest and most boring place of residence in the whole universe. I have already pointed out various circumstances which contributed to make it disagreeable for people in general and for ourselves in particular during the period of my stay. It must also be remembered that after the excitement, the animation, and the dramatic intensity of the two years 1813 and 1814, which I had spent at the one centre where events were most strongly felt, I had come to this capital, with its sadness and its monotony, to hear daily discussions on the question of the chandelier; therefore it will be understood that I might well feel some unjustified prejudice against the town.

The town of Turin is regularly laid out and the streets run in parallel lines, but the arcades which decorate the chief thoroughfares give them a deserted appearance, and the carriages are not sufficiently numerous to replace the lack of pedestrian traffic. The exteriors of the houses are handsome. A Venetian used to say that in his country the inhabitants wore masks, but that here the town itself was masked. The metaphor is entirely exact, for these beautiful frontages usually veil dreadful hovels with labyrinths of apartments inconveniently placed and poorly furnished. It is indeed astonishing to find so much poverty behind the screen of these architectural designs. In any case it is difficult to appreciate their merit because of the condition into which they are allowed to fall.

Under the pretext that repairs will be required some day, and that the solidity of the buildings might be injured by the construction of new scaffoldings, the holes originally made in the walls have never been filled up, so that every wall, including those of the King's palace, is riddled with square holes. Each of these holes provides a habitation for a family of jackdaws, which form a black cloud in every street and make a terrific uproar throughout the town. To the unaccustomed eye nothing is sadder than the appearance and the cries of these birds.

As regards one's domestic life, the rooms that can be procured do not compensate for the ennui of life outside. So few strangers stop at Turin that it is difficult to find a lodging. The fine palaces are occupied by their owners or let for long periods, and the diplomatic body have the greatest trouble in finding suitable residence. Comfort is not to be considered.

My father had taken the house of the Marquis Alfieri, then Ambassador at Paris, as he had been assured that it was laid out and arranged in the French style. It is true that it did not possess the enormous *sala* of the Piedmont palaces, and that every room had paned windows. But my room, for instance, was also fronted by a long stucco gallery; there were no means of lighting a fire, and though furnished with beautiful crimson damask, it was paved, not with flagged stones like a moderately respectable kitchen, but with cut blocks like the Paris streets. At the head of my bed a door led through an open balcony and communicated with my maid's room. My mother was little better off, and my father even worse, for his room was still larger and gloomier.

The English Minister had a superb palace, the architecture of which was remarkable and greatly admired; this was the palace Morozzi, which happily possessed the *sala* of which the Piedmontese think so much. This *sala* occupied the centre of the house from top to bottom, so that on the first floor communication was made by outer galleries which the architect had been careful to leave open, that they might be sufficiently light. Poor Mr. Hill had offered to have them closed with window panes at his own expense, but the whole town was horrified at this mark of Britannic barbarism. In order to avoid the rigours of these outside passages, he had eventually established himself in three little rooms just below the first floor, the only apartments in the building which could be heated. This was all the more necessary as winter in Turin is long and cold. For several weeks I have seen the thermometer between ten and fifteen degrees below zero, and the inhabitants did not seem surprised or inconvenienced by this temperature, notwithstanding the scantiness of their means to address it.

The Congress of Vienna presented the King of Sardinia with the state of Genoa. Notwithstanding our role in providing this important accession to his territory, the King remained no less irritated with France than before, on account of our retaining Savoy. The remarkable point is that King Louis XVIII was no less vexed by this question than the King of Sardinia, and was sincerely anxious to return Savoy to him. He seemed to regard himself as a receiver of stolen property. My father did not share the scruples of his sovereign, and was very anxious that France should retain that part of Savoy which the treaties of 1814 had left to her.

When the deputies of Genoa came to do homage from their state to the King of Sardinia, he requested Count Valese, Minister of Foreign Affairs, to give them a dinner. The diplomatic body was invited. Throughout the previous fortnight this dinner was an object of anxiety throughout the town, which discussed the origin of the fish, the game, and the cooks. The accessories were collected with infinite pains and trouble, recourse being had to the kindness of the court nobles and especially of the ambassadors. The manner in which the candles of one harmonised with the plate of another furnished a keenly interesting topic of conversation for several evenings.

At length the day of the festival arrived, and twenty of us sat down. The dinner was quite magnificent and well served. Notwithstanding the ornamentation, which made me fear some ridiculous result, nothing of the kind occurred. Count Valese did the honours with the easy manner of a born noble. The weariness and monotony which overwhelms the inhabitants of Turin induces them to eagerly grasp at anything resembling an event. This was the sole occasion on which I have seen any of the members of the diplomatic body invited to dinner at a Piedmont house.

Strangers, as I have said, were little inclined to stop at Turin: there is nothing to see, the society is not attractive, and the inns are bad. We saw Jules de Polignac for a moment on his way to Rome, where he had been sent by Monsieur. I believe the point at issue was the existence of the Jesuits and especially of the Congregation,[1] which had already been extending its ramifications throughout France under the name of the "Little Church." It was upon hostile terms with the Pope, Pius VII, as it had never been willing to recognise the Concordat[2] or the bishops appointed in consequence of that agreement. It was expecting that the persecution which it had inflicted upon the prelates whose investiture the Pope had refused during his discussions with the Emperor would compensate for its original disobedience.

It was hoped that the Pope should recognise the bishops who were entitled to sees previous to the Concordat and who had not resigned, and that they should retain their rights. Jules was on his way to negotiate this transaction. The Pope was probably extremely discreet, for Jules was highly dissatisfied upon his return from Rome. He had, however, secured his nomination as Prince of Rome, a matter of no great difficulty.

His stay at Turin was prolonged for a considerable time. The Jesuits

1. The Congregation was a religious association founded in 1801. Banned by Napoleon, it was reconstituted in 1814 and regrouped ultras of all wakes. Its different provincial branches made it a very powerful and secretive opposition. It was disbanded in 1830.
2. The Concordat was a treaty signed in 1801 between Bonaparte and Pope Pius VII. It imposed the resignation of *émigré* bishops and increased the authority of the State over the Church.

were beginning to grow powerful in that town, and he used their influence to secure his appointment as Chevalier de Saint-Maurice. I have never been able to understand why a man of his title and in his position should have been anxious to secure this scrap of ribbon.

The Order of the Annonciade is one of the most illustrious and exclusive in Europe; it includes none but full members, styled excellencies. The King of Sardinia creates excellencies as elsewhere a sovereign may create dukes or princes, with the exception that the title is never hereditary. Certain posts as well as the Collar of the Annonciade give the right to this title. It implies all the distinctions and privileges that can be enjoyed in the country. I can understand that such a distinction might be desired, though it can have but little advantage to offer a foreigner. However, the little cross of Saint-Maurice can be met at every turn in the street, and seemed to me a strange ambition for Jules. When, however, a man with the title of M. de Polignac is willing to become a Prince of the Pope, there can be no limit to his childish vanities. This fact, however, did not prevent him from conceiving higher ambitions.

Accustomed as we were to his absurdities, he still retained the capacity of rousing our astonishment. The young men of the embassy were amazed at the theories which he supported with considerable eloquence, it must be admitted, but with a total lack of common sense. One day he informed us that he was very anxious to be nominated Minister by the King, not, he added, because he thought himself cleverer than others, but because nothing was easier than to govern France. He would impose only one condition upon the King: he would demand that for ten years he should be guaranteed the portfolios of Foreign Affairs, of War, of the Interior, of Finance, and, in particular, of the Police. With these five departments exclusively in his hands he would be responsible for everything without the smallest trouble to himself.

Upon another occasion he said that since France was anxious for a constitution, she ought to be given one which was broad and satisfactory to the most Liberal opinions; that the constitution should be read before the Chamber, and that the reader should then place it upon the tribune and add:

"You have heard the reading of this constitution which ought to suit you; it remains for you to show yourselves worthy of it. Preserve peace for ten years, and it shall be published, but every revolutionary movement, however feeble, will delay for one year the moment which we desire no less than yourselves." Meanwhile, "Io el rey!" he would continually cry aloud with his hand upon a great sword which he dragged about after him. As the King's aide-de-camp, though, he had never seen a pistol fired or commanded a man, he was in uniform as often as possible.

The conversation turned one evening upon the bad feeling prevalent in Dauphiné,[3] which was attributed to the large numbers of those who had acquired the property of exiles. M. de Polignac declared:

"That is the fault of the Government. I have proposed a very simple means of solving this difficulty. I have guaranteed its infallibility, but no one will use it."

"What is this means?" I asked him.

"I have offered to lead a flying column of ten thousand men, to establish myself successively in each province, to drive out the new owners and to reinstate the former proprietors with a force in every case too great to permit any hopes of resistance. It could be done easily without the least uproar, and everybody would be satisfied."

"But, my dear Jules, you can hardly expect the new owners whom you are expropriating to be satisfied."

"Oh, dear me, yes, for they will always be worried."

These stupidities would be hardly worthy of mention were it not for the deplorable notoriety which the poor Prince de Polignac acquired at so high a cost. I could cite a long list of these incidents, but these will suffice to show the tendencies of his narrow mind.

My father had been ordered to keep an eye on the movements of the Bonapartists who were scattered about Italy, and upon their communica-

3. A province of France situated in the Alps.

tions with the island of Elba. For this purpose he had employed an English doctor called Marshall, whom the Prince Regent of England had sent to Italy to gather information concerning the conduct of his wife, who was something more than indiscreet.

In 1799 this Marshall had brought vaccine to Italy; he had been at Naples at the moment when the court exacted its cruel vengeance after its return from its exile in Palermo in the ships of Admiral Nelson. At that time he was young, and had been justifiably disgusted by the spectacle of these horrors. Hence he had availed himself of his English nationality and of the freedom which his doctor's profession allowed him to do many kindnesses to the victims of this Royalist reaction. Since that time he had remained in close connection with the revolutionary party, and had every opportunity for learning their projects without participating in their plots.

One night in January 1815 he came to my father with great secrecy, and showed him documents which proved almost beyond doubt that a movement was being prepared in France, and that the Emperor Napoleon was intending shortly to leave the island of Elba to give his personal support to the movement. My father was convinced of the gravity of this news, and urged Marshall to communicate with the French Government. He refused to impart his information to any Minister. According to him, the offices of every Minister were surrounded by Bonapartists, and he feared for his personal safety.

M. de Talleyrand had been temporarily replaced by M. de Jaucourt, who never answered any despatches; correspondence was conducted from the offices, and was purely official. My father could not have known to what Minister he should refer Marshall, who, moreover, refused to submit the documents he had secured to anyone except the King himself. He prided himself upon his personal connection with the Prince Regent, and it would seem that the lofty station of his employers dignified in his eyes the somewhat dishonourable traffic which he pursued. The importance of his revelations justified his obstinacy on this point.

My father gave him a letter to the Duc de Duras, who introduced him in the study of Louis XVIII on January 22. The King sent his thanks to my father for the zeal which had procured this precious information. No special precautions, however, were taken, and the Government did not even send a corvette to cruise off the island of Elba. The carelessness prevalent at this time was far in advance of the credulity of other years.

I have just said that my father had received no despatches from the Minister of Foreign Affairs. I was wrong: he received one despatch demanding Piedmont truffles for the King; it was four pages in length, and went into the minutest details concerning the manner of their transport with rapidity and certainty. Prince Talleyrand kept him, indeed, fairly well informed of the proceedings of the Congress, but as he was resident at Vienna, he could neither learn nor communicate any news from France.

Towards the end of February the court moved to Genoa to receive the Queen, who was expected from Sardinia. The diplomatic body followed the court. We left the valley of Turin and of Alexandria beneath the snows which had covered it since the month of November, and reached the summit of the Bocchetta. This route is no longer used. The mountain of the Bocchetta is remarkable for the fact that there is no level at the top, and a carriage has no sooner completed the ascent than the horses have begun to descend the other side.

At the time of year when we were travelling, this fact was all the more striking because we passed directly from midwinter to late spring. Upon one side the mountain was covered with snow, the streams were frozen, and the waterfalls displayed their stalactites of ice. On the other side of the mountain the trees were in bloom or in leaf, the grass was green, the streams were murmuring, the birds twittering, while nature seemed to be making holiday and anxious to obliterate the sad impressions which had overwhelmed the mind a quarter of a minute before. I have rarely experienced a more delightful impression.

After a rapid drive of several hours across delightful country, we reached Genoa on February 26, 1815. The streets were carpeted with flowers, never have I seen so many, and the weather was delightful: I forgot the fatigues of the journey and its toilsome beginning.

On getting out of the carriage I took a walk in these sweet-smelling streets, clean and well-flagged and far pleasanter to the foot than the floor of my paved room in Turin. I found them filled with a cheerful, animated, and busy population, strongly contrasting with the dirty and listless inhabitants I had just left. The women with their silken shoes and their heads covered with the becoming *mezzaro* delighted me, and the children seemed charming.

The whole of Genoese society was also in the streets, and in five minutes we were surrounded by forty acquaintances. I suddenly felt that the leaden cloak which a six months' stay in Turin had fastened to my shoulders was now raised. My joy was, however, somewhat calmed by the one hundred and fifty steps which I was forced to climb in order to reach the pleasant rooms in a great palace which had been reserved for the French Ambassador.

During my stay at Genoa the only inconveniences were the height of the staircases and the unexampled importunity of the beggars. I shall not repeat what everybody knows concerning the magnificence and beauty of the palaces, nor shall I say anything concerning the customs of the country, for I had no opportunity of observing these; a few days after our arrival political events obliged our retirement, and I saw little or nothing of society.

The Genoese took no pains to hide their objection to the reunion with Piedmont and their dislike for the King. Few of them came to the court, and they were regarded with disapproval by their countrymen. Their vexation was the keener as they had expected emancipation for some time.

Lord William Bentinck, the commander-in-chief of the British troops in Italy, attracted by the fair eyes of la Luisa Durazzo, as they say in Genoa, had authorised by his silence if not by his words the reestablishment of the former Government during his occupation of the town. The acts by which the Congress settled the fate of the Genoese seemed to them the more cruel in consequence. Master for master, they preferred a great man to the good King Victor, and if they were no longer to be Genoese, they would rather be French than Piedmontese. The decision of Vienna had made them violent Bonapartists, and the rivers of Genoa were a special starting point for correspondence with the is-land of Elba.

The English army, before handing over the town to the Sardinian authorities, had dismantled the public works and carried off every-thing from the harbour, down to the chains of the galley slaves. This outrage had exasperated Genoese sentiments of nationality.

The day following our arrival we were invited to a demonstration which an English commodore was giving to the King. He was to be shown the effect of Congreve rockets, a new invention at this time. We all went on foot, in admirable weather, to a little plateau upon a rock some furlongs from the town, whence there was a magnificent view. An old ship, moored out at sea so far as to be hardly visible to the naked eye, served as a target. A sea breeze was blowing which spoiled the rocket display, but cooled the air and made it delightful. The spec-tacle was animated upon the coast and brilliant in the harbour on our right, crowded with ships in full dress.

The firing was interrupted by the danger of striking two little ships apparently stranded by the wind. Evidently they did not wish to land, and were tacking to get out to sea; eventually they succeeded, and firing practice was resumed. In view of the facts which we after-wards learnt, there is no doubt that these two brigs were carrying Bo-naparte and his fortunes to the shores of Cannes. Had one of these rock-ets chanced to strike these boats, how great a change might have been made in the destiny of the world!

The commodore gave a well-appointed lunch served under a tent, and the company parted, well pleased with their morning's amuse-ment.

I remember the Princess Grassalcowics came to finish the day with us. I had long been intimate with her. She was sailing the next day for Livorno. During the evening we talked of the want of news, the mo-notony of the papers, and wondered whether it was worthwhile living merely to wait another fortnight for a wretched protocol of the Congress of Vienna. Half-seriously, half-jestingly, we regretted the agitations and the excitement of the previous years; life seemed to us monotonous when no great movement was in progress.

My mother observed:

"This is young ladies' talk; let me advise you not to tempt Providence. When you are as old as I, you will know that these peaceful moments which you are so childish as to call wearisome never last long."

Three days afterwards the Princess returned to Genoa, as she had been unable to disembark at Livorno, and before a hasty return to Vienna she came to our house with a downcast face and said:

"Ah, dear Lady Ambassador, you were right, and I ask your pardon for my foolishness; I am greatly ashamed of myself."

I might have shared her remorse, as I had shared her fault.

While we were at a concert my father was called away; a message was waiting for him despatched by the French consul at Livorno announcing the departure of Bonaparte from Porto-Ferrajo. My father immediately proceeded to inform the authorities. He despatched a courier to M. de Talleyrand at Vienna, and another to Paris; then he sent a secretary from the embassy to take the news to Masséna, with orders to warn all the authorities upon the coast as he went. This precaution was nullified by the rapidity of the Emperor's movements. A few hours after his departure from Genoa, M. de Château, Second Secretary to our Embassy, was crossing the bivouac at Cannes, which had been already abandoned though the fires were still burning. We spent the night copying letters and despatches which were entrusted to these various couriers.

The excitement was great the following morning. It was expected that the Emperor would disembark at some point of Italy and join the troops of Murat,* who had been raising forces for some time. The Austrians were not in a position to offer resistance; General Bubna was most uneasy, and reproached the Piedmont authorities for their anxiety to secure German evacuation before they had time to form a national army. Count Valese, on the other hand, asserted that the expenses of the occupation absorbed all the revenues of the state, and that military organisation was impossible as long as the occupation continued.

Lord William Bentinck arrived in great haste. People looked at one another, expressed their anxiety and disquietude and uttered mutual reproaches, but in view of the general uncertainty concerning the Emperor's disembarkation, it was impossible to decide any line of action or to issue any orders. General Bubna was the first to receive instructions; thereupon the Austrians, the English, and the Piedmontese were somewhat reassured, and thought they had time to look around.

Bubna demanded permission to march his troops into Piedmont. Count Valese obstinately refused, and the General was obliged to quarter them upon the frontier of Lombardy; he also issued a formal declaration that he would remain behind the Po, leaving Piedmont unprotected, if the Neapolitan army should advance. The Sardinian Government persisted in its attitude, and soon conceived the strange idea that it might be able to secure its neutrality from Napoleon and from Murat. The relations of my father with the Government were afterwards affected by this delusion. The Sardinian Ambassador was the only representative who did not join King Louis XVIII at Ghent.

M. de Château returned bringing the fairest promises from Masséna. He had seen Mme. Bertrand arrested upon her arrival from the island of Elba, and had observed everywhere as much enthusiasm for the Duc d'Angoulême as indignation against the Emperor. This news was correct, as far as Provence was concerned and for the time being. Very different news was brought in on the wings of the wind. With astonishing rapidity and by unknown channels, we learnt the success of the rapid march of Bonaparte.

One morning a French officer wearing the white cockade came to my father and handed him a dispatch from General Marchand,* which was too insignificant to have been the true reason for his appearance. He was greatly agitated and demanded an immediate reply, as the General had to arrange the moment for his return. My father urged him to go and rest for a few hours. While he was trying to find the answer to this riddle, which was the more difficult to discover, as the rumour had gone abroad that General Marchand, commander of the Department of Isère, had recognised the Emperor, General Bubna came in and said:

"My dear Ambassador, I have to thank you for the care with which you have paid the postage of my letters. I know that fifty louis have been asked of you for the letter which I have here. It is from General Bertrand, who writes to me on Napoleon's orders, bidding me to send off immediately by courier these despatches to Vienna for the Emperor and for Marie-Louise. I am never in a great hurry, and shall wait quietly for a favourable opportunity. What do you propose to do with your young man?"

My father thought for a moment, and concluded that to have him arrested would be too serious a step. He summoned him from his inn, requested him to leave immediately, warning him that if he gave the Sardinian Government time to learn the manner in which he had crossed the frontier, he would be arrested as a spy, and no Ambassador could attempt to save him. The officer was imprudent enough to say that he would have to stop at Turin, where he had letters to deliver. My father advised him to burn them, and gave him a passport prescribing a route which would carry him away from Turin. I have heard nothing more of this gentleman, who had the audacity after this explanation to ask my father for the fifty louis which General Marchand in his supposed letter had requested him to hand the messenger for travelling expenses.

Bubna kept the secret sufficiently long enough to secure the safety of the messenger. At that moment he might have been in a critical situation, for the pacific tendencies of the Sardinian Government were then nonexistent, while its horror at the Bonapartist leanings of the Piedmontese had been raised to the highest pitch.

The declaration of March 13[4] was sent to my father by M. de Talleyrand as soon as it had been signed by the sovereigns assembled at Vienna. My father had it printed without delay, and three hours after its arrival my brother started off to carry it to the Duc d'Angou-

4. A declaration in which the Allied Powers declared Napoleon to be the perturber of European peace.

lême, whom he found at Nîmes. So great had been the speed of its delivery that the effect of the document was somewhat impaired, and
doubts were cast upon its authenticity. The Duc d'Angoulême kept my
brother with him, and appointed him his aide-de-camp. Shortly afterwards he sent him into Spain to ask for help which he did not secure.
In any case, had this help been granted, it would have arrived too late.

In view of my system of noting the smallest circumstances which
in my opinion throw any light upon character, I feel obliged to relate
one incident, puerile as it may seem. My brother, as I have said, had
brought to the Duc d'Angoulême a document of the highest importance, and had displayed an energy which proved the extent of his
zeal. Everywhere he had scattered copies of the declaration along his
road, without inquiring into the political opinions of the persons to
whom he handed them, a proceeding not entirely without danger. The
Duc d'Angoulême knew this, and seemed well pleased with him; he
invited him to lunch. Rainulphe dressed himself as well as a man could
who had just ridden a hundred leagues, and accepted the invitation.

Hardly had they sat down when the Duc d'Angoulême began:

"What uniform are you wearing?"

"That of a staff officer, my lord."

"To whom are you aide-de-camp?"

"To my father, my lord."

"Your father is only a Lieutenant-General; why then are you wearing a shoulder-knot? Only the King's family and the families of the
Princes have any right to them, though they are permitted in the case of
marshals, you are wrong to wear one."

"I did not know it, my lord."

"Now that you know, you must take it off at once. In strict justice
you should be arrested, but I will excuse you. Do not let me see it
again."

It will be understood how greatly a young man such as Rainulphe
then was would be disconcerted by so public a rebuke. The Duc d'Angoulême would occasionally grow excited to the point of anger upon
small matters of military detail, and delude himself with the idea that
he was a great General.

The King of Sardinia announced that he was proposing to go to Turin. His Ministers and General Bubna accompanied him. The English Minister remained at Genoa with my father, who was more easily able to communicate from there with the Duc d'Angoulême in the south of France. We soon witnessed the arrival of all the public figures who had been driven out of the south of Italy by the movements of the Neapolitan army. The Pope, Pius VII, was the first one, and was lodged in the King's palace. I had not seen him since the time when he came to the coronation of the Emperor Napoleon; we went several times to pay our respects to him. He talked willingly and familiarly upon all subjects. I was especially touched by the calm and dignified manner in which he referred to his years of exile, to which he seemed to attach neither glory nor merit; he appeared to regard it as a circumstance which had unfortunately been inevitable and regretted that his duty had driven him to force Napoleon to the wrongdoing of persecuting a Pope. His discourses were characterised by a noble and fatherly moderation which must have been inspired from on high, for upon other subjects he was by no means as distinguished. One felt that he was a man who was beginning again a career filled with tribulations which would lead him to neither bitterness nor to exaltation. The word "serenity" seemed to be invented especially for him, and he inspired me with a very sincere veneration for him.

Shortly afterwards he was followed by the Infanta Marie-Louise, Duchess of Lucca, and better known by her title of Queen of Etruria. Genoa was crowded, and as she could not find a suitable lodging, she established herself in a large room in an inn, where with the aid of screens a sleeping apartment was constructed for all her family. She appeared to be in complete harmony with this dingy apartment. I have rarely seen a more vulgar personage than this Princess, and her conversation was no better than her appearance. As she was a Bourbon, it was necessary to pay some court to her but it was done with little enthusiasm.

She used to drag a daughter about with her who was as untidy as herself, and a son who had been so strangely brought up that he wept if he had to mount a horse, was made ill by the sight of a gun, and when he was obliged one day to cross on a ferry was overcome with an attack of nerves. The Duchess of Lucca insisted that the Spanish Princes had been brought up just as her son had been. My father attempted to re-monstrate with her upon the subject, but only succeeded in making himself disliked.

Mr. Hill came to us one morning with a face even sadder than usual; his Princess of Wales was in the harbour. Under pretext of giving up his room to her, he left her to the care of Lady William Bentinck, jumped into a carriage, and went off to Turin. Lady William would have done the same if she had been able to. Princess Caroline* established herself in Mr. Hill's rooms.

The next day we saw in the streets of Genoa a sight which I shall never forget. There was a kind of phaeton constructed like a sea shell, covered with gilding and mother-of-pearl, coloured outside, lined with blue velvet and decorated with silver fringe; this was drawn by two very small piebald horses driven by a child who was dressed like an operatic cherub with spangles and flesh-coloured tights, and within it lounged a fat woman of fifty years of age, short, plump, and high-coloured. She wore a pink hat with seven or eight pink feathers floating in the wind, a pink bodice cut very low, and a short white skirt which hardly came below her knees, showing two stout legs with pink top-boots; a rose-coloured sash which she was continually draping completed this costume.

The carriage was preceded by a tall and handsome man, mounted upon a little horse like those which drew the carriage; he was dressed precisely like King Murat, whose gestures and attitude he attempted to imitate. The carriage was followed by two grooms in English livery upon horses in the same fashion. This Neapolitan turn-out was a gift from Murat to the Princess of Wales, who exhibited herself in this ridiculous costume and in this strange carriage. She appeared in the streets of Genoa on this and the following mornings.

The Princess was then in the full fury of her passion for Murat, and wanted to accompany him to the camps. He had been obliged to insist on her departure with some sternness. She only consented to leave because she hoped to induce Lord William Bentinck to unite the English forces with the Neapolitan arms. On this subject she spared neither demands, supplications, nor threats. Their influence upon Lord William can easily be imagined, and he, moreover, went away two days after her arrival.

She was also a highly zealous Bonapartist, though she showed some fear that the Emperor might compromise the King, whose title she reserved exclusively for Murat. She speedily became the centre of every Opposition element in Genoa, and went so far that after some days the Sardinian Government begged her to find another refuge.

During the previous carnival, which she had just spent at Naples, she had conceived the idea of inducing the resident English to give a subscription ball to Murat. The scene took place in a public hall. At the moment of Murat's arrival, a group of the prettiest Englishwomen, dressed like goddesses from Olympus, advanced to receive him. Minerva and Themis then took possession of him and conducted him to a platform where the curtains opened and showed the spectators a group of symbolic figures, including Renown, a role played by one of the pretty Harley ladies. Glory, who was represented by the Princess, even more ridiculously dressed than the others, tripped forward, took a feather from the wing of Renown, and wrote, in large golden letters upon a panel which she held, the names of the different battles in which Murat had distinguished himself.

The spectators roared with laughter and applauded, while the Queen of Naples[5] shrugged her shoulders. Murat had sufficient good sense to feel vexed, but the Princess took this masquerade seriously, as a glorious ovation for the object of her affections and for herself, who was so well able to do him honour. I heard the story of this performance from Lady Charlotte Campbell, the last of the ladies of honour to abandon her. She wept with vexation as she spoke, but her story

5. Caroline Bonaparte, third sister of Napoleon.

was consequently more comical. It was necessary to see the heroine to appreciate the ridiculous element to the fullest.

To assuage the grief which she felt at her separation from Murat, the Princess of Wales had conceived the idea of dressing one of her men who slightly resembled him in precisely similar fashion. This living portrait was Bergami,[6] who afterwards became famous, and who even then, according to the captain of the ship which had brought him from Livorno, assumed the rights of Murat over his royal mistress as well as his costume. This, however, was regarded as nothing more than a sailor's bad joke.

Her position required that we go and pay our respects to this merry-andrew. She hated us, as she considered us hostile to Murat, and gave herself the petty pleasure of great rudeness. We went with Lady William Bentinck at a day and hour fixed by her. She kept us waiting a long time, and at length we were admitted to a green arbour where she was lunching, dressed in a very open dressing-gown, with Bergami to wait upon her. After a few words to my mother she attempted to speak nothing but English to Lady William. She was somewhat disconcerted to find us also taking part in the conversation, from which she had hoped to exclude us, and was thus reduced to speaking of the virtues and the royal and military talents of Murat.

Shortly afterwards she gave an audience to my father and began a long speech upon the infallible success of Murat, his approaching union with the army of the Emperor Napoleon, and the triumphs which awaited them. My father began to laugh.

"You are laughing at me, Ambassador?"

"Not at all, Madame; it is your Royal Highness who is trying to throw me off the scent by your serious air. Such a conversation between a Princess of Wales and an Ambassador of France is so frivolous that your Highness can hardly expect me to take it seriously."

She showed herself much offended and cut short the interview. We were in no way tempted to renew the acquaintance. She insisted that

6. Bartolomeo Bergami, overwhelmed with favours from the Princess, was made corespondent in the action George IV brought against his wife.

my father had helped to secure the order for her departure, an utterly false assertion. If the Government had been urged by anyone, it was rather by Lady William Bentinck, who was greatly weary of her. Lord William and Mr. Hill were spared these annoyances.

We were in a most unpleasant situation. Nothing is more painful than to be abroad in an official position in the midst of such a catastrophe and obliged to display a calmness which one does not feel. No one shared our feelings in a satisfactory manner. Some proclaimed the certain success of Bonaparte, others his rapid downfall before the Allies and the humiliation of the French armies. It was rarely that the language of these predictions was so well chosen as not to wound our feelings. Consequently, as soon as the undeniable seriousness of events relieved us of the painful necessity of pretending an assurance which we had not felt for a moment, we shut ourselves within our house and went out no more.

The Marquis de Lur-Saluces, aide-de-camp of the Duc d'Angoulême, arrived with dispatches. The Prince ordered my father to ask the King of Sardinia for the help of troops which would enter the country at Antibes and join him in Provence. He had just secured a considerable success at the bridge of the Drome, and had also displayed before the eyes of both armies a personal bravery which had greatly raised his reputation. He felt the need and the desire for vigorous action.

When the Duc d'Angoulême could be roused from his fatal predilection for passive obedience, he was not wanting in energy. He was by no means so great a nonentity as certain foolish actions with which a volume might be filled would induce one to believe. He was an imperfect but by no means an incompetent person.

My father made ready a carriage and went off to Turin with M. de Saluces. From the latter we had learnt that my brother had been sent into Spain. A few days later the *Moniteur* published letters from the Duc d'Angoulême to the Duchesse which had been intercepted; the letters stated that young d'Osmond was the bearer. We had every reason to fear that he had been arrested, and our anxieties continued for twenty-seven days.

Communications with the south had been interrupted; our only knowledge of events was derived from Paris newspapers which arrived at irregular intervals. Thus it was that we learnt of the defeat of the Duc d'Angoulême, of the agreement made with him, and of his departure from Cette. The name of my brother was nowhere to be found, but eventually we received letters from him written from Madrid. He was about to leave this capital to rejoin his Prince, whom he thought was still in France, and after a circuitous journey, he found him again at Barcelona.

The Duc d'Angoulême had proposed to send my brother to Madame, as he told him in his letter, and had then changed his plan and despatched him to the Duc de Laval, Ambassador at Madrid. This is the fact that had caused us such great uneasiness, our anxiety being entirely justified by the outbreak of civil war, when it was impossible to foresee what would be the fate of the prisoners or what vengeance would be taken upon one side or the other. The event showed that political passion had been exhausted as well as anger, and that personal interests were all that remained of the early Revolution years.

Murat was advancing so rapidly in Italy that people were already packing up at Turin. My mother and I were both anxious to go and rejoin my father, but he daily opposed the plan. The question of money was becoming important, and affected our prospects of security enough to dissuade us from a double journey at an uncertain time.

The demands of M. de Saluces had been received with great coldness by the Sardinian Government. Their success in any case was out of the question, as the news of the disaster and withdrawal of the Prince arrived immediately afterwards. However, my father observed some embarrassment in the Minister's reception of M. de Saluces, and noticed a tendency to keep the Ambassador at arm's length while overwhelming the Marquis d'Osmond with politeness.

At the same time all Austrian or English help was rejected, and it became plain that the Government hoped to conduct negociations independently and to maintain the possibility of securing its neutrality from the Emperor if he succeeded in establishing himself. Bubna was greatly amused by this policy and used to speak of King Victor as the august ally of the Emperor Napoleon. My father was not in a position to laugh, but he also believed that these ideas were entertained by the Sardinian Cabinet.

Murat was defeated at Occhiobello by the Austrian armies and ceased to advance, and the embargo upon our movements was removed. It was officially announced that the arrival of the Queen from Sardinia was indefinitely postponed and we returned to Turin.

Before leaving Genoa, I wish to say a word about two men whom we saw there as they passed through. The first was the Abbé de Janson. He had heard of the departure from the isle of Elba while on the coast of Syria, where he was making a pilgrimage to Jerusalem, and the wind had so entirely seconded his own energy that he had reached Genoa with almost inconceivable rapidity. He stayed only two hours to learn the course of events, girded up his loins, bestrode a posthorse, and went off to join the Duc d'Angoulême.

This Abbé in his ecclesiastical costume excited much ridicule among the soldiers; but when they saw him walking amidst grape-shot during the battle on the bridge of the Drome, carrying the wounded upon his shoulder, and giving them every kind of consolation and help with as much coolness as a grenadier of the Old Guard, the vicar, as they called him, stirred their enthusiasm to the highest point. The Abbé de Janson afterwards threw his energies with regrettable zeal into the service of intrigue. He became Bishop of Nancy, and one of the most active members of the Congregation which proved so fatal to the Restoration; he then made himself so unpopular that he was driven from his episcopal town during the Revolution of 1830.

The other personage whose passage through Genoa I wish to recall was Henri de Chastellux. He was twenty-five years of age, master of a considerable fortune, and attached to the embassy at Rome. It was there that he learnt of the treachery of his brother-in-law, Colonel de Labédoyère. He was even more horrified because he had a tender affection for his sister and understood her deep need of consolation, situated as she was amid a family whose Royalism was no less extreme than her own. M. de Chastellux immediately obtained leave of absence from his Ambassador, and after putting his papers in order, packed up his books and effects and started in a hired carriage, having struck a bargain with the owner to carry him to Lyons in twenty-seven days.

Revolutions do not usually proceed at this pace. On arriving at Turin, M. de Chastellux was informed that he could not continue his journey. He went to Genoa to consult my father upon his future action. It was decided that he should go to join the Duc d'Angoulême. My father told him that he would give him despatches to carry. Two hours later a secretary went to take him the despatches, and found him lying on a bed, reading Horace.

"When do you start?"

"I do not know. I have not been able to settle yet with the owners of conveyances which have been sent to me, and am expecting others."

"You are not going, then, by the Corniche?"

"No; I intend to hire a felucca."

The secretary brought back the dispatches, which were sent off by courier.

Henri de Chastellux embarked the next morning, but as he had arranged to sleep ashore every night, he did not reach Nice until five days later. There he heard disquieting rumours concerning the position of the Duc d'Angoulême: M. de Chastellux waited patiently for their confirmation, and after ten or twelve days, we saw him reappear at Genoa, having gone no farther than Nice.

This singular apathy in the case of a young man who was by no means unintelligent, and should have been urged forward under the circumstances by his social position and his family connections, formed an extraordinary contrast with the prodigious activity displayed by a man whose calling might have dispensed him from action. It was a contrast which struck us greatly at the time, and which I have never forgotten.

My father was in continual correspondence with the Duc de Narbonne, Ambassador to Naples, the Duc de Laval, Ambassador to Madrid, and the Marquis de Rivière, commander at Marseilles. He sent them the news which came to him from Germany and from the north of France. The embassy at Turin was very ill provided with secretaries and attachés, and when my father left Genoa he made me responsible for this correspondence. The duties were confined to sending a resumé of the news which came in to us, distinguishing official news from the common rumours with which we were inundated. Several of these letters were intercepted, and some, I believe, were printed in the *Moniteur*.

Harmful gossip has seized upon this puerile incident to assert that I usurped the duties of Ambassador. My own anger at this absurdity readily induced me to remain ignorant of the diplomatic business which my father has since handled, and my ignorance is probably greater than it would have been but for this ridiculous invention. Politics amuse me, as I have already said, and I gladly take an amateur part in them to occupy my spare time. As I never felt the need to talk about matters confided to me, my father would happily have communicated any business to me had I so desired.

In Piedmont we continued to lead the retired life which we had adopted at Genoa. My father did not wish to change anything in the outward appearance of his establishment, but circumstances forced him to lessen any unnecessary expenses. Our only amusement was to take delightful walks every day upon the beautiful hills which border the Po beyond Turin and extend to Moncalieri.

This amusement would have been a real pleasure if the roads had been less disagreeable; even on foot they were difficult and most fatiguing to cover. The paths serve as water-courses in the rainy season and are steep and filled with loose pebbles. Walking is difficult and even painful, and the ladies of the country hardly ever venture upon these paths. Fatigue, however, is compensated by admirable and infinitely varied views over a delightful countryside.

We learnt in succession circumstantial details of what had happened at Chambéry and at Grenoble. All these accounts coincided in pointing to M. de Labédoyère as chiefly to blame. I was the more inclined to believe the assertions that his action was premeditated because before my departure from Paris, I had heard him use entirely Bonapartist language wholly hostile to the Restoration.

The family of his wife, Mlle. de Chastellux, had been foolish enough to almost force him into the King's service, and he had been weak enough to agree. I cannot state at exactly what time this weakness became treason, but this is certain: a few days after he had rejoined his regiment, as he was going from Chambéry to Grenoble, he stayed to lunch with Mme. de Bellegarde, and told her that he did not doubt the success of the Emperor Napoleon, and earnestly desired his good fortune. As he was mounting his horse he called out to her:

"Good-bye, Madame; in a week I shall either be shot or be a marshal of the Empire."

He seems to have begun the movement among the troops who joined the Emperor, and to have misused the weakness of General Marchand, who was entirely dominated by him. The gratitude of the Emperor for the service he had rendered was not repaid as highly as he had hoped, but his premonitions in the other direction were realised only too sadly.

It was impossible not to be struck by the grandeur, the decisiveness, the audacity, and the prodigious skill which the Emperor displayed during the march from Cannes to Paris. It is not surprising that his partisans were electrified, and that their zeal was reconfirmed by the touch of his genius. It was, perhaps, the greatest personal achievement accomplished by the greatest man of modern times. I am persuaded, moreover, that it was not a prearranged plan. Nobody in France was wholly in on the secret, and it is not likely that anyone in Italy knew more.

The Emperor had left a great deal to chance, or rather to his own genius. Proof of the fact is the case of the commander of Antibes, who was first called upon to surrender and refused to recognise the imperial eagles. The flight of these eagles was thus entirely dependent on the attitude of the men whom they met upon the road, and the fine expression which speaks of them as flying from steeple to steeple, though justified by success, was a hazardous enterprise. Once more the Emperor had trusted in his star, which had not failed him, though it was to serve as a torchlight at his vast obsequies.

On arriving at Paris, he learnt of the Declaration of Vienna on March 13 and felt at the same time a coldness and a reticence on the part of those people who had been most devoted to him in the Civil Government. His political instinct immediately understood that these people represented public feeling much more than the soldiers. He would perhaps have been tempted to govern by the sword if the sword had not been occupied in resisting foreign opposition. There was only one means to crush the constitutional spirit which had so rapidly developed in France: this was to give full rein to those popular passions which quickly produce the most frightful tyranny in the name of liberty and nationality. To do the Emperor justice, no one ever had a deeper hatred of such measures. He certainly desired absolutism, but in such a way as to ensure public order, peace, and national honour. When he fully understood the nature of his position, he despaired of success, and the resulting despondency probably influenced the discouragement which he showed at the time of the Waterloo catastrophe. I have reason to believe that a very few days after his arrival at the Tuileries he ceased to display the energy which he had exhibited from the time of his departure from Elba. Possibly, if he had found among his former civil servants the same enthusiasm which inspired the military, he would have been better able to accomplish the gigantic task which lay before him; perhaps, again, this task was impossible to accomplish.

I return to affairs at Turin. The Pope had preceded us thither, and his presence gave occasion to a somewhat curious ceremony, at which we were present. Piedmont is in possession of the Holy Shroud. Christianity attaches such value to this relic that the Pope alone can order its exhibition. It is enclosed in a box of gold, which again is enclosed in one of copper, which again is enclosed—in short, there are seven boxes, and their seven keys are in the hands of seven different persons.

The Pope keeps the golden key. The box is placed in a magnificent chapel of a splendid church, called the Church of the Holy Shroud. Canons who bear the same name perform the services. The relic is never displayed to the eyes of the faithful except under special circumstances and with most imposing of ceremonies. The Pope usually sends a special legate, whose business it is to open the box and to bring him back the key.

The presence of the Holy Father at Turin and the importance of current events aroused the desire to give the soldiers, the population, and the King the satisfaction of beholding this precious relic.

Notwithstanding the hopes which the Sardinian Government secretly cherished of obtaining recognition of its complete neutrality, it had nonetheless quickly raised a considerable number of troops who appeared highly competent. These new bodies were assembled in the castle square, and after the Pope had blessed their new flags the Holy Shroud was displayed.

The King and his little court, those members of the diplomatic body who were Catholic, the Knights of the Annonciade, the other excellencies, cardinals, and bishops, were the only spectators admitted to the room where the ceremony was prepared. There were not more than thirty of us: the only ladies were my mother, Mme. Bubna, and myself, and we thus gained excellent places. The box was brought by the chapter in charge of it. Each box was opened in succession, the high personage who keeps the key handing it over in his turn, and a report upon the state of the locks was drawn up with great length and detail. This part of the ceremony proceeded like taking the seals off any property, with no religious context, except that the cardinal who opened the locks recited a prayer upon each occasion.

When the last of these caskets, a brilliantly shined gold box of considerable size, was reached, prayers and genuflections began. The Pope approached the table on which the casket had been placed by two cardinals. Everybody knelt down, and many forms and ceremonies were expended in opening the casket. These would have been more in place in a church than in a drawing-room, where they seemed somewhat undignified, especially from a close vantage point. At length the Pope, after approaching and withdrawing his hand several times, as if he feared to touch the casket, drew from the box a large piece of coarse, stained cloth. Accompanied by the King, who followed him closely, and surrounded by the cardinals, he carried it out to the balcony, where he unfolded it. The troops fell on their knees, together with the population, which filled the streets behind them. All the windows were thronged, and the spectacle was fine and imposing.

I have been told that it was possible to see distinctly the blood-stained marks of the face, the feet, the hands, and even of the wound upon the Holy Shroud. I was unable to judge for myself, as I was placed at a window near that in which the Pope was standing. He exhibited the relic in front of him, to the right and to the left, during which time the most solemn silence prevailed. At the moment of his withdrawal the kneeling crowd arose, uttering loud cheers: the firing of cannon, the rolling of drums, the cheers announced that the ceremony was concluded. When he returned to the drawing-room the prayers began once more.

The Holy Father was kind enough to ask us, through Cardinal Pacca, if we would like to have any object blessed and touched with the Holy Shroud. As we had not foreseen this favour, we were not provided with any suitable article. However, we gave our ring and the chains which we wore around our necks. The Pope made no objection and gave us a glance full of kindness and paternal goodness. We had recently seen him on many occasions at Genoa. He alone and the cardinal whom he was obliged to appoint legate extraordinary for this occasion had the right to touch the Shroud itself. They had much trouble in folding it up, but no one was allowed to offer them any help. When the first casket was closed the Pope took the key, and the cardinals then placed the box in the second shell. After this ceremony, the Pope, the King, and those who were invited went into a room where lunch had been laid, or rather where refreshments were ready, for there was no set table. There, the two sovereigns held a reception. They waited until all the boxes had been closed and the canons had resumed their procession to the church, after which everyone withdrew.

I do not remember whether Jules de Polignac was present at this ceremony, but he arrived about this time invested with full powers by Monsieur, who had been appointed Lieutenant-General of the kingdom by Louis XVIII. He asserted that he was ready to raise a French Legion of the White Cockade on Sardinian territory, but the Government would not hear of this plan. After much trouble he obtained permission to establish himself on the frontier, in order to keep a closer eye upon his connections in the south, and settled in the house of a priest. He was in almost daily correspondence with my father, and gave him all kinds of unpleasant news.

My father's information from other sources led him to expect soon an outbreak of hostilities. He advised Jules de Polignac to take measures for his safety; Jules replied on June 15 that he was certain to receive a warning at least ten days before the opening of the campaign, which could not begin for four or five weeks. While thanking my father for his precaution, Jules begged him to set his mind at rest, as he was certain to be earlier and better informed than anyone else.

The same messenger brought a letter from the parish priest—we seemed to be beset by priests—of Montmélian, who informed my father that, after taking his letter to the post, Jules had gone back to the house to get his horse, and that at the moment when he had his foot in the stirrup the house had been surrounded by a company of French soldiers, who had entered the town without striking a blow, and that Jules had been taken prisoner. The priest was the more uneasy as the saddle-bags were filled with correspondence which would compromise Jules and all his connections. The priest had sent the letter across the mountains to an office which was not yet seized; Jules's letter, however, which bore the postmark of Montmélian, arrived at the same time. It was one more occasion on which poor M. de Polignac was betrayed by that lack of foresight which seemed to be his special quality. It was invariably accompanied by self-confidence pushed to a fabulous extreme. Since to this he added great rashness and remarkable courage, which had often been put to the test, nothing warned him of danger, and he blindly plunged into it. It must be said in fairness that when the consequences had happened, he would contemplate them calmly and undergo the results of his errors with unusual fortitude.

We were horrified to hear that he was a prisoner. His gentleness and courtesy in ordinary life made him very attractive. I forgot at that moment that I had always accused him of being guided by ambition and of using the fald-stool as a stepping stone; I remembered only the pleasant and obliging character whom I had known from the time of our joint childhood, and wept bitterly for his fate. It was impossible to foresee the Emperor's policy in treating prisoners such as Jules. He was in a special and very dangerous predicament because the Restoration had freed him from his captivity under the Imperial Government.

My father made many efforts to hear from him, but for a long time without success. However, he obtained a declaration from all the Ministers at Turin announcing that their sovereigns would take reprisals if M. de Polignac was treated other than as a prisoner of war. The Sardinian Cabinet was the most obstinate, but eventually consented to sign last of all. These efforts were useless. Marshal Suchet had no intention of making capital out of this conquest. He sent M. de Polignac to Fort Barraux, advised him to keep perfectly quiet, and seemed to forget all about him, though he saw that he was well-treated. He received orders to send him to Paris, and ignored them. I do not know how long he could have continued this benevolent indifference, but events were proceeding apace.

The Government of Piedmont had shared so entirely the assurance of Jules that when the French were seizing Montmélian another branch of the army crossed the mountains and was able to carry off at Aiguebelle an excellent Piedmontese regiment, which had been quietly drilling with blank cartridge. The best part of this adventure is that the same thing had happened in the same place and in the same way at the outset of the preceding war. This caused a great sensation at

Turin. M. de Saint-Marsan was speedily appointed Minister of War, although he had served in the French Government. The authorities begged for Austrian help with as much zeal as they had hitherto refused it. General Bubna, however, informed Count Valese that he would have to pay for his obstinacy: he had warned him long ago that hostilities were about to break out, and that his secret and personal negociations with the French Government to secure neutrality would be unsuccessful. He had not been willing to believe him, and he therefore now gave him formal notice that if the French should seize the Mont Cenis before he could occupy it, an event which seemed highly probable, he would withdraw his troops into Lombardy and abandon Piedmont.

No sooner had he uttered this threat than he displayed prodigious energy in order to nullify it. Bubna was a strange character. Tall, stout, lame from a wound, idle when he had nothing to do, he spent three-quarters of every day lying on a bed or on the straw in the stable, smoking the foulest tobacco from the lowest public-house. When he was pleased to enter the drawing-room he was the best company in the world, apart from the smell of his pipe: a witty story-teller, caustic and cynical, understanding and using every nuance of a language. If civil or military affairs demanded his attention he took not a moment's rest, and the Bubna who had spent six months almost entirely in a horizontal position would spend seventy-two hours on horseback without appearing fatigued.

He told me in confidence that he was somewhat exaggerating his anxiety and his intentions in order to punish Count Valese for his hesitation. As I was very angry with the Count for the coldness he had shown to the French Ambassador, I was highly pleased by this attitude. My father, with his superlative wisdom, did not participate in this joy: he approved of the success of Count Valese in saving his country from weeks of Austrian occupation, and sympathised with the desire of a little kingdom to try and secure its general neutrality, although he thought the effort hopeless.

It is certain that the resistance which the Cabinet had offered to the reoccupation of Piedmontese territory by the Austrians was regarded in the eyes of the inhabitants as compensating for many of the errors with which the Government was reproached. The population had conceived a hatred for the Austrians, who had taught them to miss the French troops. "The French," they used to say, "extorted much, but what they took they ate with us in our houses, while the Germans take even more and carry everything away."

This saying was true, both of the administration and of the officers and soldiers. The authorities imported everything from Austria, even horseshoes, and bought nothing in the territory which they occupied; on the other hand, they carted everything away, even the hinges and the locks from the doors and windows in the barracks which the troops were evacuating. The wagons following an Austrian regiment evacuating an "allied" country were a curious spectacle, both for their fabulous number and for the huge number of every kind of object with which they were crammed. These convoys aroused the anger of the Italian peoples, who suffered under this system of general spoliation.

The news of the opening of the campaign at the Belgian frontier and the battle of Ligny, fought upon the 16th, came to us with great rapidity through France by means of a telegraph which had brought it to Chambéry. We were obliged to await the arrival of a regular courier to receive the news of Waterloo. Thereupon events which we were obliged to call good news followed as rapidly as bad news had occurred three months before. We were forced to rejoice, but there were some heartbreaks.

The King of Sardinia's head was entirely turned by the sight of the Piedmontese troops entering France with the Austrian army, and he already saw himself as a conqueror. His magnanimity was contented with the Rhône as his frontier. He manifested some desire for Lyons, but consoled himself with the thought that it was a disloyal town.

I have already said that he was easily accessible; he was at home to everybody and was very talkative, especially at this exciting time. There was not a monk or a peasant whom he did not buttonhole to relate his military projects. At the time when he was Duke of Aosta he had served in a campaign in the valley of Barcelonnette, and had kept a great admiration for the agility and courage of its inhabitants; he therefore wished to capture Briançon by storm at the head of his "Barbets," as he called them. He presented this plan to General Frimont when he came to take up the chief command of the Austrian army. Bubna, who was present at this interview, used to relate in a most ridiculous manner the calm astonishment of the Alsatian Frimont, who vainly attempted to catch his eye to learn what he thought of these extravagances, and was forced by Bubna's obstinacy to answer for himself. Fortunately, the King tumbled off the chair on which he had climbed to take by assault a jar of tobacco on the top of a wardrobe, and hurt himself rather badly, dislocating his wrist, and Briançon was saved.

The physical appearance of this poor Prince made his plans the more ridiculous. He was an ugly copy of the Duc d'Angoulême. He was smaller and more stunted; his arms were longer, his legs thinner, his feet flatter; his grimace was broader; in short, he approached more nearly that particular type of monkey which seemed to be the model for either one. He suffered terribly from his wrist, which was badly set by a kind of bonesetter brought over from Sardinia. Rossi, one of the cleverest surgeons in Europe, was turned out of the castle because he had entered it under a French Government. However, pain had its way, and at the end of ten or twelve days Rossi was called in, the wrist was properly set, and the King's sufferings were relieved.

The boasts of the King and of his party, absurd as they were, were by no means agreeable to our ears. Some weeks later my father was able to seize the opportunity for a most happy retort. The Duke of Modena came to see his father-in-law, upon which occasion a court reception was held. My father was present, and happened to be near a group of men at the moment when the First Chamberlain of Modena was loudly asserting the case and necessity of dividing France in order to secure the peace of Europe. My father intervened, and observed in the politest manner:

"May I venture to ask you, Comte, from what historical document have you derived the information that France can be disposed of as if the Duchy of Modena were in question?"

As may be imagined, the First Chamberlain was highly disconcerted. This counterthrust, so strongly in contrast to my father's usual politeness, was widely reported at Turin where the claims of the German Duke of Modena were far from popular.

The course of events in Belgium stopped the march of the French armies in Savoy, and gave the Austrians time to concentrate at Chambéry too large a force to allow for the possibility of resistance. The occupation of Grenoble, where none of the Piedmontese troops were left, completed the pride of these extempore conquerors. I cannot say whether our vexation or our anger was the greater when we thought of our cannon in the hands of the "Barbets" of the King. Although Fort Barraux continued to hold out, means had been taken to permit the escape of Jules de Polignac, who rejoined the troops at the headquarters of General Bubna, and took part in the attack upon Grenoble.

These recollections are too painful, and I would not willingly recall them to memory. I prefer to relate two incidents which were in my opinion more honourable to our old captains than any of those military successes which are so familiar to them. These incidents are proof of their patriotism.

The Allies announced that wherever they might find the Government of Louis XVIII in force before their arrival, they would insist upon no kind of confiscation. Any towns, however, which they might enter by force of arms or through the town's capitulation were to be treated as conquered countries, and the munitions of war were to be carried off. They were, indeed, expert at the work of dismantling fortifications, as what happened at Grenoble can testify.

The advance guard under the orders of General Bubna was advancing upon Lyons. Monsieur de Corcelles, commander of the National Guard, went to the General and offered to induce the townspeople to assume the Austrian cockade or the Sardinian cockade, or indeed any colour rather than the white cockade. Bubna, kind as he was, was by no means inspired with a sacred respect for the property of others, and

was too clever to authorise the "patriotic" intentions of M. de Corcelles, though he did not entirely reject them. He told him that deci-
sions upon such important points could not be made off-hand, and that
he had no instructions upon this point, but that he would ask for them,
and that doubtless it would not be impossible for the House of Savoy
to transfer its capital to Lyons, and Piedmont to be reunited with Lombardy. This was a question for consideration, and in the meantime no
precipitate action could be taken; his advice, therefore, was that the
tri-colour cockade should be retained. The Austrian army would be in
the town the next morning, and then would be the time to discuss the
accommodation of mutual interests.

M. de Corcelles returned to Lyons and reported the steps which he
had taken, and the interview which he had had to Marshal Suchet.

The General treated him with the utmost contempt, told him that
he was a villain and a bad citizen, and that he himself would prefer to
see France reunited under any kind of government rather than lose a
single village. He drove him out of the house, deprived him of his command in the National Guard, and immediately sent for M. de Polignac,
M. de Chabrol, M. de Sainneville (the one being prefect and the other
chief of police before the Hundred Days), installed them himself in the
exercise of their duties, and did not withdraw until he had seen the
royal colours displayed. Bubna found these colours flying the next day,
to his great disappointment, but did not venture to complain.

At the same time, similar results influenced the course of events at
Toulon under slightly different circumstances. Marshal Brune was in
command of that town. The garrison was wildly enthusiastic for the
imperial system, and these sentiments were shared by the town. One
morning, when the gates were open, the Marquis de Rivière, Admiral
de Ganteaume, and an old *émigré*, Comte de Lardenoy, commander at
Toulon for the King, who was followed by one gendarme, arrived
wearing the white cockade. They passed the sentinels, galloped into
the square, and reached the Marshal's house before the astonishment
which their sudden appearance had caused could permit any movement for their arrest. They reached the study where the Marshal was

busy writing. At first he was surprised, but immediately recovered himself, held out his hand to M. de Rivière, whom he knew, and said to him:

"I thank you, Marquis, for this proof of confidence, which shall not be disappointed."

The new arrivals showed him the Declaration of the Allies, and informed him that an Austro-Sardinian body of troops was advancing from Nice, and that an English fleet was sailing upon Toulon. It was impossible to defend the town with any success, as the whole of France was occupied, and the King already at Paris; if, however, the Marshal insisted on flying his colours, his action would cost the country the vast amount of naval and military stores contained there. The Allies would spare nothing, and were hastening to reach the town before the King's Government had been recognised. These gentlemen, trusting to his enlightened patriotism, had come for the purpose of explaining the situation, and were ready to swear upon their honour to the accuracy of the facts.

The Marshal carefully read the documents, which confirmed their words, and added:

"The fact is, gentlemen, there is not a moment to be lost. I can answer for the garrison, but am by no means certain what terms I can obtain from the town. In any case, we shall all perish together, but I will not lend myself to any foolish obstinacy which would deliver the harbour to English plunderers."

He immediately took steps to assemble the officers of the troops, the authorities of the town, and the most influential members of the Bonapartist party. He harangued them to such effect that shortly afterwards the white cockade was adopted, and the old Comte de Lardenoy was recognised as commander.

The Marquis de Rivière was well able to appreciate the loyalty of the Marshal, by which he was greatly touched. He advised him to remain with his friends during the first moments, when the excitable passions of the southern population would reach their height. Marshal Brune insisted upon withdrawing; possibly he feared that he might be accused of treason by his own party. Whatever his motive was, he went away, accompanied by an aide-de-camp of M. de Rivière. He sent this companion back when he thought he was beyond the area where he could be recognised or meet with any danger.

The conduct of Marshals Suchet and Brune has inspired me with even more respect for the reason that I cannot pretend their example would have been followed by Royalist leaders. Few of the latter would have placed their commissions in the hands of a foreigner, risking immense loss to their country, and they would have shrunk from restoring the tri-colour with their own hands; and had there been any found adopting these measures, our party would have branded them as traitors.

In the early days of March the King of Sardinia issued orders for the expulsion of all the French from his states. The rapid success of the Emperor so impressed him that he did not venture to secure the execution of these orders. However, as soon as his fears were somewhat calmed by the battle of Waterloo, his orders became peremptory and his agents pitiless. Frenchmen who had been domiciled for thirty years in Piedmont, who were landowners and had married in the country, were driven from their homes by the royal *carabinieri*, were conducted to the frontier as if they had been malefactors, though no one took the trouble to utter the slightest reproach against them; their wives and children came weeping to the embassy, and we were overwhelmed with their complaints. We could do nothing but share their lamentations and their deep indignation.

My father made every possible official protestation, with the other members of the diplomatic body supporting his efforts and displaying their disgust and their disapproval of this cruel measure, which, however, nothing could stop. At length my father received a message from Prince Talleyrand, informing him that the Government of Louis XVIII had been reconstituted. He immediately presented himself to Count Valese, and told him that if this unjustifiable persecution of the subjects of his Majesty were continued, he would at once demand his passports, would inform his own court of his intention, and knew he could rely upon their approval. This step saved some of the unfortunate wretches who had obtained a respite, but the majority had either gone, or were at any rate ruined by this precipitate display of fear and of childish animosity against a body of innocent inhabitants.

These circumstances completed my dislike for absolute and arbitrary governments; my homesickness had increased to such an extent that I could no longer breathe in the gloomy environment of Turin. It was a real relief to leave the town, at any rate for a period of time. I therefore resolved to spend a few weeks in Paris, where personal business had summoned me. My father consented the more readily to my departure as he was himself anxious to secure more exact information about the course of events in France than he could derive from the newspapers. Despatches arrived irregularly, and often gave only scanty details, whereas my correspondence would be both detailed and daily. I was intended by Nature for the post of onlooker, and he could have no observer better suited to his requirements.

I have said that my brother had rejoined his Prince at Barcelona; he spent some time there, and accompanied the Prince to Bourg-Madame. The Duc d'Angoulême sent him to carry his despatches to the King as soon as he knew that his Majesty was in Paris. The King sent my brother back to his nephew, and he was therefore obliged to make his way through the Army of the Loire upon two occasions, a matter of some danger in those early days. He was, however, successful in accomplishing his double mission, and was rewarded by permission to join his relatives. After spending several days with him, I preceded him upon the road to Paris, where he was to rejoin me immediately.

I left home on August 18, Saint Helen's Day, after wishing my mother many happy returns of her feast day; my absence could not be replaced as far as she was concerned, and she was much depressed. The next day she was to accompany my father to Genoa, where the Queen disembarked without difficulty. When the Queen arrived from Sardinia, her dress and manners recalled the charming and fashionable Duchess of Aosta as Piedmont remembered her. Her unpopularity in that province was extreme; I cannot say if it was justified, as I have had no further connection with that country, and only an inhabitant can pass a correct judgement upon this matter. The accounts given of the affair by the Piedmontese were always characterised by extreme reticence.

I stayed for several days at Chambéry, where I learnt the exact circumstances of the treason committed by the troops, and especially M. de Labédoyère. It was obvious that he had been working beforehand to influence his regiment, and that the events of Grenoble were very far from unpremeditated. Public feeling in Savoy was highly excited. The old nobility earnestly desired the restoration of the dynasty of Savoy. The middle classes, the manufacturing and commercial element, preferred to remain Frenchmen. The peasants were ready to shout "Long live the Sardinian King!" as soon as their priests gave the order. Hitherto wishes, sighs, fears, and prejudices had been merely whispered, and the parties had confined themselves to mutual hatred.

Shortly before the Hundred Days, Monsieur had made a tour in the south, where his charming and affable manners had brought him high popularity. At Chambéry he lodged with M. de Boigne, who showed him much kindness. The day before his departure, the Duc de Maillé handed him from the Prince six Crosses of Honour for distribution in the town. M. de Boigne made no bad choice, though the responsibility was entirely his. The accompanying documents had been filled in with the names which he suggested, with no further information.

Throughout this tour Monsieur seemed to have been in the habit of thus returning the hospitality which he received. It has been supposed that his recklessness in scattering Crosses of Honour during 1814 was dictated by political ends and by a wish to bring the Cross into disrepute. This, in my opinion, was not the case: the Cross was regarded as valueless by our Princes, and they gave it away as something of no importance. It will be understood to what degree this action irritated people who had shed their blood to secure it. By such ignorance of popular feeling, rather than by malice aforethought, the Princes of the House of Bourbon often trampled unsuspectingly upon interests and national prejudices which had grown up during their long absence. They never took the trouble to learn any of these sentiments, persuaded as they were that their restoration had been accomplished. They were never able to understand that they occupied a responsible position, implying work to be done and duties to be performed.

I arrived at Lyons on August 25. With the assistance of the Austrian garrison, an uproarious celebration of the Festival of Saint Louis was then in progress. The town was illuminated, fireworks were going off, and the whole population seemed to be occupied in these celebrations. One could only ask what had become of that other crowd which formerly had received Bonaparte with such enthusiasm. I have seen so many reversals of popular favour that I have often asked myself this question. I think that the mass of people are the same, but that they are differently influenced by a small nucleus of leading figures who change and are carried in different directions. The same crowd, however, is fully convinced of the honesty of its applause, to whatever object it might be directed.

I now arrive at a painful admission, which I might omit, since it concerns only myself and my personal feelings. I have promised, however, to tell the truth concerning everyone, and can make no exception in my own case. It is only right that people should know how far natural good feeling can be destroyed by partisan passion.

On arriving at the Hôtel de l'Europe, I asked for the newspapers, and when I read of the condemnation of M. de Labédoyère I was seized with a dreadful feeling of delight.

"At last," I said to myself, "one of these wretched traitors has been punished."

This feeling was only fleeting, and I was immediately horrified by my sentiment. It was, however, sufficiently definite to weigh upon my conscience. From that moment, in view of the disgust and remorse with which it inspired me, I have foresworn to the utmost of my power all party spirit or the vengeance which it exacts. I might, indeed, have been able to justify myself with the information concerning the conduct of M. de Labédoyère which had just been received at Chambéry. There were the gloomy results of his guilty treachery: the country torn by faction and invaded by a million foreigners. In a woman's heart, however, nothing can excuse bloodthirsty thoughts of vengeance, and this dreadful feeling must be ascribed to its proper origins, party spirit, which is a monster whose advances can never be too energetically repulsed if one lives in revolutionary times and wishes to preserve elements of humanity.

I spent two days at Lyons, where several persons had met with whom I was connected through both Frenchmen and foreigners. I heard some information of events in Paris. Opinions differed on the part which Fouché had played in these events, but everybody agreed that he had entered the council of Louis XVIII at the request of Monsieur and under the influence of the most enthusiastic members of the *émigré* party. It was at Lyons that I learned the facts I have mentioned concerning the conduct of Marshal Suchet. I also heard another incident which struck me greatly.

When Monsieur made his sad expedition at the moment of the return from Elba, he was obliged to leave town by the Paris route, while the garrison and inhabitants rushed down the Grenoble road to meet Napoleon. Only two gendarmes of the escort which had been ordered prepared to accompany his carriage. The next day they were denounced to the Emperor. He sent for them and promoted them. It cannot be denied that he had every right political instinct.

My stay at Lyons had been unduly prolonged: it was necessary to wait until the roads were free or, in other words, entirely held by foreign garrisons. I still preserve the passport with which I travelled through my sad country during those melancholy days. These formalities were painful, but the roads offered a spectacle consoling to a French heart, notwithstanding its bitterness. This was the magnificent attitude of our disbanded soldiers. In bands of twelve or fifteen, in uniforms as clean and neat as if on parade, with white sticks in their hands, they were going to their homes, sad but by no means crushed, and preserving a dignity in the hour of misfortune which showed them worthy of their former successes.

I had left Italy infested with brigands as a result of the petty campaign of Murat. The first group of soldiers in the Army of the Loire which I met inspired me with some fear, in view of these recollections. However, as soon as I looked them in the face, my only feelings were those of sympathy, and this they seemed to understand. The nearest of these groups which I passed scrutinised me closely as if to see to what party I belonged, but the last comers invariably saluted me. They inspired me with that kind of pity which a poet has termed bittersweet, and which magnanimity imposes on anyone not devoid of generous sentiment. I do not think that there is anything finer in history than the conduct of the army and the attitude of individual soldiers at this time. France has every reason to be proud of them. I did not wait for the day of reckoning to begin my enthusiasm, and from that time on I regarded them with respect and veneration. It is, indeed, remarkable that at a moment when more than one hundred and fifty thousand men were disbanded and sent into the country without provisions, there should have been no single crime or misdemeanour committed throughout France which can be laid to their charge. Public security was preserved unbroken. The châteaus were left in peace, the towns and villages received useful citizens, intelligent workmen, and interesting storytellers. There can be no higher praise for conscription than this noble conduct on the part of the soldier, which had brought forth conduct, I believe, unique in the course of history. I was the enemy of the soldiers of Waterloo, and had stigmatised them with reason as traitors for the last three months, but I had not been a single day upon my journey than I began to be proud of my glorious countrymen.

CHAPTER SIX

Paris

1815

*A*s if to impress upon my mind the horrible cruelty of my feelings concerning M. de Labédoyère, I found that the sensation of the moment in Paris was his execution.

In 1791, when the Comte and Comtesse de Chastellux had followed Madame Victoire to Rome, two of their five children, Henri and Georgine, had remained in France, where their grandmother brought them up in a little Normandy château. On her grandmother's death, Georgine went to join her parents in Italy, and they soon returned to Paris. She was never able to overcome the extreme shyness which she had contracted in the solitude in which she had been brought up until the age of eighteen. She had known Charles de Labédoyère from childhood, as the properties of their respective mothers were situated in the same area. From childhood the affection between these two neighbours was reciprocal. Georgine became very pretty and M. de Labédoyère was very much in love with her. Henri de Chastellux, whose schoolfriend he had been, encouraged his feelings. The family of Labédoyère was delighted with this prospect of seeing their son settled in life; the Chastellux gave their consent, and the marriage took place shortly before the Restoration.

Charles de Labédoyère was extravagant, fond of gambling and

women, and especially of war. In other respects he was a good man: witty, cheerful, loyal, frank, generous; he promised to amend his faults, and really expected to succeed. Georgine adored him in spite of his shortcomings: her affection, however, was rarely shown; she was so shy about displaying her feelings that one might have lived with her for months without discovering them. She was undoubtedly the most modest and retiring creature that I have ever met.

At the time of Bonaparte's return she was reduced to despair by her husband's action. Though she had hardly recovered from her confinement, she left her house and took refuge with her parents, declining to see her husband when he arrived in the Emperor's suite. The course of events brought about a reaction, and she resumed relations with him as soon as he was in trouble, and attempted to recover her fortune in order to provide him with the means of escape. She proposed to rejoin him with their child, and I think that it was in order to complete these arrangements that he returned to Paris, where he was arrested.

This timid woman immediately became heroic. Audiences, prayers, supplications, and importunities—nothing deterred her. She begged her family to use their influence to support her efforts, but no one would accompany her or take a step of any kind. Deprived of all help, she did not abandon hope, but knocked at every door, forced her way in where admission was refused, and even secured an interview with the Duchesse d'Angoulême, though she could not move her sympathy; in short, she displayed the courage of a lion.

When all means were exhausted, she had recourse to Mme. von Krüdener.* This last visit gave grounds for some feeble hope, and the poor young mother, with her child in her arms, went to the prison of the Abbaye to communicate her success to her husband. She found the square full of people, a cab surrounded with troops before the door of the prison, and a man in the act of entering the vehicle. A terrible cry was heard, for she had recognised M. de Labédoyère: the reason of this scene was all too obvious. The child fell from her hands; she threw herself into the fatal carriage, and fainted. Charles caught her in his arms, embraced her tenderly, confided her to the care of a faithful servant who had picked up the child, and took advantage of her fainting to close the carriage door. His death did not belie the courage which he had often displayed on the battlefield. Mme. de Labédoyère was taken home before she had recovered consciousness. From that moment on her native shyness returned. For a long time she refused to see her family, and could not forgive their cruel callousness.

Twenty years have elapsed from that day to this, but her sadness has not been relieved for a single day. On the other hand, her Royalist sentiments have become more than enthusiastic. The blood of the victim sacrificed to the Restoration seemed to her a holocaust which must definitely assure its permanence and its glory. She educated her son with these ideas; for her, Legitimism was a religion.

I think I have referred to the great deliberation with which her brother Henri was accustomed to travel. I do not know where he was at the time of the catastrophe, but his absence had given Georgine some basis for hoping that he would have helped her in this dreadful crisis if he had been in Paris; she therefore expended upon him all the tenderness which was not absorbed by her son and by her grief. It was only upon the occasion of the marriage of Henri with Clara de Duras, daughter of the Duc de Duras, that she consented to see her family again. She afterwards lived in the most absolute seclusion.

The name of Mme. von Krüdener has been mentioned above; my relations with her did not begin until somewhat later, but I may as well relate them here.

I was taken to her house by Mme. Récamier. I found her a woman some fifty years of age, with traces of extreme beauty. She was thin and pale, and her face showed a strong capacity for emotion; her eyes, though hollow, were beautiful, and her look expressive. She had that sonorous voice, with its sweetness, flexibility, and resonance, which is one of the greatest charms of northern women. Her grey hair was parted simply on her forehead and she dressed with extreme neatness. She wore a black dress with no ornaments, which, however, showed a certain distinction.

She inhabited a large and fine suite of rooms in a residence on the

Faubourg Saint-Honoré. The mirrors, decorations, and ornaments of every kind, as well as the furniture, were all covered with grey cloth; the very clocks were enveloped in covers which only allowed the dials to be seen. The garden extended as far as the Champs Elysées, and it was through this garden that the Emperor Alexander, when lodging in the Palace of the Elysée used to visit Mme. von Krüdener at any hour of the day or night.

Our arrival interrupted a kind of lesson which she was giving to five or six people. After the usual formalities, in which she displayed the ease and readiness of one accustomed to the highest society, she resumed her occupation. She was speaking on the subject of faith. The expression of her eyes and the tone of her voice alone marked any change as she took up the thread of her discourse. I was astounded by the eloquence, the readiness, and the style of her extemporaneous address. Her look seemed at the same time vague and yet inspired. At the end of one and a half hours she ceased to speak, her eyes closed, and she seemed to fall into a kind of a stupor. The initiated informed me that this was the signal for retirement.

I was considerably interested, but I did not propose to be present at a second performance. These discourses were given upon regular days, and I thought it advisable to choose another day for leaving my card upon Mme. von Krüdener. To my surprise, I was admitted, and found her alone.

"I was expecting you," she said; "'the Voice' had announced your visit to me. I have hopes of you, and yet I have been so often deceived!"

She fell into a silence which I did not attempt to break, not knowing how to begin. At length she resumed and informed me that "the Voice" had told her that she would have, in the line of prophetesses, one successor whom she would form, destined to approach nearer than she herself to divinity, for she could do nothing but hear, and this successor would see!

"The Voice" had announced to her that this predestined successor would be a woman who had preserved her purity in the midst of high society. Mme. von Krüdener would meet her when she least expected her, and with no warning to prepare her for their intimacy. Her dreams, which she did not venture to call visions, for she, who alas I was not called to see, had pictured this successor to her with some resemblance to my features. I protested with sincere modesty that I was not called to this high glory. She pleaded my cause against myself with the most attractive warmth, and touched me so that my eyes filled with tears. She thought she had secured a disciple, if not a successor, and strongly urged me to come and see her often. During that morning, for the fascination of her company kept me with her several hours, she told me how she had come to Paris.

In the course of 1815 she was on her way to the south of Italy where her son was waiting for her. Between Bologna and Siena her sufferings warned her that she was leaving the road which she ought to have followed. After struggling for a whole night against this strong influence, she gave way and retraced her steps, and from that moment the improvement in her condition showed her that she was on the right path. The improvement continued as far as Modena, but some leagues upon the road to Turin, her sufferings renewed, but ceased as soon as she started for Lausanne. When she reached the town, she learnt that her cousin, a childhood playmate, and an aide-de-camp to the Emperor Alexander, had fallen dangerously ill in Germany. Thus the wishes of "the Voice" were explained; doubtless she was intended to bring light into this soul and to comfort her suffering friend. She crossed Tyrol, encouraged by pleasanter feelings, and went to Heidelberg, where she found the allied sovereigns; her cousin was lying ill in another town. She learnt where he was, and started off the next morning without seeing anybody.

Hardly, however, had she left Heidelberg when her illness recurred with greater violence than before. At length she gave way, and after several stages retraced her steps to Heidelberg. Her peace of mind returned, and it became impossible for her to doubt that her mission was in this town, although she had not yet discovered its nature.

The Emperor Alexander took a trip lasting some days, and the pains which she experienced during his absence showed her to whom she was called to bring the light. She vainly struggled against the wishes of "the Voice": she prayed, she fasted, and begged that this cup might be taken from her, but "the Voice" was pitiless, and she was obliged to obey.

The Baroness von Krüdener did not inform me how she had become intimate with the Emperor, but her success was assured. She had invented a new form of flattery for him. He had grown weary of that kind of flattery which represented him as the greatest potentate of earth, the Agamemnon among kings, et cetera, and she did not, therefore, speak to him of his earthly power, but of the mysterious power of his prayers. The purity of his heart gave to his prayers a strength which no other mortal could attain, for no other had so many temptations to resist. In overcoming these temptations he showed himself the most virtuous of men, and consequently was the most powerful of men before God. It was by means of this clever flattery that she led him as she pleased. She made him pray for her, for himself, for Russia, for France; she made him fast, give alms, undergo self-mortification, and renounce all his favourite pursuits, and obtained everything from him through his hope of increasing his influence in heaven.

She hinted rather than explained that "the Voice" was Jesus Christ. She never spoke of it except as "the Voice," but admitted with floods of tears that the errors of her youth had forever cut her off from the hope of seeing. It is impossible to say with what rapture she depicted the happiness of one called to see. Doubtless, reading this cold narrative, the reader will say that she was a madwoman or an intriguer. Possibly one of those who thus judges my account may themselves have been personally under the charm of this brilliant enthusiast. As for myself, though little disposed to enthusiasm, I became so suspicious of the influence which she might exert that I only visited her at distant intervals and on days when she was at home to everyone, as she was then less attractive than in individual intimacy.

I have sometimes thought that M. de Talleyrand, when he found that he had quarrelled too deeply with the Emperor Alexander to regain any personal influence over him, invented this means of influencing him. It is certain that the Baroness von Krüdener was working on the side of France during this sad year of 1815. After she had spent several hours praying to the Emperor Alexander that a cloud which she had discovered on the star of France might be removed, and after she had asked him to use his heavenly influence for this task, and had assured him that "the Voice" declared that his prayer would be answered, it was highly probable that at the next day's meeting, if some condition disadvantageous to France was demanded by the other Powers, the Emperor Alexander would come to the help of his suppliant, and would support his mystical prayers with the weight of his earthly greatness.

It was not only for public business that Mme. von Krüdener used Alexander. This is what happened concerning M. de Labédoyère. His young wife, as I have said, came to ask the Baroness to request a pardon through the Emperor Alexander. The Baroness received her with benevolence and emotion, and promised to do all that would be permitted. She therefore shut herself up in her oratory. Time passed, and the Emperor found her in tears and in a dreadful state. She had just fought a long combat with "the Voice," without obtaining permission to present the request to the Emperor. He was not allowed to act in this affair, and the sentence was the more rigorous as the soul of M. de Labédoyère was not in a state of grace! The execution took place.

Then Mme. von Krüdener persuaded the Emperor that he had one more great duty to fulfill. It was necessary for him to use his great influence before God in favour of this unhappy wretch whom he had been obliged to abandon to the vengeance of man. She kept him for eight hours by the clock in her oratory at prayer kneeling upon the marble. At two o'clock in the morning she dismissed him, and at eight o'clock a note from her informed him that "the Voice" had told her that the Emperor's prayer had been heard. At the same time she wrote to the despairing Mme. de Labédoyère stating that after spending several hours in purgatory her husband had an excellent place in paradise owing to the influence of the Emperor's prayers, and that she took great satisfaction in being able to assure her of this fact, being persuaded that it was the best possible relief for her sorrows.

I had heard of this letter, and of the outburst of grief, rising to the point of fury, which it had inspired in Georgine. I ventured a question to the Baroness upon this subject, which was readily opened, and she told me everything as I have related it.

I can remember a somewhat amusing incident which I witnessed at her house. There were seven or eight of us in her room one morning. She spoke to us in her inspired language of the high virtues of the Emperor Alexander, and praised the courage with which he abandoned his intimacy with Mme. de Narishkine, thus sacrificing to duty his dearest affections and an intimacy of sixteen years.

"Alas!" cried Elzéar de Sabran, with an inimitable expression of sympathy, "Alas! Sometimes in these matters it is easier to give up an intimacy of sixteen years than one of sixteen days!"

We all burst into laughter, and the Baroness von Krüdener set the example. Soon, however, she resumed her role and withdrew to the end of the room, as though to apologise to "the Voice" for this incongruity.

Whatever motives guided the Baroness von Krüdener, and I myself believe that her good faith was absolute, she had succeeded in playing a most important part. She had supported the claims of France throughout the peace negociations, and had been the leading influence in bringing about the "Holy Alliance." She accompanied the Emperor to the famous Camp of Vertus, and the Declaration signed there by the sovereigns, since called "The Convention of the Holy Alliance," was drawn up by Bergasse, another enlightened member of the confraternity, under her eyes and by her orders.

The Russians and those in attendance upon the Emperor were greatly vexed by the ridicule aroused by his connection with the Baroness von Krüdener, and Count Nesselrode reproached me with some impatience for visiting this intriguer, as he called her.

Benjamin Constant seems to have been one of her most ardent disciples. I say "seems," because it has always been extremely difficult to discover the real motives which underlie the actions of M. Constant. She made him fast and pray and mortify himself until his health suffered in consequence and he was terribly changed. When someone mentioned this fact, the Baroness replied that it was good for him to suffer, for he had much to expiate, but that the time of his probation was drawing to its close. I am not certain whether Benjamin was anxious to secure the favour of "the Voice," or whether he required the special protection of the Emperor, for at this period his position in France was so equivocal that he thought of emigrating.

Mme. Récamier had discovered the fountain of youth during her exile. In 1814 she had returned from Italy almost as beautiful as she had been in her early youth, and much more amiable. Benjamin Constant had known her intimately for a number of years, but he suddenly became inspired by an extravagant passion for her.

I have already said that she always had some sympathy and much gratitude for all the men who fell in love with her.

Benjamin drew heavily upon this general fund of affection. She listened to him, sympathised with him, and regretted that she was unable to share sentiments so eloquently expressed.

This frenzy of his was at its height when Napoleon returned. Mme. Récamier was overwhelmed, and feared further persecution. Benjamin was too enthusiastic to avoid adopting the feelings of the woman of whom he was enamoured, and under this influence he wrote a lampoon full of venom and brilliance against the Emperor, announcing his eternal hostility. This composition was printed in the *Moniteur* of March 19, the night when Louis XVIII abandoned his capital.

When poor Benjamin learnt this news, terror seized his heart, which was not nearly as lofty as his intellect. He hastened to the post. There were no horses; diligences and post-carriages were full; and it was impossible to leave Paris. He went and hid himself in a retreat which he thought was undiscoverable. His terror may be imagined when he was sent for the next day by Fouché. More dead than alive, he obeyed the summons. Fouché received him very politely, and informed him that the Emperor wished to see him at once. This seemed to him strange, but he felt somewhat reassured. He reached the Tuileries, and all doors opened before him.

The Emperor received him with the utmost graciousness, requested him to sit down, and began the conversation by assuring him that his past experiences had not been wasted. During his long waiting in the island of Elba he had reflected deeply on the situation and upon the needs of the age; men evidently desired liberal institutions. The mistake of his administration had been to neglect publicists such as M. Constant. The Empire required a Constitution, and he intended to apply to the chief lights of the Empire for the composition of it.

Benjamin thus passed in the space of half an hour from the fear of a dungeon to the joy of being summoned to the part of a miniature Solon, and nearly fell ill with emotion when he found that the dream of his life was accomplished. Fear and vanity fought for possession of him, and vanity remained triumphant. He was overwhelmed with admiration for the great Emperor who could do such ample justice to the merits of Benjamin Constant. And the author of the article in the *Moniteur* of the 19th became a State Councillor on the 22nd and Bonaparte's chief advocate.

Somewhat ashamed of himself, he called upon Mme. Récamier, but she was not the kind of woman to show any displeasure. Perhaps, also, she was glad to find herself relieved of a responsibility which would have weighed upon her if he had been persecuted for opinions which were more the result of sudden enthusiasm than of calm conviction. Political parties were less charitable. The Liberals never pardoned Benjamin for his panegyric on the Bourbons and legitimacy, the Imperialists declined to forgive his sarcasms towards Napoleon, while the Royalists hated him for his rapid recantation between the 19th and 22nd of March, and for the part which he played at the end of the Hundred Days, when he went to ask of the foreign sovereigns a master of any kind, provided the choice did not fall on Louis XVIII.

These continual changes had made him the object of universal contempt. He became conscious of the fact and consequently despaired. In this frame of mind he came into the hands of the Baroness von Krüdener. Whether his object was worldly pleasure, or whether he wished to change the course of his diseased imagination, I will not venture to decide. He continued to go to Mme. Récamier for consolation, and she treated him with gentleness and kindness. He was, however, somewhat vexed with her on account of the article which she had inspired, and this circumstance marked the crisis of his great passion.

I have never known anyone who was better able than Mme. Récamier to sympathise with all misfortune, and to understand the weaknesses of human nature without showing any irritation. She would no more display vexation with a vain character drawn to some inconsistency, or with an afraid man who committed some cowardice, than with a gouty man for having the gout or with a lame man for the inability to walk. Moral weakness inspired her with as much and perhaps more pity than physical infirmity. This moral weakness was tended to with a light and gentle touch which secured her the keen and tender gratitude of many unhappy people. Her power was the more readily realised because her soul, as pure as it was lofty, merely drew upon that abundant source of compassion which Heaven had placed in her most womanly breast.

Some weeks later Benjamin Constant conceived the idea of writing a letter to Louis XVIII explaining his conduct; it was a difficult task. Full of this idea, he called upon Mme. Récamier and discussed it at length. The next day there were some people at her house, and she asked him quietly:

"Have you finished your letter?"

"Yes."

"Are you satisfied with it?"

"Entirely satisfied. I have almost persuaded myself."

It was not so easy to convince the King. I believe, though I am not sure, that the letter was printed. Only the Royalist party was foolish enough not to take a man of talent seriously. At the end of a few months Benjamin Constant was one of the leaders of the Opposition.

I return to the day of my arrival in Paris in September 1815. Ready as I was to share in the general joy evoked by the King's return, my pleasure was spoilt by the presence of the foreigners. Their attitude was much more hostile than during the preceding year. As the conquerors of Napoleon in 1814 they had shown themselves generous; as the allies of Louis XVIII in 1815 they pushed their demands to the point of insult.

The strength and prosperity of France had aroused their surprise and their jealousy. They thought the country had been exhausted by our long wars, and saw it rise, to their astonishment, from its disasters so fair and powerful that at the Congress of Vienna M. de Talleyrand had been able to secure a leading role for France. Ministries and nations were alike alarmed, and as the opportunity for a further crusade against us had been provided, everyone was determined to turn it to their best advantage. Their hatred, however, was entirely blind: although they wished to humiliate France, they were anxious at the same time to consolidate the Restoration. The humiliations, however, of this period inflicted a wound upon the new Government from which it never recovered, and became one of the reasons for its downfall. The nation never entirely pardoned the royal family for the sufferings imposed upon it by those whom the Crown called allies. Had the foreigners been styled enemies, animosity would have been less keen and less permanent.

Excusable as these feelings were, they were at the same time entirely unjust. It is inconceivable that Louis XVIII found any satisfaction in beholding Prussian cannons trained upon the Palace of the Tuileries. The sight of the white Austrian cloaks enclosing the entrance to the Carrousel and the Arc de Triomphe stripped of its ornamentation was far from agreeable for him. Nor was he any better pleased that foreigners should make their way as far as his private apartments, and carry off the pictures which decorated his palace. He was obliged, however, to bear these outrages, and to swallow his disgust in silence. Moreover, it was his personal firmness which preserved the bridge of Iéna, which the Prussian General, Blücher, wished to blow up, and the column in the Place Vendôme, which the Allies desired to throw down and divide. In his efforts towards the latter purpose he was sup-

ported by the Emperor Alexander. This sovereign was always generous. Notwithstanding his dislike for the royal family, and the inclination which he had shown at the beginning of the campaign to refuse
any support to the Restoration, he now used his influence with the
coalition to modify the sacrifices which the Allies wished to impose
upon us.

I never knew exactly what his plans were at the time of the battle of
Waterloo. Possibly he had no definite policy, and was thrown into the
indecision whose consequenses had been so strikingly shown by Pozzo
to Bernadotte, the Crown Prince of Sweden, in 1813. I propose to recall this incident, although it belongs to an earlier date.

During the campaign in Saxony, Pozzo and Sir Charles Stewart
had been sent to the Swedish army as commissaries. The Allies were
invariably afraid that Bernadotte might declare in favour of the Emperor Napoleon. He eventually decided to come into line, and took
part in the battle of Leipzig; the rout of the French army was complete.
Immediately the Gascon mind of Bernadotte began to entertain wild
dreams, and to regard the throne of France as a possibility for himself.
He opened a conversation with Pozzo upon this question. Not daring
to begin the subject directly, he expounded a long theory, the result of
which went to prove that the throne should belong to the worthiest,
and that France should choose her King.

"I thank you, Sire," said Pozzo.

"Why, General?"

"Because I shall be the choice."

"You!"

"Certainly; I believe myself the worthiest. By what means will
anyone prove the contrary? By killing me? Then others will come forward. But enough of this 'most worthy' theory! The man most worthy
of the throne is, for the peace of the world, the man who has the best
right to it."

Bernadotte did not venture to carry the conversation further, but he
never forgave Pozzo.

The latter gave a similar lesson to his imperial master in 1815 in a different manner. When the Emperor Alexander heard of the victory of Waterloo, he requested General Pozzo, who was with the Duke of Wellington,* to object to the advance of the army, and to try to gain time, so that the English should not enter France until the Austro-Russian and Prussian armies were in line. In his opinion Louis XVIII should be obliged to await the decision of his fate in Belgium.

Pozzo found himself in the utmost embarrassment upon receipt of this despatch. He knew the Emperor's dislike for the House of Bourbon, a dislike which increased with the discovery of a proposal for an alliance between France, England, and Austria, concluded during the Congress of Vienna by M. de Talleyrand, with hostile intentions towards Russia. A copy of this treaty, which had been left forgotten in the King's study, had been sent by M. de Caulaincourt to the Emperor Alexander during the Hundred Days. The Emperor attached no great importance to it, believing it to be an invention of Napoleon to withdraw him from the Alliance, but a second copy was found among papers taken from M. de Reinhard, the French Minister in Frankfurt, and further doubt was impossible. To this new reason for dissatisfaction was added the King's treatment of him in the previous year, and he was by no means inclined to desire his restoration. Hence he had shown no disinclination to listen to the negociators sent from Paris, and it was difficult to foresee the result.

Pozzo was by no means in love with Russia, and was anxious to create a nation to his own taste in France by preserving a sovereign who was under a personal obligation to himself. After some small hesitation, he went off to find the Duke of Wellington.

"I am about to entrust to you the care of my head," he said. "Here is the despatch which I have received, and here is the answer which you have given."

He then read what he had written to the Emperor concerning the Duke of Wellington, whom he represented as insisting on an immediate march upon Paris, taking Louis XVIII with him.

"Would you mind," he said, "making this answer and continuing these arrangements in spite of the objections which I presumably have offered?"

The Duke held out his hand.

"Rely upon me; the conference has taken place exactly as you have reported it."

"Then," said Pozzo, "there is not a moment to be lost, and we must act accordingly."

No one was taken into their confidence. The King was at the centre of small intrigues, and M. de Talleyrand was sulking. But he had another plan, which contained certain special points, although its principal object was to keep himself at a distance from the Emperor Alexander. He did not know that the papers of M. de Reinhard had been captured, but had continually feared some indiscretion. Pozzo did not trust him sufficiently to explain the real situation. The Duke induced him to rejoin the King, who for his part agreed to a separation from M. de Blacas.

Paris was reached with the utmost speed, and the King was rushed into the Palace of the Tuileries, to use the picturesque language of Pozzo in telling the story. No sooner had this been accomplished than he jumped into a carriage and hastened to the Emperor. The Emperor's quarters were by arrangement at Bondy; Pozzo drove with great rapidity, and found the Emperor some leagues beyond there. He came to inform him that Paris had yielded, and that the Palace of the Elysée was ready to receive him. The Emperor asked him to take a seat in his carriage. Pozzo gave him an animated description of the battle of Waterloo, attaching huge importance to the manoeuvres of Blücher. He then related the entry into France, the ease of the march, the warmth of their reception, the impossibility of stopping when there were no obstacles, and finally the measures taken by the Duke for securing Paris. The Emperor listened with interest.

"The next thing," he said, "is to settle the political situation. Where have you left the King?"

"At the Tuileries, Sire, where he was received with universal enthusiasm."

"What! Louis XVIII in Paris! Apparently it is the work of Providence. What is done is done, and there is no use in attempting to undo it. Perhaps it is for the best." The relief which the Ambassador felt on hearing this pious resignation will be understood. Notwithstanding his absolute confidence in the loyalty of the Duke of Wellington, he had been greatly anxious as to how the Emperor would receive the news of this event. Liberal as this despot was, he did not always forget his estates in Siberia when he thought he had been badly served. The Emperor continued his journey, and slept at the Elysée. His displeasure was reserved for M. de Talleyrand and Count Metternich. The Austrian was able to overcome this obstacle, but the Frenchman was defeated by it shortly afterwards.

My uncle, Edouard Dillon, had accompanied the King to Belgium. He gave me an account of all the hardships of the departure, the journey, and the residence abroad. Monsieur and his son, the Duc de Berry, had left in the mud of Artois such scanty military reputation as the pity of the exiles would have wished to preserve for them. The King's household had been dismissed at Béthune with unparalleled curtness and harshness; several of its members, however, had been able to cross the frontier. Voluntarily and at their own expense, they united at Ghent and formed a guard for the King, who accepted their services with as much carelessness as he had displayed at the Tuileries.

M. de Bartillat, an officer in the Life Guards, told me that he had been at Ghent and had commanded a considerable number of guards of his company who had come together in pure zeal, and that neither he nor they had ever secured a word from the King or had ever been able to find if he knew of their existence. My own opinion is that the Princes were afraid to commit themselves to their partisans or to make promises, in case the new exile should be of long duration.

Shall I tell the story of the Camp d'Alost under the command of the Duc de Berry, which was so unfortunately broken up at the moment when the battle of Waterloo had begun? The Duke of Wellington expounded his views with cruel publicity for the Prince, whom he reproached with breaking down the bridge. The Duc de Berry excused himself upon the ground that false rumours had made him believe the battle was lost.

"The worse for you, sir. When you run away you should not place obstacles in the way of brave men who may be obliged to make an honourable retreat."

I prefer to relate the fierce energy of a certain soldier. Edouard Dillon had been ordered by the King, after the battle of Waterloo, to relieve the wants of the French wounded who were collected in a hospital at Brussels. He came to a bed occupied by a noncommissioned officer in the Imperial Guard, whose arm had just been amputated. In reply to his offers of help the soldier threw the bleeding arm at him, and said, "Tell the man who sends you here that I still have an arm left for the service of the Emperor."

One of my first duties on reaching Paris was to visit M. de Talleyrand. I had been ordered by my father to fully explain the painful situation of the French in Piedmont. I accomplished my mission somewhat clumsily; I had never been at ease with M. de Talleyrand. However, he received me very graciously, and when I told him towards the end of the month that I would take his orders for Turin, he urged me not to be in a hurry to pack up. I understood that my father's transfer was being proposed, but did not venture to ask for further information.

I have always been extremely shy in my dealings with officials, except when I had the moral support of knowing that I required nothing from their kindness. As long as my father was a subordinate official, I felt myself in a dependent and therefore a disagreeable position, notwithstanding the kindness which the authorities invariably showed me.

Our hero, the Duke of Wellington, took it upon himself to carry out the spoliations demanded by the Allies. Under pretext that the English had no claims of this kind to make, he was so generous that he came and took down the pictures from the walls of our museums with his own victorious hands. This is not mere rhetoric, but a description of the facts. He was seen on a ladder setting the example. When the Horses of Venice were taken down from the Arch of the Carrousel, he spent the morning perched on this monument opposite the King's windows supervising the work. In the evening he was present at a small reception given by Mme. de Duras for the King of Prussia. We could not hide our indignation, but he laughed at us, and jested upon the subject. At the same time he was wrong, for our resentment was justified, and was more politic than his conduct.

The foreigners had represented themselves as allies, and had been received as such, so that the discredit for their actions fell upon the reigning family. The Duke's conduct was the signal for his subordinates to display their impertinence. The blood still boils in my veins when I remember the remark of a certain vulgar animal called Mackenzie, an army paymaster.

The conversation had turned with sad and serious earnest upon the difficulty which France would find in meeting the enormous indemnities imposed by the foreigners.

"Oh, nonsense," he said, with a loud guffaw; "they may cry out a little, but the thing will be settled. I have just come from Strasburg; I passed through the town on the day when the Prussian General had demanded the contribution, which was said to be enormous; his contribution was paid. But everybody was dining." I could have killed him with a look.

The Duc de Duras, First Gentleman of the Chamber, was on duty for the year. Of the various positions at court, this one alone was held for more than three months. Mme. de Duras was lodging in the Tuileries. As I was an old friend of hers, and had no house of my own for the moment, I was constantly with her. Her position obliged her to give large parties from time to time, but her salon was usually open only to certain regular comers. The conversation there was freer and more reasonable than elsewhere. Probably the conversations which we then held would astonish us now, and we should consider them extravagant if they were repeated to us. Nonetheless, they were the most sensible among the views of the Royalist party. Mme. de Duras was much more liberal than her position would seem to allow. She was ready to listen to any opinion, and her judgements were untainted by party spirit. She would lend an ear to any generous idea which was not calculated to compromise her position unduly as a great lady, which she enjoyed all the more as she had waited for it a long time.

She could not console herself that M. de Chateaubriand had not been allowed to share in the return from Ghent. His influence had gained him the post of Minister of the Interior to the fugitive King, and she could not understand why the King did not reconfirm his nomination at his restoration. Hence there was a tinge of opposition in her language which was entirely to my taste. Her daughter, the Princesse de Talmont, did not share her mother's views; her enthusiasm was exaggerated, but she was so young and pretty that even her foolishness was graceful. In 1813, at the age of fifteen, she had married the only heir of the family of La Trémoille. Adrien de Montmorency declared that it was a historical marriage, and that the birth of her first child would be a national event. The annals of the country have not, however, recorded this event; M. de Talmont died in 1815, leaving no child.

The Duc de Duras exclaimed at the funeral:

"It is a terrible thing to be a widow at seventeen when one cannot marry anyone but a sovereign Prince."

The Princesse de Talmont declined to be bound by this condition, against the wishes of her father, and even of her mother. The death of the Prince de Talmont had caused us no personal grief, but our circle was deeply affected by the misfortune of the La Tour du Pin* family.

Hombert de La Tour du Pin-Gouvernet had reached the age of twenty-two. He was a gallant and most distinguished person, though his handsome face and the fact that his parents had spoiled him terribly made him appear somewhat ineffectual. During the disturbed period when people enlisted in the colonels, to use the angry phrase of the old soldiers, Hombert had been appointed Officer Extraordinary, and the Marshal, the Duc de Bellune, had taken him on as aide-de-camp. It cannot be denied that these marks of favour caused much vexation among comrades who had won their promotion at sword's point. Hombert had a discussion on the rules of service with one of these men:

the young man argued in a light and the other in a grumbling tone, but the matter went no further. However, upon reflection, Hombert felt some scruples. The next day he went to his father, and told him precisely what had happened, except that he gave his own role in the matter to one Donatien de Sesmaisons, another of his comrades. He added that this friend had requested him to consult his father as to the advisability of carrying the matter further.

M. de La Tour du Pin heard him attentively, and replied:

"This is one of those matters where advice is hardly called for."

"You think, then, Father, that they ought to fight?"

"It is not unavoidable. And if Donatien had been in the service longer, the matter might well be concluded by shaking hands. But he has only just entered the army. The captain has seen much service, and you know what jealousy there is against you newcomers. In Donatien's place I should fight."

Hombert left his father's room to go and write a challenge. The necessary consent arrived, and the meeting was arranged for midday in the Bois de Boulogne.

Before the family met for lunch, Hombert informed his father that he was acting as second for Donatien. His anxiety was obvious. He overwhelmed his mother with caresses, and insisted that she should herself pour out a cup of tea for him. She agreed, laughing at his obstinacy. His sister Cécile used to tease him upon the importance which he attached to a certain lock of hair which fell over his forehead, and now resumed this family joke.

"Well, Cécile, to show you that it is not the dearest of all my possessions, as you say, I give it up, and you can take it."

Cécile pretended to fence with a pair of scissors. Hombert did not wince, and she merely kissed his forehead.

"Why, my dear Hombert, it would grieve me as much as you."

Hombert caught her, embraced her tenderly, and went away to hide his agitation. Mme. de La Tour du Pin reproached him for this display of sentiment, which made them all melancholy. M. de La Tour du Pin, believing that he knew Hombert's secret, helped him to hide his distress. When Hombert had gone out, his sister found in her work-basket the lock of hair, and cried out:

"Oh, mamma, Hombert has certainly given in to that piece of foolishness. See what a sacrifice he has made! But after all, I am sorry."

Mother and daughter exchanged regrets, but felt no alarm. M. de La Tour du Pin was uneasy concerning Donatien, and went for a walk in the Champs Elysées. He soon perceived Donatien himself, whose gloomy countenance spoke of misfortune. Unfortunately, he had been the second, and Hombert had received a bullet in the forehead in the very spot recently covered by the lock of hair, which now became a most precious relic. He was dead. M. de La Tour du Pin had condemned his son that morning.

The first aide-de-camp of the Marshal, a man of influence, had been anxious to settle the quarrel. Hombert had offered objections. However, the reasons for the quarrel were so slight that the arrangement was almost made in spite of Hombert's resistance, when unfortunately he used a slang expression, saying that his adversary's ill temper had seemed to him somewhat mad since he had been so far from any desire to give offence. By the word "mad" he meant somewhat unreasonable.

Hombert's opponent responded: "What! You call me a madman!"

Hombert shrugged his shoulders. Two minutes afterwards he was dead.

M. de La Tour du Pin never recovered from so dreadful a shock; and it might even be said that his reason was affected. I shall not attempt to describe the despair of this bereaved family; we shared their sorrow, and the salon of Mme. de Duras, where the family had been constant visitors, was saddened for a long period by this cloud.

The elections of 1815 went entirely for the Royalists, and the nobility secured an immense majority. It was the best chance which the nobility had had for forty years to recover some superiority in France. Had the nobles shown themselves calm, reasonable, generous, and enlightened, had they displayed a desire to work for the country and to protect its members—in a word, had they played the part which the aristocracy of a representative government should play at the moment of its supreme power—these services would have been recognised, and the throne of France would have found a real support in the influence of the nobility. But this Chamber, which the King characterised as *introuvable*[1] in its early days, now showed itself extravagant, ignorant, factious, reactionary, and entirely dominated by class interests. It cried aloud for vengeance, and applauded the bloodthirsty scenes of the south. Upon this occasion the nobility made itself increasingly unpopular, even as ten years later it lost its last claims for respect in the disgraceful debates concerning the indemnity to the *émigrés*.[2]

When the deputies took their seats they had not yet reached the exaggerated pitch they afterwards attained. Nonetheless, their animosity drove Fouché out of office even before the opening of the session. They displayed an equal repugnance to M. de Talleyrand. He might have ventured to fight them if he had been supported by the court. But Monsieur permitted the Duc de Fitz-James to say:

"Well, sir, that wretched hobbler is going to dance," and smiled in approval of this comment concerning a man who had placed the House of Bourbon on the throne twice in twelve months.

It is said that Louis XVIII felt that such services were a heavy burden, and regretted the sacrifice which he had been compelled to make in removing the Comte de Blacas. Moreover, the Emperor Alexander, who had been a zealous protector of M. de Talleyrand in 1814, had now become his principal enemy. The Minister yielded to this accumulated opposition, and his resignation was accepted with more readiness than he had perhaps expected.

I went to his house in the evening, when he came up to me and told me that the last act of his Ministry had been to appoint my father to the London ambassadorship. His nomination, in fact, though signed by Richelieu,* had been secured by M. de Talleyrand. He had asked the

1. The King meant the Chamber was too good to be true. His majority was overwhelming.
2. A law voted in 1825 that indemnified the *émigrés* for their properties seized and sold during the Revolution. The sum amounted to one billion francs. The law was hugely unpopular.

King for this nomination in 1814, but the Comte de La Châtre had been First Gentleman to Monsieur the Comte de Provence; he had been promised this position in the King's household, and as he bored the King to despair, his most Christian Majesty preferred having an incompetent Ambassador in London to a disagreeable servant in the Tuileries. At length, however, he yielded. Notwithstanding the immense advantages which M. de La Châtre derived from his appointment as peer, Duke, First Gentleman of the Chamber, a large pension from the Peers' Chamber, and another from the Civil List, he was greatly vexed by this change.

With his nomination my father received a letter from the Duc de Richelieu, recalling him to Paris. He did not, however, wish to leave Turin until the fate of our compatriots was definitely settled. This business kept him at Turin for several weeks. It was during this interval that my disagreeable relations with M. de Richelieu began.

Upon my first evening at the salon of Mme. de Duras I saw a tall man with a handsome face, whose youth contrasted strangely with his grey hair, come in. He was very short-sighted, and continually blinked in a manner which made his expression by no means attractive. He wore boots, and his bad taste in dress was almost an affectation in itself; nonetheless, he preserved the dignity of the highest rank. He threw himself upon a sofa, and talked with a shrill and squeaky voice. A slight foreign accent and somewhat outlandish expressions convinced me that he was not a Frenchman. At the same time his language and the sentiments which he expressed refuted this idea. I saw that he was familiar with all my friends, and racked my brain to conjecture who this well-known stranger might be: it was the Duc de Richelieu, who had returned to France after my departure from Paris. The impression which he made upon me at this first meeting has never changed. His manners always seemed to me as disagreeable and displeasing as possible. His fine and noble character, and his real business capacity, together with his enlightened patriotism, commanded my approval, I might almost say my devotion, but it was an approval more forced than voluntary. Our relations have always felt the effects of this bad beginning. I was heart and soul a member of his party, but knew little of his friends and nothing at all of his intimates. We would meet daily without speaking.

The acrimonious manner of M. de Richelieu often made him political enemies among people less reasonable than myself, if the foolishness of the observation may be permitted.

M. de Talleyrand sometimes boasted that he had retired in order to avoid signing the cruel treaty imposed upon France; the fact is that he succumbed to the accumulated weight of the animosity to which I have already referred. M. de Richelieu had been brought into power by the Emperor Alexander, and hard as the terms were to which we were forced to submit, they would have been far worse had any other Minister been in office.

As soon as M. de Richelieu had been nominated, the Emperor Alexander loudly proclaimed himself the champion of France. Thus, when he distributed presents to each of the diplomats upon his departure, he sent M. de Richelieu an old map of France which had been used at the Conference. Upon it were traced the numerous territorial claims which the Allies had raised, and which their representatives hoped to secure. He added an autographed note, stating that the confidence inspired by M. de Richelieu had alone been able to avert this enormous sacrifice from his country. The Emperor added that this present had seemed to him most worthy of his noble character, and he would no doubt appreciate it more than any other. Such a gift does honour to the sovereign who conceives the idea of it and to the Minister who is so exemplary as to inspire the idea.

Notwithstanding this success, which M. de Richelieu was not the man to proclaim, and which was not known until long afterwards, his heart, with all its French patriotism, was overwhelmed by this terrible treaty. The tone of voice in which he read the treaty to the Chamber, and the gesture with which he threw down the paper on the desk when this painful duty had been accomplished, have become historic, and began to reconcile every thinking man in the country to a nomination which at first appeared somehow too Russian. Nothing in the

world was more unjust, for M. de Richelieu was the purest of Frenchmen, by no means an *émigré*, and as little an aristocrat as circumstances
allowed him to be. He was a Liberal and a patriot in the best sense of
the two terms.

During his first Ministry his ignorance of people caused him some
drawbacks; for a Prime Minister, knowledge of persons is quite as important as knowledge of affairs. It was this ignorance that induced him
to accept without opposition a colleague proposed by Monsieur, the
Comte de Vaublanc. He speedily displayed an ineptitude so delightfully foolish that it would have evoked roars of laughter if he not been
supported by the Princes and the Chamber. Any absurdity was contagious in those latitudes. M. de Vaublanc promptly attempted to fo-
ment an intrigue against M. de Richelieu, which was discountenanced
by foreign influence.

At about this time, Monsieur gave M. de Vaublanc a large white
horse. He used to pose on it in the garden of the Minister of the Interior
for a statue of Henri IV. No one, in his opinion, could sit a horse so
perfectly as himself. If his claims had ended there, it would have been
possibly better for him, but his demands were carried to incredible
extremes and expressed with a want of tact and a bluntness wholly
inconceivable.

My father had somehow or other concluded the business concerning the French who were domiciled in Piedmont, and had handed over
the rest of Savoy to the King of Sardinia according to the terms of the
Treaty of Paris.[3] In the Tuileries, Louis XVIII was as pleased at this
event as anyone in Paris could be. His Minister did not share this satisfaction, and this last portion of his duty was so disagreeable to him
that he refused, with some temper, the Grand Cordon which was offered to him upon the occasion of this restitution. The fact is that my

3. The first treaty of Paris was signed between the Allies (Great Britain, Austria, Prussia, and Russia) and France on May 30, 1814. France abandoned its recent conquests and
accepted the frontiers of 1792. The second treaty, signed on November 20, 1815, imposed on France a hefty fine, the restitution of all the works of art seized by Napoleon,
and an occupation army of one hundred fifty thousand men.

father was then expecting to obtain the Order of the Saint-Esprit, and if the prejudices of his youth made him desire it somewhat too anxiously, they also inspired him with a great disdain for all foreign decorations.

Upon his arrival, M. de Richelieu overwhelmed him with marks of confidence. The preparations that were necessary for his removal to London kept him in Paris so long that he was unfortunately summoned to sit at the trial of Marshal Ney.

I do not propose to give the full details of this deplorable affair, which caused us great anxiety. During the last days of the trial the peers and all their connections received threatening letters. It was virtually recognised that the peers were bound to condemn the Marshal. The King has been greatly reproached for not pardoning him. I doubt whether he had either the power or the will to do so.

When we judge events of this nature after a lapse of many years, we do not give sufficient weight to the impressions prevalent at the time. Everyone was afraid, and nothing is more cruel than fear. An epidemic of vengeance had set in, and of this no other proof is necessary than the words of the Duc de Richelieu when he sent the case to the Court of Peers. That so fine and noble a character as the Duc was unable to avoid the contagion, it was bound to become universal, and I doubt if he could have denied popular clamour the victim which it claimed without driving it to greater excesses.

At a later date another King was seen to interpose his influence between the fury of the people and the victims which it demanded.[4] But in the first place this King was, in my opinion, a character high above average, and consequently the more reasonable members of his party appreciated and encouraged this moderation. He ran the risk of a popular uprising, in which his life, but not his power, might be lost.

In 1815, on the other hand, it must be admitted that those who demanded an example to deter future traitors were the honourable

4. Allusion to the attitude of Louis-Philippe during the trial of the Ministers of Charles X.

members of the party, the Princes, the bishops, the Chambers, and the court, in addition to the foreigners. Europe told us that we had no right to be generous or indulgent at the expense of European blood and treasure. The Duke of Wellington's attitude and his refusal to invoke the capitulation of Paris is further evidence of the fact. The Marshal's pardon depended much more upon him than upon Louis XVIII; we must also remember that the death penalty for political reasons was then regarded as natural by all, and also that moderation in the Restoration Government was a dreaded influence which secured the growth and general dissemination of a more enlightened Liberalism.

I do not wish to offer any excuse for the madness which prevailed at that time. I was as angry then as I should be now to see members of high society readily offering their personal services to guard the Marshal in the prison cell, and to sleep there for fear he should escape; I have seen others offer themselves as a guard to take him to the place of punishment; while the Life Guards begged as a favour and obtained as a reward permission to put on the uniform of the police in order to guard him the more carefully and to give him no chance of seeing a sympathetic look on the face of any old soldier.

All this is as true as it is hateful. My object is to point out that more than kindness was required to secure the pardon of Marshal Ney; his pardon would have been an act of the highest courage. Louis XVIII was by no means a bloodthirsty character, but he was too entirely and exclusively a prince at heart to give undue weight to the life of one man when balancing contrary interests. Moreover, the poor Marshal, who was thus piteously sacrificed to momentary passion, and who has since been deified by other passions of like nature, could never have been anything more to the Imperialists than the traitor of Fontainebleau, the deserter of Waterloo, and the denouncer of Napoleon. In the eyes of the Royalists the guilt of his conduct was even more pronounced.

These wrongdoings, however, have been wiped out in his blood, and all that now remains to memory is his military courage, so often and so recently employed with superhuman vigour in the service of his country. The proverb says, "The dead alone never return." I should prefer to amend the saying, and write that "In times of revolution the dead are the only ones who return."

I remember one day during the trial I was dining at the house of M. de Vaublanc. My father arrived at the expiration of his period of duty from the Luxembourg, and told us that a postponement had been granted at the request of the Marshal's lawyers. M. de Vaublanc jumped up, flung his napkin against the wall, and called out. "If those peers imagine that I will consent to be a Minister to a body which shows such weakness, they are greatly deceived. One more display of such cowardice, and all honest men will be forced to hide their heads."

There were thirty people at table, including several deputies, and all joined in the chorus. Yet the only issue was a legal postponement, which could not possibly be refused unless an extraordinary court were appointed. The excitement of partisans might well be understood when the temper of Government Ministers was so cruelly hasty.

My father and I expressed our indignation as soon as we were in our carriage; if we had expressed it in the house we should have been stoned. We were already catalogued as malcontents, but it was not until after the Ordinance of September[5] that my opinions were stated to be "those of a pig." I will ask my nephews not to laugh; it was the literal expression used by ladies of high rank, and used frequently.

I used to meet the Duc de Raguse constantly, especially at Mme. de Duras's, where he was an intimate friend. I felt towards him some of the general prejudice, and though I had never been a supporter of Napoleon, I did not like the Duc the better for his betrayal. Foreigners, who were well informed upon this matter, were the first to explain to me to what extent the loyalty of the Marshal had been calumniated. I also observed that the Duc remained faithful to his old comrades, notwithstanding the insults with which Bonaparte's party overwhelmed him. Whenever they were attacked, he supported them keenly and vigourously, addressed them without the smallest reticence, and was

5. The Ordinance of September 5, 1816, pronounced the dissolution of the *Chambre introuvable.*

the zealous and active protector of all who suffered through interference. These facts began to arouse my respect, and enabled me to better appreciate his distinguished mind and his lively and extensive conversational powers, which were undeniable merits. The day was approaching when my affection for him was to become real.

Another trial aroused passions at that time. M. de La Valette,* conscious of his innocence, and persuaded that, according to the letter of the law, he had nothing to fear, surrendered to justice. He would have been acquitted but for a certain document which originated as follows. Old M. Ferrand, the Postmaster-General, was seized with such terror upon the Emperor's return that he was both afraid either to remain at his post or to abandon it. He asked M. de La Valette, his predecessor under the Emperor, to sign for him a permit for post-horses. M. de La Valette objected for a long time; at length he yielded to the tears of Mme. Ferrand, and in order to calm the fears of the old man he signed his name to a permit drawn up by M. Ferrand in his study surrounded by his family, who were loud in their protestations of gratitude. This was the only proof which could be exhibited to show that he had resumed his powers before the legal term. I presume that the surrender of this document must have cost the Ferrand family dearly. I admit that such Royalist devotion has always seemed horrible to me, and M. de Richelieu was disgusted; he hated persecution in any case, and the more he learned of the business of government the more his political partisanship decreased. As he could not prevent the trial of M. de La Valette, he did his best to secure his pardon in case he should be condemned.

It is said that M. Pasquier, though he had previously been the *Garde des Sceaux*,[6] came to give clear and conscientious evidence in his favour. M. de Richelieu requested the King to pardon M. de La Valette. The King replied that he could not venture to face the fury of his family, but that if the Duchesse d'Angoulême would consent to say a word for this purpose, he would grant the request readily. The Duc de Richelieu

6. Minister of Justice.

went to see the Duchesse, and secured her consent after some difficulty. It was agreed that she should ask the King's pardon after lunch
on the next day, and the King was forewarned. When the Duc de Richelieu came to the King the next day, his first words were:

"Well, my niece never spoke, and you must have misunderstood
her."

"No, Sire; I had her absolute promise."

"Go and see her, then, and try and induce her to act. I will wait for
her if she is ready to come."

An event of vast importance had, however, occurred in the Palace of
the Tuileries: the previous evening the usual custom had been changed.
Every day, after dining with the King, Monsieur used to go down to
his daughter-in-law at eight o'clock, returning to his own rooms at
nine. The Duc d'Angoulême used to go to bed, and Madame to the
rooms of her lady of the bedchamber, Mme. de Choisy: it was there
that the closest, that is to say the most violent, members of the Royalist
party used to meet.

Upon the evening in question Madame found them in full force;
they had heard of the project for securing the King's pardon. She admitted her share in the plot, and said that her father-in-law and her
husband approved of it. There were immediate outbursts and cries of
despair. The danger to the Crown which such an act would involve
was pointed out to her, and, breaking through all usual custom, she entered the carriage of a lady present at this meeting, and went to the Pavillon de Marsan, where she found Monsieur, who had been similarly
lectured by his own circle, and was much inclined to recall the consent which had been extorted from him. It was resolved that Madame
should do nothing, and that if the Minister and the King desired their
own dishonour, the rest of the royal family would at any rate keep their
hands unsullied. Hence the reason for Madame's silence. M. de Richelieu obtained an audience, but found her resolution immovable; she
had pledged her word too far. Their hatred of one another dates from
this moment.

M. de Richelieu went off to relate these circumstances to the King.

"They are inexorable, as I had foreseen," said the monarch, with a sigh. "But if I were to defy them I should never have a moment's rest."

While these events were taking place in the royal household the Duc de Raguse was asked what he would be willing to do on behalf of M. de La Valette. "Anything you like," was the reply. He went first to the King, who gave him what he himself called his wooden countenance, allowed him to speak as long as he liked without showing a single sign of interest, and dismissed him without answering a word. The Marshal[7] understood that M. de La Valette was lost. Unaware of the attempt which had been made to use the influence of Madame, he set all his hopes upon her, and went to warn Mme. de La Valette that it would be necessary to have recourse to this final possibility. But the danger was foreseen: all approaches were closed, and she was unable to see the Princess.

The Marshal was on duty as Major-General of the Guard; he concealed Mme. de La Valette in his apartment, and while the King and the royal family were at mass he passed all the sentinels, and brought her to the Hall of the Marshals, through which the royal family had to pass on their return. Mme. de La Valette threw herself at the King's feet; he vouchsafed only the words, "Madame, I am sorry for you."

She then besought the Duchesse d'Angoulême, and caught hold of her dress; the Princess tore it away with a violence for which she has often been reproached, and which was attributed to anger and hate. This I believe to be entirely unjust. Madame had pledged her word, and could not retreat; probably her movements upon this occasion were made with her usual brusqueness. I should be rather inclined to believe that she was actuated by pity, even by the vexation that she could not dare to yield, than by anger. The misfortune of this Princess consisted in the fact that her intelligence was wholly disproportionate to her strength of character.

The conduct of the Marshal was as loudly blamed by the courtiers as it was approved by the public. He received orders not to reappear at

7. Mme. de Boigne generally uses the term Marshal to identify the Duc de Raguse.

court, and went away to his estates. The officer of the Life Guards who had allowed him to pass the sentinels was imprisoned. When these preliminary facts have been understood, there will be less astonishment at the general cry of execration which arose throughout the party when the escape of M. de La Valette was known. The King and his Ministers were suspected of complicity; the Chamber of Deputies roared, and women howled like a pack of hyenas deprived of their whelps. They even desired to take proceedings against Mme. de La Valette, and it was necessary to keep her in prison for some time to allow the storm to subside. M. Decazes,* who had hitherto been a favourite of the Royalists, now inspired them with a distrust which speedily became hatred.

Though the Government had done nothing to facilitate the escape of M. de La Valette, I believe that it was secretly delighted. The King shared this satisfaction. He speedily recalled the Duc de Raguse, and showed him much favour on his return. But his party was less indulgent, and treated him with as much coldness as it had previously shown him kindness. I must make an exception in the case of Mme. de Duras, who stood apart from this extravagant aristocracy; her enthusiasm was confined to generous ideas, and the disgrace of the Marshal was a merit in her eyes. Notwithstanding this attitude on the part of the mistress of the house, his isolation in her salon often threw him into my company, and we used to talk together. It was not until his conduct at Lyons had brought his quarrel with the ultra-Royalist party to a head that he took refuge in a small circle of which I became the centre, and of which he was one of the supports until further storms brought new upheaval to his adventurous life. I shall probably have occasion often to speak of him hereafter.

My father started for London at the outset of 1816, and my mother followed him. I did not rejoin them until the spring.

The foreigners had retired to the garrisons which had been assigned to them by the Treaty of Paris. The Duke of Wellington alone, as Generalissimo of all the armies of occupation, resided in Paris, and did the honours of the town at our expense. He frequently gave parties, at which attendance was obligatory. He was anxious to see much of society, and as our future prospects largely depended upon his good humour, it was necessary to bear with his caprices, which were often strange.

I remember that upon one occasion he conceived the idea of making the diva Grassini, who was then at the height of her beauty, the Queen of the evening. He seated her upon a sofa mounted on a platform in the ballroom and never left her side; had her served before anyone else, made people stand back in order that she might see the dancing, and took her in to supper himself in front of the whole company; there he sat by her side, and showed her attentions usually granted only to Princesses. Fortunately, some high-born English ladies were there to share the burden of this insult, but they did not feel the weight of it as we did, and their resentment could hardly be compared with ours.

Generally speaking, the Carnival was a gloomy function, as was indeed entirely fitting. None of our Princes appeared. The Duc de Berry was entirely eclipsed by his brother, and the difference in their respective attitudes during the Hundred Days justified their present positions. However, the Duc d'Angoulême was displaying moderate tendencies which made him somewhat unpopular, and the ecclesiastical party would not pardon his dislike for the politics of the confessional.

The character of the Duc d'Angoulême is somewhat difficult to describe. He was a mixture of such various and extraordinary contrasts that at different periods of his life he might have been represented with equal truth as a wise, pious, and courteous prince, conciliatory and enlightened, or as a wild and almost insane figure. I have described him as I have seen him when circumstances brought him before me. But to understand his character it must first be said that he was always dominated by the idea of unlimited obedience to the King. The nearer he was to the throne, the more, in his opinion, was he bound to set an example in this respect. While Louis XVIII was alive, this passive obedience was somewhat modified, at any rate in form, by the obedience which he owed to Monsieur, but when the authority of father and king was centred in Charles X,* his devotion was unbounded, and we will see the sad results to which it led.

The marriage of the Duc de Berry was now a leading question; it already had been discussed in 1814. The Emperor Alexander had wished him to marry his sister, and had been greatly irritated by the manner in which she was rejected. The Duc de Berry was anxious for this marriage to take place, but the King and Monsieur considered the Russian family insufficiently ancient to provide a mother for the Children of France.

The Duchesse d'Angoulême shared these views. Moreover, she had no desire for a sister-in-law whose political connections would have given her complete independence, and who would therefore have been a personage of importance. She was also afraid of a Princess whose personal accomplishments might have gathered around her people distinguished for their intellectual powers, for whom Madame herself always felt an instinctive repugnance, whatever their political opinions.

The Princess of Naples, a Bourbon by birth, belonging to a little court and uneducated, secured all the family votes. She was forced upon the Duc de Berry, who showed no interest in the affair. M. de Blacas was instructed to undertake these negociations, which did not occupy his diplomatic talents for long. At the same time the idea of marrying Monsieur was conceived. This was a reasonable project, although Madame objected as much as she could. She could not have borne to see any Princess holding court and taking precedence over her. Monsieur, who loved her tenderly, apart from other motives would not have wished to cause her this vexation. This recalls an apt remark from Louis XVIII. He was a gouty invalid, in a terrible state of health. One day, when he was speaking seriously to Monsieur as to the advisability of getting married, the latter said to him, with a slightly ironical laugh:

"Brother, as you preach so well, why not get married yourself?"

"Because my children would all be first-born," replied the King dryly. Monsieur could find no reply. Life within the Tuileries was neither intimate nor agreeable. At that time, however, the King used to talk with his family of public business, for the rupture was not yet complete.

The English Ambassador, Sir Charles Stewart, had married the daughter of Lord Hardwicke. The presentation of the new Lady Ambassadress became the occasion for the first time since the Restoration of what is known in court language as a *traitement*. A dozen ladies, most of them bearing titles, were summoned to be present at the residence of the Duchesse d'Angoulême at two o'clock. My father's position as Ambassador to the English Government secured me this distinction. We were all assembled in Madame's drawing-room, when the usher went to inform Mme. de Damas, who was taking the place of her mother, Mme. de Sérent, as lady of honour, that the Ambassadress was arriving.

At the same moment Madame, who had probably been looking through her window, as was her habit, came in through another door, magnificently dressed in court costume, as we all were. She hardly had time to greet us and sit down when Mme. de Damas returned with the Ambassadress, accompanied by the lady who had been to fetch her, the masters of the ceremonies, and the introducers of the Ambassadors who remained by the door.

Madame rose, took one or two steps towards the Ambassadress, resumed her armchair, and placed Lady Stewart in a high-backed chair which was standing ready on her left hand. The ladies of title sat down behind them on stools, and the rest of us remained standing. This stage of the proceedings was somewhat long, and Madame sustained the conversation alone. Lady Elizabeth, who was young and shy, was too embarrassed to answer except in monosyllables, and I admired the way in which Madame discussed England and France, Ireland and Italy, from which country Lady Elizabeth had arrived, in order to fill the time which the slow and painful approach of the King prolonged unduly.

At length he came in. Everyone rose, and the deepest silence reigned. He broke this silence when he had reached the middle of the room by uttering in the gravest and most sonorous voice, without mov-

ing a muscle of his face, the futile observation which formality had pre-
scribed since the time of Louis XIV.

"Madame, I did not know that you were in such good company!"

Madame replied with another phrase, no doubt equally conven-
tional, which I do not remember.

The King then addressed some words to Lady Elizabeth. She continued to reply in monosyllables; the King remained standing, as did
everyone else, and after a few moments he withdrew.

All then resumed their seats, to rise immediately upon the entrance
of Monsieur.

"Ought I not to observe that I did not know you were in such good
company?" said he with a smile; he then went up to Lady Elizabeth
with the utmost grace, shook hands with her, and complimented her.
He refused to accept the chair which Madame offered him, but bade
the ladies sit down, and stayed much longer than the King. The ladies
rose as he went out, and sat down again, to rise once more at the entrance of the Duc d'Angoulême; upon this occasion, after the first compliments, he took a chair and entered into conversation. It seemed to
me that the shyness of the Ambassadress gave him courage. I do not rec-
ollect seeing the Duc de Berry at this ceremony. I do not know if his
presence was unnecessary, or if his absence was fortuitous. Nor did I
know how matters stood with respect to the Duchesse de Berry, as I
had no opportunity of being present at any similar reception.

The exit of the Duc d'Angoulême was again accompanied by rising
and sitting down as before; I was irresistibly reminded of the genuflections on Good Friday. At the end of a few minutes a lady of honour
informed the Ambassadress that she was ready to receive her orders.
Madame observed that she feared to fatigue her if she detained her
longer, and she went away, escorted as she had come. She entered the
King's carriage, accompanied by the lady who had been to fetch her.
The King's coach, with six horses and in full dress, followed her
empty. Madame spoke to us for a moment concerning the presentation,
and went back to her rooms, to my great satisfaction, for I had already

stood for two hours and was getting weary of the honour. It was necessary, however, to be present at the dinner after the *traitement*.

The Ambassadress returned at five o'clock. On this occasion she was accompanied by her husband and by several English ladies of high rank. All the French ladies who had been present at the reception were invited, and gentlemen of both nationalities were also present.

The major-domo at that time, the Duc d'Escars, and Madame's lady of honour did the honours of the dinner, which was excellent and magnificent, but by no means well-appointed, as was the case with every function at the court of the Tuileries. Immediately afterwards everyone was glad to be allowed to retire and go to rest after all this etiquette. The men were in uniform, and the women in full dress, but not in court dress. Neither the King, the Princesses, nor the Princes were there, but I noticed behind a screen Madame and her husband, who amused themselves by looking at the table and the guests before going up to dinner with the King.

I have never been able to understand how foreign sovereigns, who receive French Ambassadors at their tables upon intimate terms, can be willing to endure in the person of their representatives the arrogance of the House of Bourbon. It was far from courteous not to invite the Ministers to their own residence, but to make them come with all these people, and this in *fiochi*[8] to a servants' dinner, has always seemed to me the last degree of impertinence. This dinner was no doubt attended regularly by people of good family, but it was the table of second-rate importance in the Palace, since it seems that the King's table held first place. The entertainment did not even take place in the rooms of the First Chamberlain, where it might have been regarded as a social meeting, for the rooms were too small and he lived on too high a floor. The guests met in the waiting-room to the apartments of Madame, and dined in the anteroom of the Duc d'Angoulême. Hence they seemed to be relegated to the outer apartments, as if the place had been

8. Italian for "finery."

let to some stranger for an entertainment. I could have imagined that the old-time dignity of Versailles and of Louis XIV might have continued without interruption; it is hard to imagine that anyone would have dared revive these formalities. Louis XVIII clung to them rigidly, and had it not been for his health and the humiliation of his infirmities, we should probably have seen a revival of the King's rising and going to bed, with all the ridiculous ceremonies that these functions required.

Monsieur cared much less for them, and when he ascended the throne he continued the custom which his brother had established, and confined the *coucher* to a short reception of those courtiers who had the right of admission, and to the heads of departments who came to receive the password. The customary phrase was no longer "I am going to the *coucher*," but "I am going to receive the password." This was more dignified and decent than the customs of the old court which poor Louis XVI exhibited every evening.

INDEX

Montmorency, Mathieu de, xxvii, 64

Montpensier, Duc de, 31

Moreau case, the, 46n 6

Morozzi Palace, Turin, 162

Mortefontaine, M. de, 106

Mouchy, Duc de. *See* Noailles, Charles de

Munich, *émigré* society in, 33

Murat, King of Naples: attempts to help Napoleon, 171; defeat at Occhiobello, 181; in *Dictionary of Characters*, xxvii; gift to Princess Caroline, 176; subscription ball at Naples, 177

Nantouillet, M. de, 35

Naples: the Royalist reaction in, 167; the subscription ball to Murat, 177

Naples, Queen of. *See* Charlotte

Narbonne, Duchesse de, 9

Narishkine, Mme. de, 212

National Assembly, 13

National Guard, the, 12, 114, 123

Necker, M., xxviii, 8

Nelson, Admiral Lord, 20

Nesselrode, Count: acquaintance with Comtesse de Boigne, 71, 105–106, 109, 113; declaration of the Allies, 105; mentioned, 212; Minister of Foreign Affairs, 103

Neuchâtel, Prince of, 72

Ney, Marshal, xxviii, 126; trial and execution of, 230–231, 232

Nîmes, 174

Noailles, Alexis de, 82–86

Noailles, Charles de, 83–84

Noailles, Marshal de, 83

Novant-ott, system enforced by Victor Emmanuel I, 147–148

O'Brien, Mr., 68

Occhiobello, Murat defeated at, 181

O'Connell, Mr., 28, 29

"Old Guard" in procession of Louis XVIII, 123

Opera, the visit of the Allies, 109–110, 117

Orange, the Prince of, 12

Ordinance of September 5, 232, 232n 5

Orléans, Duchesse d'. *See* Marie-Amélie of Naples, Princesse

Orléans, Louis-Philippe, Duc d': attitude on trial of the Ministers of Charles X, 230n 5; character of, 31; in *Dictionary of Characters*, xxv; marriage with Princesse Amélie, 137–138; policy, 140; repugnance of Mme. de Angoulême for, 138–139

Orléans, Princesse Adélaïde, xv, 138

Orloff, Michel, 105

Osmond, Abbé d', 7

Osmond, Antoine Eustache, Bishop of Cominges and afterwards of Nancy, 54

Osmond, Marquis d': appointed French Ambassador in London, 226–227; audience with the Princess Caroline, 178–179; at Compiègne, 121–122; in *Dictionary of Characters*, xxix; distribution of the Declaration of March 13, 173–174; education of daugh-

Produced by Wilsted & Taylor Publishing Services
COPYEDITING: Caroline Roberts
DESIGN: Melissa Ehn
COMPOSITION: Sarah Lowe
PRODUCTION MANAGEMENT: Christine Taylor

Printed by Transcontinental Printing Book Group